RENA'S PROMISE

RENA'S PROMISE

A STORY OF SISTERS IN AUSCHWITZ

RENA KORNREICH GELISSEN

WITH HEATHER DUNE MACADAM

**EXPANDED
EDITION**

*Love
Rena*

BEACON PRESS
BOSTON, MASSACHUSETTS

BEACON PRESS
Boston, Massachusetts
www.beacon.org

Beacon Press books
are published under the auspices of
the Unitarian Universalist Association of Congregations.

18 17 16   8 7 6 5 4 3

This book is printed on acid-free paper that meets the uncoated paper
ANSI/NISO specifications for permanence as revised in 1992.

Text design and composition by Kim Arney

Some dialogue has been created.

Library of Congress Cataloging-in-Publication Data
Gelissen, Rena Kornreich, 1920–2006.
Rena's promise : a story of sisters in Auschwitz / Rena Kornreich Gelissen ;
with Heather Dune Macadam. — Expanded edition.
pages cm
Includes bibliographical references.
Summary: "The inspiring story of one woman's struggle to survive during
the Holocaust. An expanded edition of the remarkable story of Rena
Korneich, one of the few women who survived the first Jewish transport
to Auschwitz and more than three years in the Nazi death camp. Rena's
Promise is a compelling story of the fleeting human connections that fostered
determination and made survival a possibility. Moving from the bonds
between mothers, daughters, and sisters to the links between prisoners, and
even between prisoners and guards, this memoir reminds us of the humanity
and hope that survives inordinate brutality" — Provided by publisher.
ISBN 978-0-8070-9313-9 (paperback) — ISBN 978-0-8070-9509-6 (ebook)
1. Auschwitz (Concentration camp) 2. Holocaust, Jewish (1939–1945)—
Personal narratives. 3. Gelissen, Rena Kornreich, 1920–2006.
I. Macadam, Heather Dune. II. Title.
D805.P7G45 2015
940.53'18092—dc23
[B]
2014037297

Dear Mama and Papa:
This book is for you. For fifty years I've been telling
you this story in my mind. Now it's finally written
down and I won't have to tell it anymore.

—Love, Rena

❧

And for Danka:
Without you there would be no story.

Human beings are more alike than we are unalike.

And no human being can be more human than another.

—*Maya Angelou*

Leviticus 19:33–34

When a stranger sojourns with you in your land, you shall not taunt him.

The stranger who sojourns with you shall be as a native from among you, and you shall love him as yourself . . .

וְכִי יָגוּר אִתְּךָ גֵּר בְּאַרְצְכֶם לֹא תוֹנוּ לג.
אֹתוֹ:

לד. כְּאֶזְרָח מִכֶּם יִהְיֶה לָכֶם הַגֵּר | הַגָּר
אִתְּכֶם וְאָהַבְתָּ לוֹ כָּמוֹךָ כִּי גֵרִים הֱיִיתֶם
בְּאֶרֶץ מִצְרָיִם אֲנִי יְהֹוָה אֱלֹהֵיכֶם:

Contents

PREFACE

The heart is only so big, so I do not hate.
To hate is to let Hitler win.
—Rena Kornreich Gelissen

"What is it to you?"

That was the question the woman asked me while we stood on the rooftop of a Brooklyn apartment building enjoying a cookout and celebrating the release of *Rena's Promise* twenty years ago. She had just been introduced to me as someone important in the Holocaust community (I won't say who), and her question was no doubt due to the fact that I was an American Gentile—a shiksa no less!—who had just coauthored this book.

Until that moment, it had never occurred to me that the Holocaust was something that should be private or unshared by the rest of the world.

When I was writing the first edition, I was too poor to travel to Poland, and after the book came out in 1995—though I was invited to make the trip to Auschwitz by Peter Matthiessen and the Zen Peacemakers—I did not feel mentally or emotionally ready for the physical reality of the camp. It would take me almost another twenty years before I was ready. In 2012, I finally made that journey, going first to Poprad, Slovakia, where the first transport of 998 girls originated.[1] I arrived on the eve of the seventieth anniversary of the first transport's departure from that train station and found that I was not alone in remembering

---

1. History has always referred to 999 women being on the first transport, but when the lists (there are two: the transport collection list and the camp registration list) were compared, I found that there were actually 998 women, due to a clerical error.

those girls. There were candles and flowers and stones placed under a commemorative plaque that states: *On this site stood the railway station from which, on March 25, 1942, the first transport left for Auschwitz death camp, carrying a thousand Slovak Jewish girls.* The seventieth anniversary of the first transport was an unprecedented event in Slovakia. The government sponsored a memorial train carrying survivors, students, scholars; even the Slovak prime minister, Iveta Radičová, and deputy prime minister, Jan Figel, traveled from Poprad to Oświęcim, Poland, in honor of these girls. In much of Eastern Europe, the history of the first transport is widely recognized, but time and again I meet people in the West who have no idea that the first transport of Jews to Auschwitz was composed entirely of women, as were the first four transports from Slovakia. By April 3, 1942, 4,760 Jewish women had been registered in Auschwitz.

Something else happened the night I arrived at the train station in Poprad, Slovakia. I discovered the family of Adela Gross, and they discovered me. Adela's surviving family made an annual sojourn to Poprad to honor their seventeen-year-old sister and their aunt, who vanished in 1942. On the seventieth anniversary, they finally discovered what happened to Adela in Auschwitz—seventy years later—all because of this book.

Since my journey in 2012, I have found other families whose mothers, sisters, and/or cousins were with Rena on the first transport. One of those family members led me to the original list in the archives of Yad Vashem, in Israel. This extraordinary document lists the 998 names of the first transport and has informed this new expanded edition, which reflects the latest information about the first Jewish women in Auschwitz. Today we know that on the first transport there were 297 teenagers, 521 women in their twenties, 151 women in their thirties, 40 women in their forties, and one woman (Etela Jagerova) who was fifty-eight years old. Was she a mother or grandmother taking the place of her daughter or granddaughter? We may never know for sure; we do know that she died on September 5, 1942.

One of the most astounding revelations of the list is how many of the girls were related, which is why the subtitle of *Rena's*

Promise is *A Story of Sisters in Auschwitz*. This is not simply a story of Rena and her sister Danka. There were many other sisters in camp: Erna and Fela Dranger, also from Tylicz, Poland; and the Schwarzova sisters (Mimi, #1066; Celia, #1064; Regina, #1065)—all three of whom miraculously survived.

Lydia Marek, who helped me find the list through Yad Vashem, is the daughter of Marta Mangelova (#1741), who survived with seven of her cousins all because one of them was appointed a block elder and was able to bring her family into her block and watch over them. There are other amazing instances of survival, but the lives of many of the girls taken from their families in March 1942 ended in Auschwitz.[2]

So why is this history so important today? Why should we pay attention to the history of these young women? What is it to you? I hope that by reading this book you will find the answer to these questions.

Since 1995, many more survivors, like Rena, have written accounts of surviving the Holocaust in order to pass on their stories to future generations. Among these testimonies, Rena's story is still unique for not only the length of time she was in the camps but because she was on the first transport (historians now refer to it as the first mass registered transport).[3]

It is because of the length of time that she was in Auschwitz, that I have chosen to use footnotes rather than endnotes to create a timeline. I used this method when I was organizing Rena's narrative, which was impossible to place in time without any historical context—sometimes the only thing we could go by was the weather to give us an idea of when an event happened. By giving you, the reader, a similar timeline to follow, you will have a

---

2. Though death records for women were not kept accurately and the Auschwitz Death Records were partially destroyed, today we know that more than two hundred women on the first transport died in the first six months in Auschwitz/Birkenau. More than fifty were teenagers. (Source: Yad Vashem and the *Partial Death Records of Auschwitz Death Camp*)

3. Meaning first registered in the "Final Solution of the Jewish question" (Strzelecka, "Women").

historical perspective that Rena did not have while in the camps. I have also done what I could to stay true to the climate conditions at the time—in those spots where there are actual dates—and gathered that data through historical weather records.

TWENTY YEARS AGO, when this book was first written, we did not have access to any of this information. We had Rena's narrative; the work of historians Danuta Czech, John Roth, and Carol Rittner; and little else. Irena Strzelecka, then director of research at the Pánstwowe Muzeum at Auschwitz, had never met anyone from the first transport before she met Rena, and she used parts of Rena's story in her own contribution to *The Tragedy of the Jews of Slovakia*.

Part of that tragedy included being sold into slavery by the Slovakian government to the RHSA (the Reich Main Security Office of *Reichssicherheitshauptamt*) and subsequently disappearing from history, as well as from family. Today we can write these women back into history. We know who they were, and we can honor their memory by remembering their names.

Among the survivors are countless inspiring stories of sisters, cousins, and friends who helped each other to survive. However, this was largely a generation of women who chose to keep quiet about their ordeals, either to protect their children or husbands, or because they simply did not wish to remember more than three harrowing years in the camps. I met one such woman who was married to a rabbi but never told anyone in her synagogue that she was on the first transport to Auschwitz.

There are many reasons Rena chose to share her story, but first and foremost she wanted to honor all those who helped her. It was that altruistic desire that caused me to dedicate myself to her story. Our collaboration agreement started with a handshake, not a legal document, and because I was a poor student with a barely above minimum-wage job in a copy shop, Rena and her husband, John, used to give me a monthly stipend of fifty dollars to help pay for gas in my car. That's how it started. Every Saturday morning, after my regular work week, I would drive one hundred sixty-five miles to their home and listen to Rena's story.

Years after the book came out, I would still drive to visit Rena and her husband for birthdays and holidays or simply because we missed each other.

WHAT RENA WANTED you to know, more than anything, were the many tiny heroic acts that saved her life. Many of the people who helped her were peasants, POWs, and Gentiles. Whether it was the Polish woman who snuck two potatoes and two hard-boiled eggs to her on the Death March or the medicine smuggled to her by fellow prisoners drying the laundry, each gesture was as important to her as the monumental acts by people like Oscar Schindler or the King of Denmark are to history. The potato that the Polish woman furtively slipped to her gave Rena the courage to continue, not only because it gave her physical nourishment but because it gave her spiritual sustenance. That gesture said: I see you. You are hungry. You are human.

By telling her story to us, Rena also hoped that the pain of her experience would lessen. She had many nightmares while we wrote the book and would often call me first thing in the morning remembering some incident she had forgotten to tell me over our weekend together. The pain of her memories never went completely away, but she often remarked that the notes she received from readers did help. Whenever she felt depressed or sad, she would read them with her husband, John. In fact, they would often call me up and read her fan mail aloud, along with the personal notes they wrote back to each person. She always signed each of her letters to readers "Love, Rena," which we've reprinted in the front of the book. These two simple words encapsulate Rena's ethos and what she hoped to accomplish by telling her story: *Rena's Promise* is her letter to you.

One of my favorite stories of Rena happened after she was interviewed by psychology students at Brown University. "I felt so stupid around all of these smart people," she told me. "They asked me how I got over Auschwitz, and I said, 'I had babies.'"

Rena was not stupid. She may have only had an eighth-grade education and have been embarrassed by her "peasant" status among more educated individuals, but she knew that the only way to survive genocide is to create life and to replace hate with love. That is her legacy to us.

I was at her deathbed when Rena passed away in 2006 and delivered one of the eulogies at her funeral. I miss her almost every day of my life, and wherever I am in the world, I collect pink stones to place on her grave when I visit. She loved the color pink.

I still hear her voice in my heart and my head, and I hope that you can hear her voice as you read her story. Meeting Rena, writing her story for her, made me a better person. It did not matter who you were, Rena was always the first person to defend the downtrodden. She knew how the tiniest act of kindness acknowledges another's humanity, and that is why compassion is so important.

"WHAT IS IT TO ME?" I repeated the question and smiled at the woman standing in front of me, all those years ago. "I am a woman. I am a human being."

Rena's favorite photo of us together,
taken in the room where she told me her story.

∞

In 2011, the Rena's Promise Foundation was created as a promise to create a more ecumenical world unhindered by prejudice, racism, or hatred. For more information about the Rena's Promise Foundation and to help carry Rena's message, please visit Rena's Promise, www.RenasPromise .com. There you can find an interactive timeline about women in Auschwitz, our blog chronicling historical anniversaries, and information about the Promise Project, which is dedicated to learning more about what happened to the first women in Auschwitz.

PROLOGUE

I touch the scar on my left forearm, just below the elbow. I had the tattoo surgically removed. There were so many people who didn't know and so many questions: "What do those numbers mean?" "Is that your address?" "Is that your phone number?"

What was I supposed to say? "That was my name for three years and forty-one days"?

One day a kind doctor offered to remove it for me. "This is not charity," he assured me. "It is the least I can do as an American Jew. You were there. I was not."

So I chose to have the questions excised from my arm, but not my mind—that can never be erased. The piece of skin the doctor surgically removed rests in a jar of formaldehyde, which has turned the flesh to an eerie green. The tattoo has probably faded by now; I haven't checked. I need no reminders. I know who I am.

I know what I was.

I was on the first transport to Auschwitz. I was number 1716.

—Rena Kornreich Gelissen,
January 1994

Rena's passage through wartime Europe.

RENA

IT IS A CRISP Saturday morning in January, and my car wends its way from the foothills of North Carolina toward where the Blue Ridge Mountains crest a blue-gray horizon, like waves caught in time. As I come around the last of the hairpin curves and pass the eastern divide, my breath catches. Sunlight shatters a cloud bank above the valley of Asheville, like a good omen.

I love this drive. Without fail it always rejuvenates my spirit and my heart. That is a good thing because I am about to make this journey every weekend for the next four months, and the place I am heading will be anything but light. I am going to meet one of the few survivors from the first transport of Jews and the first transport of women to Auschwitz, a woman who after almost fifty years of silence has finally decided to tell her story.

I have only spoken to Rena twice, and it seems we have been putting off this meeting for months now, but with the holidays finally over and the snow storms finally passed, we have no more excuses. My thoughts tumble across one another; I am uneasy about the task I'm about to undertake. Helping Rena tell her story without either of us drowning in the undertow of painful memories would be a tall task for a psychologist—I am merely a writer.

However, I have my reasons for wanting to work with Rena. My family was Quaker and hid slaves just north of the Mason-Dixon Line, before and during the Civil War; my grandmother was the first restaurant owner to openly welcome members of the NAACP when they came to town to promote civil rights. I grew

1

up knowing that if my family had been in Europe during World War II, we would have risked our lives to save the Jews and probably anyone else targeted by the Nazis. Over the past year, I have volunteered at a hospice grief-counseling center, where I helped children who had lost parents or significant caregivers write a book about grief. Now I am about to attempt a similar story on a much larger scale. That is, if Rena likes me. I am secretly afraid that I will come up wanting in her eyes because I am not Jewish, because I am not Polish, because I am American, because I am young. Maybe I'm not the best person for this job.

The first time we spoke on the phone I was cooking pierogies and kielbasa for dinner.

"Are you Polish?" she asked excitedly.

"No," I told her. "I just love pierogi. We used to eat them at an all-night diner called The Kiev, on the Lower East Side in New York."

"I think I'd like that place!" We bonded over pierogi.

RENA'S HOUSE LIES in a small valley, with a pasture full of grazing cows behind it. Trussed across the horizon, hemming us in on all sides, are the voluptuous curves of the southern mountains. In the driveway, I organize my thoughts and my book bag before stepping out of the car—it has taken me just under two hours to get here from where I live in North Carolina's Piedmont. The air is cooler up here, but the sun is strong and the wind, though it has a nip of winter, has none of its cruelty.

Inside I am greeted warmly by Rena's husband, John. We shake hands and he calls out, "Mama! A beautiful lady is here to see you!"

Rena bustles down the hall toward the kitchen, a tiny dynamo of energy. She is not at all what I expect. She is lively, cheerful, chatty. "Papa, invite her to sit down. Oh, you're so tall!" She smiles up at me.

"I am? I'm the short one in my family."

"I'm the tall one in mine." Her eyes twinkle.

"Heather, come see Rena's linen closets!" John waves to me to follow him down the hallway.

"Jan, no!" She starts to reprimand him in Dutch, then, for my benefit, adds in English, "You're embarrassing me."

"Mama, you spent all day yesterday straightening them. At least let Heather see your hard work. How else will she know?"

"That's not true. They're always this neat," she says with pride.

Showing me the beautiful linens she has collected over the years, she says quietly, "I didn't have any linens or heirlooms from my family. So I collected my own at yard sales. I have stayed up til three in the morning scrubbing stains out that somebody else thought were impossible to remove."

"There. Now Heather knows how neat and clean you are. Heather, are you going to clean out your linen closets when we come to visit?" John teases.

"I don't have linen closets," I tell them and joke, "You'll be lucky if I dust."

Rena takes my arm. "Don't you dare clean for me! I clean too much. When I get nervous I can't stop."

Our banter is light-hearted and friendly. There is no ice to break. It is like we have known each other forever. And this meeting, which was supposed to be probationary, quickly turns into acceptance. Within thirty minutes of meeting Rena I know I will do whatever I can to help her, and within the same amount of time, she has accepted me into her heart, for the rest of her life.

"I just want my children to read my story someday," she says. "I can't tell it to them. I tried, but it's too hard." And that first day I know that if nothing else I will do that for her—she deserves that much.

IN THE BASEMENT, where we will spend many hours over the next year exhuming the past and embracing ghosts, there is a gas fire flickering. The room has a rosy glow from the pink sheers she has hung over the windows. From the pink room with its fire, she leads me into an adjoining room, where the family photos are on display. The wall is divided into two sections: the Gelissen family, from Holland, on the left and the Kornreich family, from Poland, on the right. In the middle are Rena and John's wedding photo and pictures of their children. Rena tells me that she wouldn't have any prewar photos if her eldest sister, Gertrude, hadn't immigrated to America before the war.

Her mother's wedding portrait reveals a beautiful woman with doe brown eyes. A Victorian lace collar wraps high up her neck and her hair is piled so gracefully on top of her head that one cannot tell she's wearing a wig. "Hi, Mama . . ." Rena kisses her hand, touches the face in the photo.

"What was her name?" I ask.

"Sara."

Next to Mama is a black-and-white photo of the Kornreich family long before the war. "You know, when we moved to North Carolina, I thought to myself, I've had my number removed, no one here knows me, I can leave it all behind," says Rena. "That's when I decided I'm not going to talk about it ever again. It's not worth it."

"So why did you tell Corrine?" I name our mutual friend.

"I don't know!" Rena laughs. "It was the strangest thing." Her eyes widen as she recounts the story that led to this meeting. "I dialed a wrong number but the voice on the other end of the line

Mama

From left to right: Danka, Mama, Zosia, Papa, Rena

sounded familiar. 'Is this Corrine from the tennis club?' I say. 'Is this Rena?' she asks."

Rena does the voices, acting out their conversation so it seems it's occurring in front of me.

"I was calling somebody else but got her instead. We both thought it was so funny, because she had been out of town for several weeks. 'How're you doing?' I say. 'I haven't seen you in a while.'

"'I've been going through a tough time,' she tells me.

"She said something about her past being painful and the next thing I know I'm saying, 'I know all about that. I was in Auschwitz.' She was shocked and asked me all about it, so I told her I'd been writing my story for fifty years in my head but I couldn't get it on paper. 'I need someone with kind eyes to sit across from me, listen to the whole thing and help me write it down.' And Corinne says, 'I know just the person.'

"And here you are! All because of a wrong number." Rena pats my knee. "Did I tell you what I thought the very first time we spoke on the phone?" I shake my head. "That you eating pierogi was a sign that you're the right person for my story." She laughs and I join her. Rena has a surprisingly happy nature and bright demeanor. Even her eyes smile.

❧

ORIGINALLY, I THOUGHT all I needed to do to write Rena's story was tape record our interviews and then transcribe the tapes. It was a good plan: She would talk. I would listen with my eyes, my ears, and the prickling of my skin. I would record and write it all down for her. Interviewing Rena about her story was not an easy task though.

I thought she would tell me her story from the beginning of the war and go to the end, from point A to point B. But memory does not move through time in a linear way. It plays hopscotch and jump rope. Point A was not so simple to locate, and somewhere during our year of excavating, sharing, and writing, point B became point Z. Rena had a magnificent memory, but it was richly and profusely associative. A mishmash of vignettes cascaded down on me, one after another. On the surface, there did not seem to be any organizing principle. The fantastic rate at which she spoke and her thick accent did not help matters. I had my work cut out for me, and the plan to transcribe the recordings would not work. Early on, I made the mistake of sending a few pages of direct transcription to Rena. She was very upset: "I don't speak such bad English!"

And so I learned how difficult it is to reproduce an oral storyteller's voice to the written page. How could I make it sound like Rena was speaking to you while you were reading? I had to do more than type—I had to find a way to convey Rena's spirit as she revealed it to me through the syncopated rhythms of her speech and gestures, the evanescence of her voice.

The most powerful memories and the most painful were often the shortest—thirty seconds before her narrative became nothing but tears. Like an emotional archaeologist, I dug gently around those memories. Part of that digging took me to the historical records that the Nazis kept, where I was able to find the actual dates for many of Rena's experiences. I spent weeks going through the archives at Wake Forest University and delving into the two volumes of Danuta Czech's *Auschwitz Chronicle*, looking for the cold details and corroborating evidence in official documentation. Finding them. . . . Those moments were chilling. Silence engulfed me. I sat at my cubicle in the Wake Forest library, stared at the Nazis' records, and felt the world stop. Time and again, I had to face the reality that my little Rena—the tiny dynamo who knew every person at the grocery store in her town by name and who greeted strangers on the street—had details so accurate that there was no doubt she had witnessed the systematic annihilation of women and children for three years and forty-one days. How did she do it? How did she come through it all and still have a heart?

These details would help me map her years in prison. Rena had no access to a calendar, and most survivors' stories chronicle their last few months or last year, at most, in the camps. I had found no other story like Rena's. So, finding a way to place her memories into a historical context was essential not only because the documentary record supported Rena's account with uncanny accuracy but because it gave her story a timeline she had never actually had access to.

What are *not* recorded in the historical record are the remarkable acts of humanity, by Jews and Gentiles, by Germans and Poles, which Rena not only witnessed but of which she was the recipient. Her written story, begun as an autobiographical gift for her children, evolved into a testament to the humanity and the courage of all those who helped her survive. She wanted to acknowledge each and every person.

∾

ON THAT FIRST DAY on a sunny weekend in January, we settled on the couch in front of the fire and I quietly clicked on my tape recorder.

"I have a lot of books on the Holocaust." Rena jumped up. "You want to see them?"

She was nervous.

"Let's talk first." I used a deep calm voice to soothe her nerves, the same voice I might use with a child woken by nightmares in the middle of the night.

She looked at me warily. Sat back down reluctantly, smoothed her pants, straightened the doily on the coffee table in front of her. Straightened it again. I felt like a dentist about to extract a tooth.

Her eyes were wide open when she asked, "Where do you want me to start?"

Tylicz

PAPA BELIEVED THAT a woman's place was to bear children, keep a kosher kitchen, and know how to pray, but Mama was determined that we know Hebrew. "I'm not going to have my girls embarrassed like I was, when they get married in temple, because they can't read from the prayer book."

She made such a fuss that in order to placate her, the elders of the synagogue decided that in this one instance they would allow me to attend the *cheder*, the Hebrew school for boys, after my regular school day. Mama paid the *melamed*, the teacher, with eggs, butter, and milk so that I could sit on one side of the room, while the boys sat on the other side, so in that way I learned Hebrew, and after class I would take the lessons home to teach Danka.

∞

"OY VEY! WHAT am I doing?" Rena exclaims suddenly, jerking us both back to the present. "I'm starting in the middle without the beginning!" She shakes her head. "I think you know everything already."

"It's okay." I pat her leg and smile. The room is bathed in pink light, and the warmth between us is tangible as Rena begins her story again, more slowly this time, backtracking to her beginnings. . . .

∞

8

WHEN MAMA WAS in her late thirties and Papa was in his late forties, I was born. It was 1920, and our family was split between the two children of their youth and the two children of their later years. Gertrude was the eldest and sixteen years older than me. Then there was Zosia, who was two years younger than Gertrude. And last there was Danka, the baby, who was born when I was just two years old.

Papa was very strict, but oh how he loved our baby. He cradled her in his arms when she was an infant and held her, rocking back and forth while *davening.* He had the most marvelous voice, and his prayers filled our house with blessings.

When I looked into Danka's cradle with Mama, I had never seen anything so delicate, so small. Oh, how I loved her little feet, her tiny hands. She was just a few months old when she got the croup though. It was awful. She coughed and coughed all day and all night; then there was no more coughing. The silence was terrible. Mama began to lament. I had never seen her so distraught.

She covered Danka's head with a white sheet and her baby blanket. The stillness in our house was so sad. . . . We had lost our baby. I wanted to wipe away Mama's tears, and so I prayed to God in heaven to bring my baby sister back to Mama. I prayed and prayed to our Lord to bring us the baby back.

Then there was a wail from beneath the blanket. First there was terror—a *gayst,* a ghost, an apparition, something unknowable had entered our house. But the wailing did not stop. Mama ran to Danka's side, threw back the blanket, and there she was, red-faced and breathing and not at all happy about being covered up.

Our baby was alive!

No wonder Papa held her and prayed. She was a blessing, an answer from God. And from that time on, even though I was just two years older than Danka, I was the big one and Danka was the little one. She was always more fragile, and Mama fussed over her because she had come back from death's portal. "Watch the little one," Mama would say. "Take care of the baby." It was my favorite job.

I WAS JUST five years old when Andrzej Garbera pushed a wagon over the mud pies Danka and I had made. Needless to say all our hard work was ruined, and being a boy, he didn't care in the least, preferring instead to laugh at our misfortune. His sole purpose, as a boy, seemed to be to torment us girls. He used to throw snowballs at us on our way to school, but I would defend my sister and throw snowballs right back. I had very good aim. "Don't you hurt my sister, Andrzej!" I threatened. Then one day he was not throwing snowballs or being a general irritation anymore; instead he just said, "Hi."

So I said hi back, and that was the beginning of Andrzej and me. . . .

Of course, we were Orthodox, and my parents were very strict about keeping company with boys, but Frania—who was a Gentile, like Andrzej—was one of my best friends. She often came over to our house to play, and her parents let her celebrate *Sukkot*, the harvest festival, with our family. We'd build an open-air shelter that we decorated with little baskets with chestnuts or apples in them, colorful rings of paper, and nuts from the roof, which was made of tree branches. Then at Christmastime, Mama would let us go over to Frania's house and help her family decorate their Christmas tree. You see, in Tylicz [sounds like "tillage"] nobody looked down on anyone else. We just all got along. It wasn't hard. We had more in common than we had differences. We were all Polish, and we all lived in the same place, and we all shopped in the marketplace. There was no prejudice. We had an ecumenical community.

There was only one thing that really made us stand out from the Gentiles in our village and that was our hair—Papa had long, curling ear locks and a long beard; Mama had a wig. That was Orthodox tradition. When Zosia got married, she begged Papa to let her keep a little bit of her hair. She cried and cried when she was shaved, and I questioned why married women had to shave their heads. "It is a promise not to be attractive to other men," Mama told us, "an acknowledgment of commitment to one's husband."

Every few weeks Mama would take off her wig and I would shave her head in the washbasin, as was our custom. With Papa's clippers I guided the teeth across her scalp, careful not to catch the delicate skin with the sharp teeth of the clippers. Mama would close her eyes as if in meditation, and I'd take that moment to study the serenity in her face. Then I'd wipe her scalp as if it were porcelain china. It was so clean and shiny, soft as a baby's.

She would let her eyes remain shut for just a few seconds after I was done, then she'd call out to Papa so I could shave his head. As they changed places their eyes would lock together for an instant and Mama would smile affectionately.

I dreamt of the day that I would have my head shaved as a solemn vow to my husband. It was a rite of passage that we feared yet longed for. Still, like Zosia, I worried about being ugly. To lose one's hair was not such a wonderful thing, but to be married, that was what we yearned for, to be married like Mama and Papa.

Danka, Dina Dranger, and Rena
in Krynica with bear.

Every time Papa passed Mama he reached out to touch her. His hand would fall between her shoulder blades and drift across the middle of her back, and sometimes, when he thought we weren't looking, he would pat her behind.

THE MARKETPLACE WAS the center of our world. From there everything was down hill. The kosher butcher and the Gentiles' butcher were on the avenue, as well as the cheese shop and the city hall. And near that center is where the Garbera family lived, right next door to our best friends, Erna and Fela Dranger. Erna and Fela were Danka's and my best Jewish friends. Frania was my best Gentile friend. We spent many evenings at the Dranger sisters' house, with their cousin Dina, who was best friends with Danka. We played dominoes or sat in the parlor and confided our dreams to each other. There was one dream I never shared though.

One cold winter evening Danka and I stepped outside to go home and there was Andrzej. "I've been waiting to bring you both home. The hill is very icy and I wouldn't want you to fall and hurt yourselves."

I thought it odd, but oh well, he was a nice boy, and it was slippery, so we went with Andrzej. And after that night it became a habit for Andrzej to wait outside of Erna and Fela's and walk us home, even after the thaw. One spring night as we ambled home, for no reason at all he took my hand and slowed down. Danka was far ahead of us.

"There's no ice on the road tonight, Andrzej," I told him.

"No, there isn't." He didn't let go of my hand.

The sound of water dripping into the stone well drew us toward the side of the lane. He slowed down, as if he were looking at something, and then he murmured my name very softly. "Rena?"

"Yes?" I looked up into his face, and there, beside the village well, Andrzej Garbera stole a kiss from my lips. There was no walking from that point on; I ran the whole way home.

Mama was waiting for me at the door of our farmhouse with her lantern lit and bobbing in the dark.

"Rena?" I can still hear her calling my name. "Rena!"

"I'm coming, Mama," I call back.

"Where have you been? It's late. Come inside."

"I was studying at Erna and Fela's," I answer, wiping my feet.

"Studying, eh?" She pushes my hair back from my face, looking into my eyes. I wonder if she can read the truth in them. "Go get ready for bed."

"Yes, Mama." I kiss her cheek. She smells like challah and vanilla.

Admiring myself in front of the mirror, I brush my hair for one hundred strokes while imagining that Andrzej is stooping for a kiss. Again and again I remember how his lips felt on mine. My heart races.

"I have been kissed." I confide this enormous secret to my reflection.

We blush.

With my nightdress on I crawl between cool, clean cotton sheets and wait for Mama to come tuck me in. "Rena, you are practically glowing. What have you been up to?"

"Nothing, Mama. It's just such a beautiful night." I smile in the darkness.

"Sweet sleep." She kisses me good night.

A tiny pit of sadness that my secret can never be shared overcomes me. I have grown up going to public school with Gentiles and being taught by Catholic teachers despite the fact that we are strict Orthodox Jews. Andrzej and I have played together since we were children, but he is still a Gentile. Nothing can come of his kiss, I know that.

∞

"I KNEW THAT." Rena stops speaking. Her eyes are damp and a small smile plays shyly on her lips, like she is still that girl remembering her first kiss in front of her bedroom mirror.

A few weeks later, as she is telling me her story, the grandfather clock chimes and her body jerks. She looks shocked to see me there, then says, "There were no clocks in Auschwitz."

This is how Rena tells her story. Through a warp of past and present, with threads woven so tightly that memory becomes her "now." She gets a distant look in her eyes and forgets I am there.

As her voice changes, her verbs dissolve from past into present tense and back again, wavering between the worlds of "was" and "is," as if there were no definitive separation between the two. And perhaps there isn't.

Sometimes, it is only my presence that brings her back to the room we are sitting in, with the strands of memories as delicate as hand-blown glass hanging in the air.

THAT FIRST DAY, Rena talks for six hours straight. The sun is setting over the mountains when John calls down the stairs, "You ladies want some tea?" I am exhausted, eager for a break. But Rena is full of vigor and could probably talk all night. Energized by our first day together, she chats merrily away as John serves tea. In what will become our tradition, we eat pierogies and kielbasa for dinner. After dessert, she finally pulls out everything she wanted to show me earlier: a collection of personal notebooks, written in Polish; historical books on the Holocaust; a pamphlet in Polish on the death march from the museum at Auschwitz. Rena and her husband tell me stories of their lives together, until John notices me yawning.

"Mama, this beautiful lady needs her beauty rest." Rena jumps up, apologizing for keeping me awake. The couch we've been sitting on all day is pulled out into a bed, and like parents they practically tuck me in. The fire glows. My eyes are weary but my mind races. In front of me are disturbing images from Peter Hellman's *The Auschwitz Album.* I can hear Rena's voice as I gaze at his visual narrative. *This is real,* a voice in my head says. *Rena is real.* It is after midnight before I finally drift off to a deep but dreamless sleep.

THE NEXT MORNING, with the sun shining in through rose-colored curtains and coffee steaming in front of me, Rena confesses, "I couldn't sleep at all last night. I kept thinking about Andrzej."

I click on the tape recorder and squeeze the china cup in my hands, as a reminder to hang on because once Rena starts talking, there is no stopping her.

"I used to have this dream in Holland, after the war, every night. . . ."

Danka is in danger. Sometimes they order her to jump, sometimes they are pushing her into the pit. Always I am standing there watching.

"Danka!" I scream, running past them, grabbing her hand just before she plummets out of reach. Standing on the edge of an abyss, her fate completely dependent upon what strength I have left, I stare into the void below us that they forced us to dig. How did we ever dig a hole so deep that there is no bottom?

"Rena, help me." Her voice is muted by our palpitating hearts.

"Please, don't let go of me."

"I won't," I assure her. My muscles quiver. Every twitch and spasm threatens to betray my promise. My body tenses. This is no dream. "Don't give up, Danka." Shuddering, my nails dig into her flesh, determined to cling onto life.

From behind us Andrzej appears. He takes our hands in his powerful grip and lifts her effortlessly out of the pit. I am so relieved to see him that I cannot speak. He smiles at me, vanishing before my eyes. "Andrzej!" I call out his name. There is no answer.

He is gone.

"If you die before me"—I hear Danka's voice—"no one is going to cry more than me. But if I die before you, even if there's no one left in the world to mourn for me, I know that you will weep over my grave."

Panting like a wild animal trapped by hunters, I wake. Chilled by internal night fears, uncertain of where I am or who I am, I struggle against the sheets entangling my arms and legs. I search the night table for a candle to light, but the room remains dark.

My name has been erased from my mind. I am a number once more.

The room around us is a bright contrast to the darkness her dream conjures. My coffee has grown cold and I am at a loss for words. Under the scar on her forearm where her number used to be, I touch a small dot of gray-blue ink still embedded in her skin.

"That was the bottom part of the one," she says. It is the color of faded black. . . .

∞

ANDRZEJ WAS THREE years older than me and had started attending high school in Krynica, a larger town about seven kilometers away, so we only saw each other rarely. I was thirteen when I met him in the marketplace again. I was so happy to see him that we talked about everything—our favorite books, our favorite subjects in school. I made sure I maintained the proper distance away from him at all times, just as Mama had instructed, but I forgot to watch the time. It was almost dark when a member of the synagogue passed by on his way to temple and saw us. You see, it was prohibited for me to speak with a Gentile boy, or any boy for that matter, without a chaperone. Oh, the embarrassment when an elder of the synagogue reprimanded me in front of Andrzej and threatened to tell Papa! Andrzej's face fell—our happy, innocent moment shattered by this harsh reality.

I hurried down the hill alone to face the wrath of my father.

Andrzej Garbera

Mama wept and Papa sternly forbade me to have anything to do with Andrzej ever again. After that I avoided Andrzej Garbera. I did not speak with him when I saw him in the marketplace, but we did still exchange glances, and those glances said more than any words. For two years that was how it was between us, and then one night there was Andrzej Garbera in front of Erna's house, asking me to walk back down the hill of our youth. I made sure no one from the synagogue was passing by, then slipped outside to join him.

"I am leaving for Krakow to join the military," he said.

I nodded but did not dare to speak—I had promised my parents.

"I am going to think of a way to write you without your parents knowing."

I turned away so he could not kiss me again, even though I wanted to feel his lips on my cheek. When I turned back, he was gone.

A few weeks later, Andrzej's sister met me in the marketplace, and when no one was watching, Hania slipped me a letter from Krakow. It took me quite a few days to get up the courage to write him back, but finally I answered, and from that time on either Hania or his mother would post my letters to Andrzej so that no one in the village would know we were corresponding.

I worked for two summers in Krynica as an apprentice to a seamstress and dated a few Jewish boys. We went to the picture shows and socials, but no one caught my heart. I was about to turn seventeen and was starting to think about a future. Whom should I marry? Then, as if reading my mind, Andrzej wrote:

Dear Rena,

I just got my officer's stripes and am no longer living in the barracks on the base. I am now entitled to an apartment in the city. I've enclosed enough money for the train to Krakow.

Would you come to marry me? You can do anything you want to with the Jewish religion. You can bring up the children in the Jewish faith. I will buy you a silver candelabra so that you may light the candles on Friday night in our home just like your mother. If this is not acceptable to your parents, I will have myself circumcised and accept the Jewish religion. I have loved you since the first day I saw you when we were children. If you love me as well, why should we not be happy? If you would come to be my wife I would be the happiest man in the whole of Poland.[1]

In so many ways, Andrzej's proposal was a dream come true. How I longed to marry and raise a family, but marriage to him was an impossibility. And I had to make my heart hard to write back:

Dear Andrzej,

My parents do not want you to convert to Judaism, even that would not be enough. You must be born Jewish. I thought you understood the strict rules of our faith and our people. I'm sorry if I have led you on in any way. For me to marry a Gentile would destroy my parents. They would mourn for me as if I had died and then treat me as if I were no longer their daughter. It is impossible for you and me to be together. Despite my feelings for you, I could not bear never seeing my family again. Here is your money back. I am sorry, but I cannot marry you.

Love, Rena

Of course, I didn't even discuss Andrzej's letter with my parents. It would have been devastating to them if they knew we were corresponding, let alone that he had proposed. For my parents to approve of my husband, he had to be Jewish, preferably Orthodox, and I would never have done anything to upset my family.

∞

ONLY ONE FAMILY had a radio in Tylicz. In the afternoon they would open the window and everyone would gather outside to hear the news of the world and listen while Adolf Hitler made strange and fervid speeches threatening the Poles, the Jews, and anyone not Aryan. It was 1938, and Mama and Papa were concerned about the sudden annexation of Slovakia with Germany; they both had brothers who lived just across the border, in Bardejov. I was much more concerned about Andrzej's secret proposal. Then Germany

---

1. Though the letters from Andrzej were lost in the war, Rena seemed able to recount them word for word because she had read them so often.

and Russia made a pact between them and all of Poland trembled with fear. We had been divided too many times not to take the threat of Stalin and Hitler seriously, so Poland called up its young men to join the army and defend our country. Many of the boys in our village joined the army: Tolek, Alex, Andrzej. They were part of our defense, and we were so proud of them.

Then, on September 1, 1939, Germany invaded Poland, and there was no more innocence in our lives. Andrzej was not captured. He and the other boys snuck home and joined the underground because Tylicz had immediately been transformed from a sleepy little border town into a strategic position within our occupied homeland. German border guards, watchdogs, and guns were everywhere, and the Nuremberg Laws were put into effect. A man named Joseph, from the synagogue, was appointed as head of a new organization, the *Judenrat*, or Jewish Council, and was ordered to deliver the names of all the young Jewish people living in Tylicz. Within the first week of the Nazi invasion, we were forced to wear armbands at all times, with the Star of David embroidered on them in blue. We could no longer buy food from Gentiles, hire Gentiles to work for us, or cross the Slovakian border (where they were still allowed to trade goods with Gentiles). Any Jew or Gentile disobeying German law, it was proclaimed, would be considered a traitor and punished by death. Danka and I, along with other young Jewish men and women, were assigned to clean the army quarters, polish shoes, scrub floors, and do anything else the Germans ordered them to do.

For years a poor Gentile woman had come to our house every Sabbath morning to light the fire and reheat the meal Mama had prepared the day before. Under these new regulations she was no longer allowed into our house or to do any work for us. She cried when she came to say good-bye, and we, along with the other Jews in Tylicz, in order not to break Orthodox law, had to eat cold food and live in a cold house because we could not light a fire on the Sabbath. Papa and the other Jewish farmers, unable to hire anyone to help, resorted to working overtime to harvest their crops. Danka and I worked from first light to late in the night, dividing our chores between working for the Germans and on our own farm.

Fortunately, there was no law against trading services for goods, so we used Zosia's sewing to trade for butter, cheese, and flour. There were still Gentile farmers who would do business with Papa too because we were their neighbors and Tylicz was a close-knit community. The German laws were not respected; they were only feared.

Many of the boys from the village who had joined the army returned home, but Zosia's husband was not among them. We had heard nothing from Nathan. Then, in October, a card with a Russian postmark came in the mail. Zosia handed it to Mama, folded her hands in front of her face, as if she were saying the Sabbath prayer, and waited for the news.

Mama cleared her throat: "Dear Family. It is very cold where I am. I love you all. Nathan."

We all stared at the floor. My sister hugged her children and sobbed. "He must be in Siberia."

Nothing was going our way. And when Herschel, Zosia's young son, became very ill and needed an operation, we were at

From left to right: Rena, Herschel,
Mama, Zosia, Ester, Danka

a loss for what to do. The new regulations did not allow Jews, not even children, to see doctors. However, because of the annexation of Slovakia by Germany, the Slovakian Jews were being treated far less harshly than the Polish Jews. They were still allowed to work and earn money; they weren't being forced to wear stars; and most important for Herschel, they could be treated by doctors.

"If we can get across the border, it shouldn't be too difficult to get to Uncle Jacob Schützer's in Bardejov. At least Herschel can get treatment there," Zosia told Mama and Papa. "Who knows where Nathan is now or if he will ever be able to return home? In Slovakia I can work in Uncle Jacob's dress shop until I find work of my own, and when I'm settled, I'll send for little Ester."

"I will send a note to my brother that you are coming," Mama said, "and pray for your safety and joy." Zosia was able to get to Uncle Jacob's with the help of Gentile farmers trading in the marketplace in Slovakia. She wrote home every week, sending her letters with our Gentile friends, who still crossed the border to trade. Herschel's operation went well, one letter said. Our prayers had been answered.

A few weeks later Zosia wrote that she had been offered a position as a housekeeper in Bratislava. Bratislava was all the way across Slovakia, on the border with Austria. Mama fretted about the distance. Gertrude had already moved to America and now Zosia was moving too? She clung to Danka and me. "It is best for Zosia to move," she assured us.

"Don't worry, Mama," we comforted her. "You have us. We will take care of you."

DANKA AND I WORKED LONG, hard days and often stayed up as late as four-thirty in the morning because we had also taken over Zosia's sewing business. I was becoming well-known as the local seamstress. One Sunday, while I was busy working at my sewing machine, there was a knock at the window, and I saw an Austrian officer standing there, smiling at me.

"I am Officer Joksch," he said. "Could you make two pillowcases for me?" I was shocked. It was a question and not a command.

A week later he came to pick them up, complimented me on my craftsmanship, ordered two more, and handed me a few coins for my work.

I ran through the house to show Mama the coins. "An Austrian officer paid me for the pillowcases!"

Mama stared at the money in wonderment. "You are a miracle, Rena. Even in all this hardship, you are able to inspire kindness in those who would normally treat us with cruelty." She hugged me and hid the coins in the teapot where all of our valuables were stored. We had not foreseen protecting our most valuable asset though—the Talmud.

In early November it was ordered that the Torah, the Talmud, and all the Jewish holy books be brought to the temple. We sat on the steps of our farmhouse waiting and praying as Papa took our most precious possession to the Germans. We waited and waited. The smell of burning paper and leather filled the air. We dared not leave the house to see what was happening though. Finally, a forlorn figure appeared on the hill and came toward our home. Papa? We barely recognized him. He had no more ear locks and no more beard. Mama wept to see him so. "Papa, what happened?" she wailed.

"The Germans ordered us to put our books in a pile and line up," Papa told us. In a daze, he and the other men moved alongside one another and stood before the mound of kindling and manuscripts.

One of the officers announced, "It is against our policy for any Jew to grow these ridiculous curls or beards. Every man in this line must be shaved or shot!" Brandishing scissors like street-hardened youths carrying switchblades, the soldiers ordered the men to remove their hats and then systematically began to sever their ear locks and beards.

Then a soldier lit a torch, and in moments angry sparks began to turn pages into cinders. "You are no longer allowed to pray or to enter the temple for any reason whatsoever!" The latest list of proclamations was read over the raging pyre. "It is against the law to worship on the Jewish Sabbath and to light candles on Friday night." Helpless, Papa and the others watched our faith devoured by flames.

∾

A FEW DAYS LATER, Officer Hans Joksch's familiar voice called from outside my sewing room window. I handed him the pillowcases he'd requested, careful to keep my eyes lowered in respect and nodded politely to another officer standing next to him.

"Rena, invite us into your home," Officer Joksch said.

His request turned everything upside down. Who was I to say no? He endangered our lives by entering our house. I could not help but suspect him of some other motive, but who would have thought what his true reason would be?

I ran through the house to warn Mama and Papa. Clasping her hands over her eyes, Mama prayed, "Good Lord, my Lord, protect us." Then, taking her place in the parlor, she composed herself with unnerving stillness.

Officer Joksch and his friend were very polite and casually asked, "Have you a gramophone in the house?"

"No." I spoke quickly, too quickly.

"That is too bad."

Officer Joksch looked around our parlor. "I bet you are a good dancer, Rena."

"So-so." I stared at the floor.

"Well, if my friend whistles something would you dance with me?"

Mama and Papa's faces were ashen.

His friend started to whistle a tango and Officer Joksch held out his hand to me. I tried not to tremble as I took it. We began to shuffle awkwardly around the parlor. I was so nervous, dancing in front of my parents, wondering what he would do if I missed even a step, but I tried to look as if I were having a good time.

His friend whistled until he ran out of breath and spittle, and Officer Joksch said, "You dance beautifully, Rena."

I could barely get the words *Danke schön* out of my mouth, it was so dry.

"Nein, nein, Fraulein. Thank you. You have made this day truly memorable to me and I will never forget your good faith." He bade us good evening—without shaking hands, of course, but still very nicely paid for the pillowcases, and left.

Mama wept quietly, wringing her hands. Papa did not speak. Oh, my God, how I was shaking. I don't know why I didn't stumble or how my knees didn't just buckle completely under me. Then it occurred to me that maybe I was a good dancer.

∞

IT WAS SABBATH, and standing in front of the mirror with my dirndl on, I began to plait my long hair into a single braid down my back. Even if we couldn't go to temple we tried to carry on as if everything were normal because in our hearts we could still worship God.

Despite what had been decreed, some of the elders of the synagogue had decided to meet anyway, but no sooner had the prayers begun than soldiers barged in.

"You people are disobeying orders and for this you will be punished."

One of the officers barked commands, pushing the men against a wall. "Today we will teach you a lesson! And today's lesson shall be that every time you meet, one of you will be taken down to the river and shot. Take him!"

Two soldiers dragged a man out the door with them, and that man was my father.

"Rena! Rena!" Joseph, the head of the *Judenrat*, yelled as he ran toward our house. Running to the window, my hands tangled in my braid, I leaned out to ask what was wrong.

"They have your father and they're going to kill him!" Joseph's voice quaked. "Run to the river and stop them before it's too late!"

My feet flew down the steps before he could breathe another word. "Fly, Rena!" His voice chased me down the road.

I was barefoot. My hair was not braided. I didn't even have on my white armband with the blue Star of David, which I was always supposed to wear. This was how I ran down the dirt road toward the river—my hair heavy against my back, falling in my face, clinging to my neck—racing across the Carpathian Hills, every step a prayer to our Lord to save my father. I did not feel the stones cutting into my flesh. I did not see the trail of blood in the dirt as I ran.

There were many bodies found along the river in the mornings, because to kill a Jew was no crime, so I knew exactly where to run.

What had Joseph been thinking, though, sending me to save Papa?

I don't care to admit this, but the truth is, at that moment all I could think about was having to tell Mama, *I stood right there and watched them kill Papa—there was nothing I could do.* The thought of her pain-stricken face was more than I could bear, so while I ran I tried to come up with a plan that would save me from having to tell Mama that Papa was dead.

I could see them across the field as soon as I broke free of the trees lining the path to the river. Papa was standing against the fence as two soldiers raised their rifles level with his heart.

"Stop!" I screamed, jumping in front of him. "This is my father. If you're going to kill him, you're going to have to kill me too." I was thinking to myself, They won't kill me; I'm a young girl. I was so naive.

"*Scheiss Jude!* Filthy dog!" they hissed.

I dared not look in Papa's face, so instead I chose to look in the eyes of his would-be assassins. "I'm not leaving my father," I told them firmly.

"Look at this girl!" They laughed in my face. "She thinks we won't kill her and her dirty Jew of a father."

I turned around and pointed to Papa's white shirt. "Look how white the collar of his shirt is. He's not dirty. How dare you tell my father he's filthy!" I didn't understand what they meant. "My mother cleaned and ironed this shirt herself." I showed them his clean collar.

"You are too funny!" They laughed, cocking their guns. "You want to say a prayer, little Jew girl, before you die?" I blinked into the barrel of their shotgun. It was strange to think that such a small, dark hole could be the last thing I looked at in life.

My hands squeezed wrinkles across my freshly pressed skirt.

For a second I imagined that there was laughter coming from the river road. It sounded so good-hearted, so jovial, that I wondered if I had suddenly gone mad while waiting to die.

"What are you boys doing there?" a familiar voice shouted from the road. Behind the soldiers, two men were laughing and riding their bicycles.

Our death squad saluted him and answered, "Heil Hitler, Officer Joksch! We're just about to kill this Jew and his daughter. Would you like to do the honors instead?"

I could barely believe my watering eyes. I was not mad. I was not dreaming. There, just a few feet away, stood Hans Joksch.

"I would rather have a beer." He slapped them on the back. "Come, hop on our bikes and I'll buy you a round!"

"Let's kill them first—then we'll be really thirsty!"

"Why bother with them? Besides, I don't want to wait any longer." He got on his bike, indicating he wouldn't take no for an answer. "Come on, hurry up. I haven't got all day. I'm sure you'll find other Jews to kill tomorrow." The soldiers looked angrily at us but did as they were told because Officer Joksch was higher ranking.

Their voices seemed to carry across the field forever, making it impossible for either of us to move. It was as if my feet had taken root in the ground. I did not dare to look at Papa. He did not dare to look at me. Tears of shock smarted our eyes. Slowly we started walking toward home, but in the middle of the road we sank down clutching the dirt beneath our hands. Our legs weren't going to carry us any farther.

ACCORDING TO THE Nuremberg Laws, any Aryan having sex with a non-Aryan could be punished by death, and many of the Jewish families thought their daughters were safe because of this concept of *Rassenschamde*, or "race disgrace." Not long after the incident at the river, though, a German soldier saw me walking to work and asked Joseph's son, Alex, who I was.

It was the middle of the night when the soldier staggered drunkenly up to Alex's house. "Open up this door!" he shouted. "Alex, I insist you open up this door and take me to Rena's house!"

Joseph quickly woke up his son, sending him out the window to run and warn us. Then he stalled the SS man until Alex could return.

"Chaim! Sara!" Alex shouted outside. "Hide Rena quickly!

"There is a German soldier looking for her."

My eyes shot open.

"Papa, you keep a lookout while I hide Rena," Mama said. "Yell when you see them." I could hear Mama's voice downstairs and was out of bed before she could reach my room. "Follow me." She took my hand, leading me into the attic.

"Lie down on your stomach." Her voice did not waver, her hands did not tremble. I lay down as she covered me with straw.

"Do not move until you hear me telling you it's all right." She smoothed the straw out over my body, making it even, so it would not look as if anyone was hiding.

"Mama, they're near!" Papa's voice warned us.

"*Ribono shel olam* (Lord of the universe, protect my child)," Mama prayed before hurrying downstairs.

Lying very flat, my stomach pulsating against the floorboards, I turned my face sideways and tried very hard not to breathe. I could hear the rifle butt denting our front door and the officer yelling.

"Where's Rena? Bring me Rena!"

"She's not at home." Papa pretended that he had been rudely awakened.

"I do not believe you! *Scheiss-Jude*! You would not let your precious daughter stay out this late at night."

"She is visiting family in another town."

"We'll see about that! I know where you cursed dogs hide your favorite things!" He pushed Papa aside, barged into our home, and walked immediately up the stairs to our attic. This was the only place to hide in farmhouses, besides the potato cellars, so it was the first place he looked.

"Is she here?" He poked through the straw with his bayonet. "Perhaps you want to tell me before I stab her through her pretty eye!" The boards creaked beneath the weight of his feet; every movement he made shuddered the floor beneath me.

He dared Mama and Papa to make a move that would betray my hiding place. They were stone solid and silent.

"So she isn't hiding under that pile—but maybe here?" He stabbed the straw repeatedly, as if it were alive and he were killing it. My heart thumped against the wood flooring. I tried not to panic, but I was sure he could hear every skip and beat of the throbbing river of blood racing through my head. A flash of steel found its mark four inches from my nose.

I did not move.

"I know you're lying to me, Jew. You'd better make sure she's here the next time a German officer comes to call or I'll cut your throat!" He slammed the door of our house so hard that the china tinkled in the cabinets.

Mama came back to the loft. "Rena, are you okay?" I held her, trying not to cry, trying to be brave. But I was shaken beyond all bravery.

"You will have to sleep up here tonight"—she smoothed my hair back across my head—"in case he returns. Try to rest. We will see about this in the morning. You're not going back to those barracks to work, though, that's for sure." She kissed my forehead, squeezing me tight against her bosom while I dampened her nightdress with my tears.

THAT NIGHT CHANGED EVERYTHING. It had become dangerous for me to live in Tylicz. The village was distraught over the incident and almost everyone rallied to help. A Gentile friend took a letter to my uncle in Slovakia, saying that I would be coming to live with them just as Zosia had done, and Papa deliberated long and hard over whom to contact about smuggling me across the border.

Andrzej had been fighting the Germans when Poland had first been invaded, but he had returned secretly to Tylicz and was now working for the Polish resistance.

Who knew the border better than Andrzej?

MY FATHER HAD never met Andrzej, yet that morning he sent for the boy he had forbidden me to see, and asked him to come to our house. Not a word had been spoken to me about these arrangements. This was my father, and of course I was not consulted.

I was standing in the kitchen when I heard Andrzej's voice at our door. My knees got weak. Mama scrutinized me. I did not even look at his face.

"Welcome, Andrzej. Please have a seat." Papa offered him a chair. "Would you like a cigarette?" Mama and I watched them from the other room.

"Thank you, Mr. Kornreich." Andrzej took the cigarette with a grateful nod.

"I have a favor to ask of you, Andrzej. . . . This is very difficult for me, but I must ask. It is no longer safe in Tylicz for Rena. Her mother and I are worried for her safety every day."

"I heard what happened last night, Mr. Kornreich. I understand your concern."

"I have no money to pay you for this favor."

"Sir, I would not take any money from you. She is my friend since childhood. I will do whatever you ask to help your daughter."

"Thank you." Papa paused, stroking his chin where his beard should have been. "You seem like a man of your word. If you would bring Rena across the border to Slovakia, her mother and I might find sleep at night."

"I will see to it," Andrzej answered gallantly. "And I swear that with my life I'm going to guard her and not one hair is going to fall from her head. I give you my word of honor that I will bring her safely to Slovakia according to your wishes. I will hold only her hand because it is rough terrain, but I will not touch her, sir. You may trust me."

My father concluded their business with a handshake, but there was a look in his eyes I had never seen before, the appearance of complete humiliation and defeat.

That evening my mother kissed my brow, weeping. "Rena, be brave, be careful, be well."

I promised to write and send them food. "I'll come home as soon as things get better."

"Safe journey," Papa said solemnly. "Bless you."

I kissed him good-bye and hugged Danka. Then I walked into the dark winter night, unchaperoned, with Andrzej.

"WE WILL HAVE to walk all night. We cannot as much as whisper—not a word—because the dogs can pick up sounds for a long distance, and once they begin to bark there is no stopping them,"

Andrzej instructed me. "The search teams will be out looking for us, and the chance of slipping through their net is very slim. If I motion down, lie flat on the ground. Do not raise your head or move in the slightest until I motion you to get up." He took my hand. "I am going to hold your hand the whole way so you won't fall. It will be just like when we were children and I brought you and Danka down the hill."

It was rainy, cold, and just beginning to sleet. Whenever searchlights cascaded across the landscape, we fell face down so as not to create a shadow. It would have been hard enough walking in that slippery slush in daylight while laughing and singing winter sledding songs, but silent, under threat of death, trying not to crunch through the new crust of snow, it was nearly impossible. Along a ravine, we threaded our way between trees, using the underbrush to hide our tracks.

Andrzej stumbled, losing his grasp on my hand for a second.

Thrown off balance, struggling to keep from falling into the abyss below, I plummeted out of reach. Rolling down the steep incline, I grabbed at tree branches to break my fall as they ripped the mittens from my hands. Biting my tongue, I splashed into a stream with no cushion but ice-covered boulders. The silence of the night shrank. Icy water crept into my clothes. Our ears pricked up for the sound of rudely woken dogs in the nearby kennels. There was the sound of water dripping off my elbows. Neither of us dared move or breathe. No dogs barked.

Finally, Andrzej signaled for me to stand up. Slowly, bracing my hands against the river rocks, I stood. My legs were barely able to stand my weight they were shaking so badly with cold and fear.

Grabbing hold of a tree for an anchor, Andrzej reached toward me. My nails dug into his flesh. My muscles shuddered, but he didn't weaken as I forced myself up the embankment. Finally I stood on level ground. His hands rubbed mine, trying to warm them as I clamped my mouth shut to muffle the chattering of my teeth. He smiled, knowing how wet and cold I was, then, taking my hand more firmly than before, he led me toward our destination.

The light from the farmhouse seemed at first to be a mirage. I was sure I was dreaming; it was late, one or two in the morning, but there were these gorgeous lights shimmering out across the snow. Andrzej motioned me toward the stable. There, snuggling between the horses and cows, we waited.

"This is the connecting point between the Slovakian and Polish undergrounds," he whispered into my ear. I nodded, knowing we were now safe.

WE WERE GREETED BY KARL, a farmer, who boasted about his poker game with the border guards. His wife served us hot cocoa and gave me some dry clothes. Karl assumed that we would sleep together, but Andrzej assured him that that wouldn't be proper, so I was given the couple's bed while Andrzej slept in the attic. The next morning, dressed like Slovakian farmers, Karl, Andrzej, and I climbed into a wagon and headed for the city of Bardejov.

Outside of Uncle Jacob's, Andrzej took my hand. "I kept my promise to your father, didn't I?"

"Yes you did, Andrzej."

"I only held your hand."

I wanted him to hold it forever and never let go. I was so frightened of this big city and this strange country.

"I love you, Rena."

"Thank you for delivering me to my Uncle Jacob Schützer's house." I blushed and darted away before he could kiss me again, so I wouldn't lose my heart to him forever.

SLOVAKIA

I HAD TO HIDE in the Schützers' house until I could speak Slovakian fluently; then they had to cut my long braids off so I would look more like a city girl. It seemed I had to give up everything from my beloved homeland, and whenever I tried to tell Aunt Regina and Uncle Jacob about the horrors the Jews in Poland were experiencing, they thought I was exaggerating. They didn't believe me! My cousins, Cili and Gizzy, thought I was far too serious and tried to get me to go out and have fun. As hard as I tried, I could not forget my parents and the hardships my sister and they were suffering, but no one in Slovakia seemed to understand the severity of our situation.

I missed Tylicz and my family. I missed Andrzej. Then one day, there he was standing outside the house. He had smuggled a package from Mama with some clothes in it for me.

"Thank you, Andrzej." I was nervous and tried to cut any conversation short.

"Rena, can't we speak privately?"

I looked to see that no one was watching us, then we stepped behind my uncle's house.

"I've just heard that they're going to start taking young Jewish people to camps for forced labor unless they are a mixed couple," Andrzej began. "If you were married to a Gentile, there'd be a good chance they wouldn't take you." I wanted to stop his words before he spoke them. "I want to marry you. Tomorrow. I have it all arranged. My brother is living about fifteen kilometers away and has a room we can stay in. I would not have to go back and forth to Poland anymore, except for important people, and we could live here in Slovakia, where it's safe."

I was all alone. I had no one to talk with about this idea. I did not know what to do, but I knew I could not betray my family or my faith. He looked so full of hope. I so wanted to believe his idea was a good one, but it wasn't.

Finally I said, "I'm not actually happy in Slovakia, Andrzej. My parents are still in Poland, and I'm dying for them. I am young and strong, more assertive than they are, yet they are the ones exposed to the Germans. I don't really want to stay here. I want to go home to Tylicz, but I can't and I don't know what else to do."

My heart ached to tell him just once that I loved him too, and if it were not for the rest of the world, I would happily marry him. Instead, I said, "There is still the matter of our religions too. I'm sorry. I cannot be your wife." I couldn't look into his face any longer. "I can't talk to you anymore. My aunt and uncle might get suspicious."

"If you change your mind, Rena, send word." He grabbed my hand in his for one tender moment. "I will never change mine."

How I wanted to tell him the truth of my heart! But I remained silent and dutiful to my family. I did not know what else to do, and I stepped back into the house bewildered and confused.

UNCLE JACOB GAVE me a weekly allowance and asked Cili and Gizzy to lend me some nice clothes to wear to dances and the movies. They tried to get me to go to socials and meet boys, but I was more interested in spending my allowance on food for my parents and going to the marketplace to meet our Gentile friends from Tylicz. It was the closest I could get to home, and I waited eagerly for market days.

The Zionist organization gave those of us from the synagogue a place to meet and to talk about forming a new state of Israel, but it was really an excuse to have dances and socialize. Cili and Gizzy dragged me to these soirees. "We're going to find you a nice

Jewish boy!" they teased me, and I had to let them. I couldn't tell
them I had a *nice* boy—he just wasn't Jewish.

Uncle Jacob also approved of my socializing, which made it
difficult to reject my cousins' invitations. "I want to be able to tell
your father that you are adapting to life here and that you've found
a suitable escort." From the way Uncle Jacob said "suitable," I
knew Papa had told him about Andrzej. "I would like you to go
out with Schani Gottlobb, the tailor. Your father would approve of
Schani, and he will make a good husband." I nodded obediently. I
did not want to go out with Schani Gottlobb, but if it would make
Papa happy, how could I not? "I am going to give you money for
a new outfit." Uncle Jacob handed me more than enough to buy
fabric for a nice new dress.

"Thank you, Uncle Jacob." I turned to go.

"And Rena, when I give you money for clothes, I want you to
spend it on clothes."

"Yes, Uncle Jacob." He had found me out about that too? I
did as he asked, but I only bought enough fabric for one dress and
then went straight to the market with the rest of the money to buy
flour, sugar, and cheese to send home.

SCHANI WAS MAD ABOUT ME. He flattered me, thinking me both
daring and smart for escaping from Poland, and he didn't mind
that I spent money on my parents rather than on clothes. We
went to socials together and a few movies. I put a good face on
for everyone, but inside I was not happy. There was nothing to
be happy about.

After we'd been dating for about two months, Schani got it
into his head that I was the one for him and proposed.

"Schani, you're crazy. . . . I can't marry you!" I didn't know
how to get out of this mess.

"Why not? Your uncle approves of me, and he's your guardian
while you're away from home."

"Schani, you're real nice. . . . I like you very much. . . ." I tried
to be as kind and honest as possible without hurting his feelings. "I
like your company very much, but my heart isn't with you."

"There's someone else, isn't there?"

I nodded, biting my lip for admitting even that much. "I didn't mean to lead you on. Anyway, it doesn't matter because nothing can come of it, but I'm not over him yet, so I cannot love you. I'm sorry."

"I can wait," he said. "You'll see. I'm going to love you so much that I will have enough love for both of us. And to prove it, I'm going to make you a beautiful coat for an engagement gift, so when you're over him in your heart, I can step into his place."

THAT WEEK I received a letter from my parents saying they were very happy about my relationship with Schani, and I knew Uncle Jacob had informed them of our courtship. "Schani will make a good husband," Gizzy told me, "and he cares for you very much." There was so much pressure from my family to do what was expected that in a state of confusion, I accepted the beautiful gray coat that Schani made for me and we were officially engaged.

IT WAS A LOVELY Saturday morning in early spring. The air was still sharp though and snow clung on in the shadows, unwilling to release its winter hold on the land. Schani and I were walking to the marketplace when suddenly there was Andrzej heading toward us.

"Hi, Rena." He tipped his hat, his eyes latched onto my soul.

My heart began predictably pounding and my face flushed with heat. I wanted to do something to show him how I really felt, but I couldn't acknowledge him without embarrassing Schani, my future husband. There was nothing in the Orthodox rules or traditions about proper conduct in this kind of situation. I knew what I wanted to do—I wanted to go over and hug him and tell him how much I missed him. I wanted to tell him all that was in my heart, but I heard my father's voice forbidding me to speak to "that boy."

For all my courage I did not have enough to say "Hi, Andrzej." I never said a word. He passed us unacknowledged but not ignored.

"Isn't that the Gentile who risked his life to bring you here?" Schani interrupted my thoughts.

"Yes." I turned away.

"That's the boy you love, isn't it?"

"Why do you say that?" I said angrily.

"Rena, look at yourself. You're flushed."

Suddenly I realized that this man bore me no malice. "I'm sorry, Schani. . . . Yes, that is Andrzej." My eyes fell to the ground. I should have stood up proudly and spoken those words, but I was embarrassed by my own inaction.

"Why didn't you go over to him? Why didn't you greet him? He saved your life."

"I didn't know how you were going to take it!" I snapped.

"What do you mean, how I'm going to take it? Like a man, that's how I'm going to take it! I will shake his hand and thank him for bringing you to Bardejov, where you are safe."

"You would do that for me?"

"Rena, I would do anything for you."

Hurriedly I looked around so I could say something, anything, to Andrzej, but he was gone. The street was empty.

"Next time you will introduce us." Schani took my arm.

"Yes, next time I would like you to meet," I answered. And for the first time I felt a tenderness toward Schani that I knew might someday turn to love.

FOR PASSOVER THAT year I sent food home, but I missed sitting at the Seder table with my family. Despite all Uncle Jacob and Aunt Regina did to make me feel at home, I missed Mama and Papa and Danka, terribly. It was one of those spring days, where you are grateful to be alive because the sun is warm and the flowers are blooming and winter's cold is gone. I was at the market, meeting Gentiles from Tylicz who knew my family and looking for goods to send home, when I heard one of my old neighbors greeting me.

"Good morning, Rena. Have you heard the rumor that they are going to move all the Jews in Tylicz forty kilometers from the border?"

"But what about my parents? How will I send them food if they aren't in Tylicz?"

"Don't worry, Rena. It's just a rumor."

Another woman patted my arm. "You remember Andrzej Garbera, don't you?"

"Of course, she remembers Andrzej, you silly cow," the other woman quipped at her friend.

"We grew up together." I tried to act nonchalant.

"He died a few weeks ago."

The words fell on my head. The earth shattered from beneath my feet. I collapsed without a word at the feet of my neighbors.

Above me, I could hear a man saying, "You dummy, didn't you know they were in love? They used to write to each other secretly."

From beneath a haze of unconsciousness I wondered how these people could know something we'd kept so well hidden.

Their voices hovered above me as if they were miles away. I reached toward them, trying to bring myself around, shaking my head, covering my eyes—I couldn't cry here in the middle of the marketplace with half of Tylicz and Bardejov watching. There was no place to show my grief, no place for me to run. From that day on I didn't care to be in Slovakia anymore. I didn't care about anything but my mother's arms, my father's voice.

I said farewell to Schani and contacted Tolek, a friend of Andrzej's who also worked in the underground. "Take me home," I told him. "I cannot bear to be here anymore. I am tired of being safe." So Tolek took my hand and brought me home to my mother's arms.

It was not a happy, carefree homecoming but it was what I wanted. "Mama! Papa!" I never thought I would say those precious words again. I hugged them as if I would never let go, as if their arms could chase my pain away. Arm in arm, we entered our house.

"You heard about Andrzej?" Mama whispered.

I nodded, biting back more tears, "Yes, Mama. I would like to go pay my respects to his mother and sisters, if you and Papa don't mind."

"It is only proper that you honor him so, Rena. Let me send a loaf of challah with you."

The streets were muddy from rain. Accompanied by the smell of warm bread in my arms, I walked the same path Andrzej and I had trod together so many times. Passing the village well, I tried not to think of his laughing face, his sweet tender kiss. Swallowing hard, I knocked on the door and forced a smile upon my lips.

His mother answered quickly, as if she had been standing there waiting for me.

"Sit down, Rena. Make yourself at home." His mother motioned for me to take a chair. "Andrzej will be here any minute."

She ran to the window, looking for him. "He'll be so happy to see you." Wringing her hands, she checked the road outside. "I think he likes you, Rena. I shouldn't be surprised if he asks you to marry him some day."

Tears cascaded down my face as Hania, Andrzej's sister, pulled me into the kitchen. Hania explained that it was better for her mother not to remember. She told me that there had been a search by the border guard, with dogs. Andrzej had to climb a tree and had hidden there all night. It was so cold he froze and fell out. "Fortunately, some of our people found him and carried him home, so the Nazis, thank the Lord, never captured him," Hania explained. "He got pneumonia, though. We tried to nurse him back to health, but his lungs gave out."

I was lost in my heart for Andrzej. Wandering the streets of Tylicz, I found my way to the village graveyard. A German guard was there and he glowered at me as I paused by Andrzej's grave. I could not place anything on his headstone because it was against German law for a Jew to put even a stone on a Gentile's grave— that would be considered desecration; I would be shot. I could only water the flowers which had already been placed there with my tears, thinking of the boy I used to say hi to on my way to school, thinking how there was no one in the world to hold my hand or greet me on that hill anymore.

AFTER ANDRZEJ DIED, the law was passed expelling all Jews from towns within thirty kilometers of the Polish border. We were only allowed to take with us one loaf of bread and one change of clothes per person, and we had to leave all of our belongings, our house, and our land. My best Gentile friend, Frania, cried as my family left Tylicz. She could do nothing to help us. The only good thing was that I got special permission to bring our cow because my parents were elderly. We rented one room from a local farmer and slept on the floor, on straw mattresses. If I was late for milking, the farmer would steal the milk from our cow and pretend she was dry, but she was never dry. There was not as much sewing to do in this new town. No one knew who we were, and so they were suspicious and closed their hearts to us. God still smiled on us though. Every few weeks Tolek would show up at our door and always he would bring almonds from Slovakia. These Danka and I would take to the market in Grybow, where we could sell them to the local Jews and make a meager sum. God bless Tolek; he insisted we keep this money for ourselves.

In spite of all these troubles and hardships, I was simply grateful that our family was together. I felt useful and knew that our parents depended on Danka and me to take care of those things they were no longer able to do for themselves. It was our greatest pleasure to care for Mama and Papa in their aging years.

ONE NIGHT, WE HAD just a bite of potato left on the plate. Papa guided the potato tidbit over to Mama. Mama bowed her head and smiled sweetly then guided the plate to me. Like Mama, I bowed my head and guided it to Danka. We must take care of the little one, after all, but Danka was not so little anymore, and she guided the last bit of potato back to Papa. Not one of us touched it. How could we take from our loved ones' mouths? This morsel was too tiny to split four ways, and we could not bear to take food from each other. We would rather go hungry; that night my heart was full, and that was far more important than my stomach.

Florynka was not so bad, but the world was turning sour around us, and things were not as they had once been. The marketplace in Grybow was full of rumors—several Jewish girls had been raped by German soldiers in a nearby town. The memory of the soldier who had stormed into our attic looking for me surged back into our lives. Late into the night Danka and I listened to Mama and Papa's hushed voices as they discussed our fate. In the morning we woke to see Mama's tear-streaked face. Her voice quivered as she took our hands. "Uncle Jacob cannot take you both, so you must go to your sister Zosia, in Bratislava. Things are still good in Slovakia, and she knows many wealthy Jewish families there who are aware of the situation here. They will take you girls in and give you a place to work where you can be safe."

"I'm not going to leave you again." I hoped to weaken her resolve.

"Yes you will, Rena, because if you don't, I am going to go somewhere and just die. I never want to see my girls raped."

My arguments dried up in my throat. I had never seen such defeat or dismay in Mama's eyes.

"And I need you to take care of Danka, Rena."

"We will go, Mama."

IN THE MORNING Tolek arrives with a sleigh. "We will have to camp off the border tonight because of the full moon, but we should be close enough that the walk won't be too strenuous tomorrow night."

His friendly face is a comfort amid so much strangeness. It occurs to me that he does not think of us as Jews but as friends. I wonder why the rest of the world cannot see things the way he does, the way I do.

Danka and I hold Mama very close to us. She seems so small, as if she is shrinking under the weight of the world. My parents have always seemed ageless, but overnight they have aged. I am struck by Mama's frailty and Papa's white hair.

"Maybe you and Schani will be getting married after all."

"He's a nice boy, that Schani. Your Papa and I would be happy of a wedding." Mama tries to lighten our mood. Her eyes twinkle for just a moment. "You are such good girls. We are so proud of you."

Folding blankets around our feet and shoulders as if we are still young children she is tucking into bed, she speaks softly of faith and hope and taking care of each other. Her eyes are sad and soft.

Papa kisses both of our foreheads. He speaks a Hebrew prayer, blessing the daughters he cannot protect.

Tolek clucks to the ponies to begin their trek toward the border, and we depart for Slovakia, leaving our parents behind.

They stumble through the deep December snow, waving good-bye. Mama's babushka falls from her head. She places one hand on her wig, holding it securely to her head, while the other chases the air frantically, as if she is trying to hold onto one last glimpse of us.

"Good-bye, Papa!"

"Good-bye, Mama!"

Our voices yell repeatedly in unison until all we have left are hoarse whispers.

Long after they have become tiny specks on the horizon we wave, hoping they can still see us. I know that they are waving, too, hoping the same thing. Mama and Papa's black shapes etched against the snow are engraved in my mind as if they are still there waiting for us to return, as if they always will be there, waiting.

Tears usually taste salty, but mine are bitter, frozen to the sides of my cheeks, frozen in time.

∞

IT HAS BEEN over a year since we came to Slovakia, and months since I have seen my sisters, who are living on the other side of the country in Bratislava. I write slowly, lingering over each word as if the very act of pen on paper will bring my youngest sister closer to me.

March 20, 1942

Hummene, Slovakia

Dear Danka,

I miss you very much. I wish I could speak with you in person, but that is not possible. I know how excited you were about Schani and I finally getting married, but there is not going to be a wedding after all. With Slovakia under this martial law now, I don't see that there is any way out of this situation but to turn myself in to the authorities and go to a labor camp. The Silbers think I'm overreacting too strongly when I tell them they'll be shot for harboring me, but you and I know differently. And they have been so kind to me these past few months, I cannot bear to put them in danger.

I'm afraid this is going to be just like leaving Poland all
over again, and my heart won't stand breaking one more time.
Will the Germans ever stop ruining our lives? I don't want to
leave you alone, but I cannot risk anyone's life, and I don't think
the Slovakian Jews understand that the Germans mean business.
   Please, be careful. I will pray that things are safe for you in
Bratislava. Give my love to Zosia, and tell Herschel and Ester
their Auntie Rena sends them a big kiss and a hug. I miss you.
                                   Your loving sister, Rena

   I tuck the letter into its envelope, wishing there was something else I could send to protect Danka, but she's all the way
across Slovakia and beyond my reach. The forces that are taking
control of all our lives have accelerated like an avalanche through
a mountain pass, and everything we know and love has been swept
up into its path. There's nothing more I can do; I must trust God
to take care of those I leave behind.

   There is another letter to write. This one I truly wish to
avoid, but there is no way around it. It is the second time I have to
postpone my engagement and marriage to Schani Gottlobb.

Dear Schani,
   I'm sorry to be telling you this with the wedding just two
weeks away, but I don't know what else to do. I am obeying
the recent order and turning myself in to the authorities for a
German labor camp. Please understand why I must do this and
try to forgive me. I've told you what Poland was like before
I escaped to Slovakia, so believe me when I write Don't Take
Anything The Germans Say For Granted. Maybe I won't have
to work for more than a few months. I don't know anything yet
about where I'm going or for how long. I pray you will respect
my decision. I'll write you and Danka as soon as I arrive in camp
and know more.
   We are young enough that when I'm released we can begin
again; I'm only twenty-one years old after all—that's not too
old for you, is it? (That is supposed to be a joke, Schani. I don't
want you to cry about this.) Someday we will have a good life
and you will make a fine husband for me, but not right now. I

hope you can wait for me one last time. I do not know what to expect, but I know that the work camp will be hard. Pray that I will not have to be there for very long. Thank you for loving me through all my trials and troubles. Give my best to Aunt Regina, Uncle Jacob, Cili, and Gizzy.

Bless you.

Love, Rena

FOLDING MY WEDDING nightgown and placing it in a chest with no hope, I wonder how my fiancé will take this news. The new shoes the cobbler made for my wedding, the robe that the tailor has sewed, everything I own has been packed and, with my dreams, put away.

Leaving the letters on the table, I turn toward the wardrobe already knowing what I will wear. My green-and-white checkered suit is both warm and attractive. I want to look my best, even if I am going to a work camp, and this is my nicest outfit. Danka has a suit just like it that a kind tailor bought for us when we arrived last year in Slovakia. We had never been to a real department store, and because we were refugees he bought each of us a brand-new suit. I got some gorgeous white felt boots with red trim too.

With a warm pair of socks on, I slip the boots onto my feet. They are snug and comfortable; I know they will travel well.

I am so worried about Mama and Papa. Where are they now? How are they doing? They don't even know that Schani and I are supposed to be getting married.

At Rosh Hashanah last fall, the tailor who bought my suit knew how worried I was, so he asked one of his customers, a German officer, to make the call to Poland for me in exchange for a leather coat. Everyone barters now.

At the post office, the German officer placed the call for me and handed me the receiver.

"I am calling for Sara and Chaim Kornreich," I told the postmaster in Florynka.

"There's no one in this town by that name."

"Are you sure?" I pleaded. "Is this Florynka?"

"There's no one in this town by the name of Kornreich."

"But they were there!"

"They aren't now."

I hung up the phone, stunned.

"Maybe they've been moved," the officer suggested.

"But where?"

He shrugged.

Where were Mama and Papa? I wanted to tell them everything that had happened, everything that was happening. How was I going to tell them if I did not even know where they were?

No one paid me any mind as I turned to leave the post office, murmuring my thanks. Outside there was a lemony sun and an empty street. I was alone in this country that was not mine, my parents were alone in the country that was, and we were worlds apart.

EVEN THOUGH WE still have no idea where Mama and Papa are, Zosia, Danka, and I send them raisins, matzos, and some money for Passover, which is next week. We don't know if they will get our gifts because the border to Poland is now completely closed, but we had to try.

"I miss you, Mama." I murmur her name like a Sabbath prayer. Since I can't speak to her, I am simply going to have to remember everything, so when I see Mama again I can tell her all that has happened since we left Poland, so I can tell her all my heart.

∽

CHECKING MY APPEARANCE casually in the mirror, I give myself an approving nod before picking up the letters and the coat Schani gave me as an engagement gift.

Mrs. Silber has gone to the market, so my departure will go unnoticed. I do not want her to know I'm going to the army barracks, even though she and her husband have said they will hide me despite the consequences. I cannot risk their lives or the life of their young daughter, who has been my charge. I do what I have to do. There is no question in my mind that this is the right thing; my only desire is to protect these kind people who have taken me into their home and treated me like a member of their family. A work camp is not going to be so bad, especially if it means saving the Silbers' lives. I'm not afraid of work. I know what the Germans expect: cleanliness, promptness, order; everything must be spotless.

It will be just like working in the barracks in Tylicz.

I leave the Silbers' house, looking back one last time to seal it in my memory. I'll return, I tell myself; this won't last forever.

"Good morning," I greet our good Christian neighbor.

"Good morning, Rena. Are you all right, dear?"

"I must go away and have a favor to ask of you."

Her eyes narrow quickly. "What is it?" Everyone seems to be on their guard. I slip the diamond ring Mama gave me off my finger and place it into her palm, folding her hand around it. "I would like you to take care of this ring. It was my mother's. . . . Would you take this coat for me, too, please?"

Her eyes shift between disbelief and desire for these beautiful things. "These are valuable. Won't you need them?"

Suddenly it occurs to me that I will never see these things again. I cannot speak. Placing the coat in her arms quickly, before I can change my mind, I try to turn away before she can see me cry.

"Whoever made this for you must love you very much." She touches the beaver trim admiringly.

"I am afraid that is true." I do not want to say good-bye to our neighbors, to my friends, my sister, or anyone ever again. Saying good-bye to my mother's diamond ring is painful enough. If I never wave farewell to another person in this lifetime, it will be a blessing. I keep my head to the ground, refusing to look back.

Standing for a moment in the center of Hummene, I think about what a nice place this is and how kind the people have been to me. Slovakia has not been a bad place to live; although the past year has been wrought with trials and homesickness, there has been happiness here. I post my letters and walk resolutely toward the barracks. Erna is there ahead of me. Dina is going to risk it and hide. We hold hands and stand in line together, hoping that Dina will be safe. She is brave not to turn herself in, but we are all illegally in this country. I don't know where to hide or what else to do but turn myself in.

Erna steps forward but gives her nickname, Etela. And then it is my turn.

"Name?"

"Rifka Kornreich." I use my nickname too.

"Nationality?"

"Polish."

He smirks as if sharing a secret joke with the officer next to him.

"Do you have other family hiding here in Slovakia?"

"I am engaged to a Slovakian citizen, does that change my status?"

"Not unless you want him to join you."

I shake off a sudden chill. "I don't want him to join me."

"Wait outside tonight." I am dismissed.

"What about my things?"

"Tomorrow someone will take you for your things."

For a moment I wish I had my coat. Its warm fur would chase the chill from my neck. I wonder if my ring and coat are safe. I wonder if I am.

There are other Jewish girls sitting next to me. Shivering against the barrack walls with nothing but my wool suit on, I use my arms to hug myself and lean against Erna. The lights around the barracks are cruelly bright, shedding no warmth on those of us in line. It is going to be a hostile night.

The events that have abandoned me to this place tease my mind. Everything moves faster than usual, as if I am inventorying what should be preserved in memory and what should be discarded.

I tuck my knees up under my skirt for warmth. My stomach growls—how I would love a piece of challah. The rich smell of egg penetrates my perception. There is something so comforting about the aroma of fresh-baked bread. I sniff the air but cannot tell if the smell is real or imagined and do not care. Rolling an imaginary morsel over my tongue, smelling it from within my mouth, I slowly allow its goodness to warm me from the inside out. I recall Mama kneading the dough, preparing our Sabbath meal. I wonder if Mama is kneading dough somewhere in Poland.

Searching for a place to rest my weary mind, I shut my eyes tight, willing myself to see Mama's face in our kitchen. Like benevolent spirits, I conjure up the smells, the sounds of home. There is Mama asking me to bring in more wood for the fire. There is Papa's pipe smoke wafting in from the parlor where he studies the texts. Like fingers, the mountain peaks surrounding Tylicz pull me into their embrace. I drift between dreaming and waking until I am running barefoot across the field beckoned by the voices of my past.

Rena!

Escaping into the world of dreams, I see Mama standing at the door of our farmhouse with her lantern lit, watching out for me, calling my name.

Rena!

The grass is wet and cool, springing between my toes. I run down the hill toward home.

I'm coming, Mama, I answer her bobbing light. But the soft, flickering flame of her lantern mutates into a searing glare that burns my eyes.

Disoriented and cold, I shake myself out of a stupor. Searchlights pass over our restless bodies. It was nothing but a waking dream. I feel tired and depressed, overcome by these foreign surroundings. My mind takes the mental images of my past and begins weaving them through my subconscious. When everything else has changed, one's sole comfort lies in what is, what was, familiar.

Rena!

I swear I hear Mama's voice calling. Cautiously I drift off once more, only to be startled repeatedly by the obtrusive glare of searchlights swaying across the compound. It is a sleepless night.

My eyes may shut, my breathing may slow, my mind may shimmer like a movie picture, but I do not escape into sweet sleep. I have been snared.

THERE IS SOMETHING in the chill at dawn that cuts to the bone. It's almost as if all the warmth from the earth is being sucked into

a vacuum and dragged from the land. My jaw aches into a yawn.
I fidget with my plaid skirt. Like a wave receding from the shore,
the past leaves me lonely and forlorn.

The soldiers rouse those who aren't up yet. I stand alert,
shivering in protest at this rude awakening, then smooth my skirt
against my legs. I want to look my best today. It is important to
make a good first impression.

"Line up! Those of you who need to go back to your resi-
dences will be taken to get your things. Line up!"

I rush to the line to retrieve what few belongings I have left at
the Silbers' house. Like prisoners we walk through town with an
officer on each side of our pitiful group. My head is down, hoping
to avoid recognition. I do not know why I feel such shame, but I
do.

Mrs. Silber is in the kitchen baking challah when the guards
pound on her door. "This Jew has turned herself in and has come
for her things." They enter her kitchen uninvited; I run upstairs,
unable to look in my hostess's eyes. The aroma from the kitchen
is so pungent that I stagger under a sudden burst of hunger. In
seconds I have my suitcase and am downstairs again.

Mrs. Silber slips a loaf and a few oranges in my bag.

There is no time for gracious farewells. We barely kiss good-bye.

Back at the railway station there are many more girls standing
in line. Some are my age. Some are much younger. I see girls from
temple. What are they doing here? What am I doing here? I am
supposed to be getting married, not going to a labor camp. I have
to remind myself that I am doing the right thing, but reality is not
a comfort. Then I see Dina.

Dina's face is ashen. She has gotten arrested. We hug each
other.

Looking around us it is clear that not all the girls at the station
are illegal Poles. Most of them are Slovakian and have families
kissing and hugging them good-bye. What is going on? I thought
we were in trouble for being illegals. Why are so many Slovakian
girls being sent away too? What are they doing here?

Word has spread quickly through the town of Humenne that
there are Jewish girls being shipped off to work camps today. Our
people shout encouragement while standing by the station gates

and throwing oranges to those of us being loaded onto the train. I catch a few, sticking them in my handbag. For a moment I scan the crowd, looking for a familiar face. The rabbi is there waving to his daughter, Adela Gross. The rabbi's daughter is going to a work camp? I do not know if I should be sad or happy that there is no one from my family waving to me.

When one thinks of a train ride, one imagines benches or at least seats or, if one has a little money, perhaps a berth. It is obvious, however, that the cars they are loading everyone into are for animals—cattle cars, to be exact.

"Where are we supposed to sit?" The girls around me voice their outrage. "This is not a train for people!" No one is listening as eighty of us are piled into the car. It is standing room only. We step on each other's toes, apologize, then step on someone else's.

There's a steady buzz of dismay over our plight. The lady next to me is nursing her baby. She is not a Jew; she is a communist.

"Would you like an orange?" I ask.

"I didn't know I needed to bring food or clothing," she says in Slovakian. I tear off a piece of challah and place a piece of precious chocolate into her hands.

"Bless you, bless you." Her voice breaks.

The train starts with a lurch. There is nothing to lean against but each other.

WHEN THE TRAIN stops it is in another town, and then another: Presov, Kysak, Poprad. At each station there are more girls lined up and loaded into more cattle cars. There are more people waving and crying and wondering what is going to happen to their daughters. And then there are no towns for a long time.

There is a bucket that is supposed to be a toilet. Hours go by before an embarrassed girl has to use "the facilities." Her sister holds up her coat as a screen while she tries to squat on shaky legs.

"I'm sorry," she apologizes. "I couldn't hold myself any longer." Some girls are shocked, but sooner or later everyone must follow suit or mess themselves. It has become apparent that this will not be a short journey, and before the day is out excrement slops freely over the edge.

8.   (49)

Tábor   P o p   r s a

208.	Grinwaldová Edita	1913	Haligovce
209.	Weissová Irena	1924	Lackovice
210.	Kronovičová Jozefa	1919	Humenné
211.	Heráková Anna	1923	"
212.	Glücková Olga	1924	"
213.	Drängerová Etela	1921	2
214.	Kornreichová Rifka	1920	"
215.	Jakobovičová Irena	1923	Udavske
216.	Teslerová Peói	1919	Humenné
217.	Ehrenbergová Anna	1922	"
218.	Ehrenbergová Henia	1925	"
219.	Friedová Margita	1925	"
220.	Wilková Regina	1920	"
221.	Teslerová Anna	1915	"
222.	Baumhaftová Cecilia	1922	"
223.	Findlingová Serena	1922	"
224.	Grünfeldová Serena	1909	"
225.	Straussová Frantiska	1921	"
226.	Siegelmannová Cecilia	1911	"
227.	Winklerová Jetty	1921	"
228.	Rosenfeldová Johanna	1914	"
229.	Guttmannová Šára	1917	"
230.	Gelbová Hermina	1921	"
231.	Gelbová Etela	1919	"
232.	Gelbová Kornelia	1918	"
233.	Beckerová Margita	1922	"
234.	Landauová Ružena	1916	"
235.	Majerovičová Helena	1908	"
236.	Friedmannová Lea	1922	"
237.	Friedmannová Edita	1924	"
238.	Grossová Adela	1923	"

List of names (partial) from first transport: Rifka Kornreichova is Rena #214;
Etela Drangerova is Erna #213; Adela Grossova is #238. The number two
in the column by Erna's name is a typo. Photo courtesy of Yad Vashem
International Institute for Holocaust Research, Jerusalem, Israel.

We expect someone to come dump our refuse for us. Every time the train stops, the ones closest to the door pound against its indifference yelling, "Open the door! The smell is killing us!"

No one answers our cries. The train moves again. There is no relief.

A thin wail rises up out of the belly of a girl. My bones resonate with her voice. Staring at her mouth, I am amazed at how such sounds of pain and sorrow can emanate from such a small place. She is hysterical. Panting with panic. Sobbing. *Lamentations.* Our faith dangles before us.

Is it days or is it hours?

The train stops. The door opens. For just a split second, daggers of light blind us. Like wild animals caught by a farmer's lantern, we freeze, immobile and in shock. The air saturates our lungs. We have forgotten what fresh smells like—gentle and sweet, not acrid, as the car has become.

"Throw out your waste!" The orders are immune to our pain.

The door slams shut too quickly, severing the outside world from our senses. Now that we have something to compare it to, the closeness is more suffocating than before. The train continues its endless trek.

This journey is a blur in my mind. I have no idea if it is three days or five days since I wrote my letters to Danka and Schani. I begin to wish I could change my mind and go into hiding. I wish I could send a letter to Danka warning her. I have made a terrible mistake. I cannot think about that—there is no turning back.

There is no more food to nosh on. There never has been any water to drink. Nothing is left to relieve the growing ulcers in our stomachs.

They are not expert at shipping human cargo yet. The stops are so many I give up trying to count them, reserving my energy for more important things. My mind is as heavy as wet sand sifted through a net of unconscious daze. I think about nothing.

The woman feeds her baby. Voices around me share stories. I have nothing to share. It is as if I am in a tunnel with no light at the end and nothing to stop the onslaught of darkness. The faces around me have changed over the days until no one is far from losing control of her mind.

It is as if the world has been shorn of all color, the only hues in the spectrum being black, gray, and the white of my boots. In this dank and fetid car I determine what I must do to survive. Everything that reminds me of what once was—my childhood, my past, my life—must be locked away in the recesses of the unconscious, where it can remain safe and unmolested. The only reality is now.

Nothing else can matter.

⚮

SOMEWHERE IN THE lapse of time I hear somebody say, "Is anyone here Polish?" I do not answer at first. It takes time to register what my ears have heard. Looking across the dingy compartment of strangers, I remember. "We're Polish." Erna and Dina lean against each other and barely nod.

"Can you read the signs we're passing?" The taller girls in our car lift me up so I can see the signs along the tracks through the barred window high above our heads.

The wind whips across my eyes. I blink back the pain as I recognize my native tongue, my native land. "We're in Poland," I say from high above their heads.

"Where are they bringing us?" Speculation and theories are discussed, but mostly there are just more questions.

"What are they doing?" Our voices ice the air.

Then there is nothing but the sound of wheels against tracks, tracks against wheels; even the baby has stopped crying.

AUSCHWITZ

Was I born from a stone?
Did a mother not bear me?
If you cut me don't I bleed?
—From a Yiddish song sung by Mama

THE BRAKES SQUEAL with such finality that we know instinctively that our journey has ended. The doors are pushed open to a dull gray haze. We blink at the light stinging our eyes. The sign reads AUSCHWITZ.

"Get out of the car," the Germans order. We shift from blank stares to the business of collecting our belongings.

"Go quick!" Men in striped caps and uniforms prod us with sticks, whispering under their breath, "Move quickly. We don't want to hurt you." The SS aim their guns, forcing these poor prisoners to hit us so that we jump from the car. And we jump, half dead, with our luggage, if we have luggage.

It is four feet to the ground. My knees, cramped from being stationary for so long, feel as if they will snap as I land. I turn to help the woman with her baby. A stick taps my shoulder, "Go quick."

I look for the eyes belonging to the voice, but there are only hollow black holes staring into my face.

"Get in line!" Orders are sharp, punctuated by whips against shining leather boots.

"Throw your suitcases over there," the SS shout.

I place mine upright, neatly, next to the growing pile, then turn to ask one of the SS guards, "How are we going to find our suitcases later?" I figure I am a human being; I have a right to ask.

"Get in line and shut up!" he yells in my face, pointing his gun at me. The hair on my skin bristles. He doesn't see that I am human.

There is an odor I cannot identify. It is not from human waste or girls who have not bathed in days, although those smells are also prevalent. It is the scent of fear permeating the air around me.

It is everywhere, in the eyes of the girl-women around me, in our clothing and our sweat.

The baby isn't alive anymore, but its mother does not notice the limpness of the form in her arms. Her desperate grasp on its corpse spooks me. There is too much happening. Everything is so hurried, so haphazard, that there is no way to make sense of the situation. I look through the crowd for some direction, for someone to tell me why we are here and what will befall us. I see him.

He stands before us, superior and seraphic, taking control, directing us to go this way or that. He is so neat and refined in his gray uniform; he is gorgeous. I smile into his blue eyes, hoping he will see me for who I am.

"Do you want to give up the child?" he asks the woman with the dead baby.

"No." Her head shakes frantically.

"Go over there," he says.

How kind of him not to point out to her that her infant is dead, I think to myself. How kind of him to place her to the side.

There is madness here. My mind begins to whirl. Struggling to focus on something, anything, to keep me from screaming, I stare at the man in gray. He is so stunning I am sure he must be considerate too. His orders are always obeyed. The SS around us defer to him quickly, answering, "Heil, Hitler!"

I watch the proceedings with semi-fascination before lapsing into the fog where nothing needs to make sense. This is not day-dreaming; this is electric shock. There is a smudge on my left boot. Spitting into my palm, I stoop to wipe it away. It is white again.

"Line up! Get into rows of five! *Raus! Raus!*" The prisoners poke us with sticks. The SS aim their guns at us. We are civilians unfamiliar with military drill. We line up clumsily. "March! Stay in your rows! If you step out of line, you will be shot! March!"

Nine hundred ninety-eight girl-women step in semi-perfect time, in semi-perfect rows of five, through the iron gates of Auschwitz. Above our heads, welded in iron, are the words ARBEIT

MACHT FREI, and we believe what the sign says: "Work Will Make You Free."

"We are young," we remind ourselves. "We will work hard and be set free. We will see what happens." But on the outside we are walking as if we are doomed. It is raining, chilled like March rain. We are lost in thought, but it is too cold to do much thinking. Everywhere it is gray. My heart is turning gray.

∞

THERE ARE MEN along barbed-wire fences, in striped jackets, caps, and pants, watching us.[1] Their eyes reflect nothing. I think to myself, This must be an insane asylum, but why would they make the mentally ill work? That's not fair.

I do not comprehend my surroundings. I keep thinking, I am well brought up, well educated, well dressed. I was looking very nice when I went to the barracks in Slovakia wearing my beautiful suit, though it does not look so good now. Still, my white boots look pretty and spotless because I've been careful not to step in any mud. Walking through these gates, I forget my resolve and think for one moment about who I was at home. I'm a neat person. I should not be here. I am different. I come from a good family. The desire to curl up in a warm blanket of past memories permeates my effort to keep in step. Forget about that now, Rena, I reprimand my weakness; that's history. I stare at the acres of barbed wire around us. This is reality.

"Halt!" We freeze, complacent and obedient under the rifles and watchtowers around us. There are rows of brick buildings going down the side of the camp road, the *Lagerstrasse*, and a high wall with barbed wire. We are forced to line up so as to be going in the door of the first block. Time passes. Is it hours or is it days?

---

1. Prior to March 26, 1942, the only prisoners in Auschwitz were men, mostly Polish Gentiles serving time for their political or religious beliefs and Russian prisoners of war.

I am somewhere toward the end of this line when people start coming out of the other side with no hair on their heads.

Leaning toward Erna, who is standing next to me, I whisper, "There are more crazy people. We must be in an institution for the insane." She and Dina nod in agreement.

"Piri! It's me!" some crazy bald person shouts to one of the girls nearby.

"Magda? Is that you? What happened to your hair?" Piri yells back.

"Don't ask questions." Her bald head checks around her to see if anyone is listening. "If you have jewelry, step it into the mud."

I look down at the watch on my wrist. I can still hear Erna and Dina and Danka laughing with me as we run through the streets toward the post office in Tylicz, where I had a phone call. "Rena has a boyfriend!" they chant. "Rena has a boyfriend!" "Do you like the watch I gave you?" my current beau asked on the crackling wire. "I love it," I flirted. "I will never take it off."

"Well, you better if you go swimming or bathe," he flirted back.

I break my foolish promise, ripping the band from my wrist.

You cannot have my memories! You cannot have anything of mine! Driving it into the mud with my heel, dirtying my precious white felt boots, I smash my watch into a thousand pieces.

THE DOOR TO Block One looms before us. Inside, the unknown is happening. We can see the girl-women coming out, but we tell ourselves we will not look different when we exit this place. Digging my fingernails into my palms, I pray I will be the one girl to exit with my hair. Then I am inside the block.

In a daze I walk up to the first table, as I have just seen Erna do. "What are you?" a German woman asks.

"Polish," I answer.

She grunts and writes down my information. She does not ask me what race I am, and I do not offer the fact that I am also Jewish. All of us are Jewish, except for the communist woman. I am puzzled by the German woman's clothes. She is not SS. She is pure German, definitely *Reichdeutsche* though, but she is wearing a triangle with a number over it. It occurs to me that she may be a prisoner.[2]

"Two gold crowns," she announces.

My mind races. Why would they make a note about my teeth? Oh, my God, they're going to take my crowns and then I'll look ugly. I go to the second table pulling my upper lip over my teeth, tilting my head down just slightly so no one notices the money in my mouth.

"Get those earrings off," the next German woman barks at me.

I look around wondering who is being spoken to in such a rude tone of voice. "You there! Take those earrings off or I'll rip them out!"

"Me?" I am stunned. Touching my lobes gingerly, I realize my mistake. The earrings my Grandpa Zayde gave me when I was six years old are glistening from beneath my curls. I have worn them for so long that they are not jewelry but a part of me.

"I forgot about them," I tell her quickly, placing the last remnant of my life on a cold table, to be tossed into a box with everyone else's past.

"Take your clothes off and leave them here." They grab my suit from me before I have a chance to fold it neatly or place it in a safe corner to be retrieved later.

"*Raus! Raus!*"

We hurry forward. We have never stood naked in front of strangers before. Trying to cover ourselves with our hands, we look at the floor, hoping this will protect our modesty. Insensitive to our nudity, they prod us into a tub of disinfectant.

"They are filthy. Don't touch them." Their voices sting as badly as the solution against our bare skin. We stand for several minutes, embarrassed to look at each other, staring into a green liquid that feels as if it will eat the flesh off our bodies.

---

2. "March 26 [1942] . . . 999 German women prisoners classified as asocial, criminal, and a few as political prisoners . . . receive Nos. 1–999 and are lodged in the part of the main camp separated by the wall along Blocks 1 to 10. . . 999 [998] Jewish women from Proprad [near Hummene] in Slovakia are [also] sent to the women's section of Auschwitz. This is the first registered transport sent to the camp" (Czech, 148).

"Get out! Get out!" Orders, more orders. The guards' words jump into our brains, dislodging free thought, exiling it to the nether regions of sanity. There are no towels to dry our shivering frames. Our clothes are not waiting for us, but the line is. Our lives have become one long line moving slowly from one horror to another.

I am held by the head and pushed abruptly into a chair. The cuss of electric shears moves closer to my ears as a tough hand pushes my head forward. "Don't move!" I am spoken to roughly, handled as if my skin were sandpaper. Running from the nape of my neck to my forehead, the clippers cut and scrape against my skin, tearing the hair from my head. Digging my fingernails deeper into my arm, I try to prevent tears from falling down my disinfected cheeks. Only married women shave their heads. Our traditions, our beliefs, are scorned and ridiculed by the acts they commit.

They shear our heads, arms; even our pubic hair is discarded just as quickly and cruelly as the rest of the hair on our bodies. We are shorn like sheep and then ordered back into the vat of disinfectant.

My flesh burns like fire. I wonder if I will get my jacket and skirt back now that the ordeal is over. They can't possibly do anything more—what else is there?

A girl screams.

THERE IS A LONG table where an officer is standing. He has rubber gloves on and there are two other men holding the girl down. I hear her scream again. I have no idea what he is doing, but I know I don't want him doing it to me. There are two lines, the one I am in, going to the table with the man and his gloves, and the line facing in the opposite direction. Blood drips down the thighs of the girl-women coming away from the man and his gloves. It only takes a second for me to weigh the consequences of action against the consequences of inaction—I turn quickly around, stepping into the other line. This is my first accomplishment in Auschwitz: no one gives me a gynecological exam.

The German women prisoners, who are obviously our superiors, toss woolen uniforms at us. There are Russian insignias on the breasts of the uniforms. We fumble, then try them on, quickly discovering that they are too huge for most women to wear. There is a tall woman next to me whose pants are too short. "Here, try mine on," I suggest. We trade. Around us, other women do the same, trying to find something that won't fall off. I balk at pulling the trousers over my body without any underwear on. Sniffing my dark green woolen shirt, I am nauseated by the dampness of the fabric. There are no buttons to close the shirt, but there are holes and reddish-brown streaks and stains. "They haven't even washed these clothes!" I remark. Touching a smear of dirt, I wonder if I can scrub it out later. But this is not mud. It is sticky. It smells sweet. My stomach lurches. I stare at the women around me who are already clothed. Still damp from the disinfectant, they are simply grateful for something to put over their bodies. Like myself, they do not notice at once, preferring to think that the cloth has been eaten away by moths rather than bullets. They do not see that the streaks are not dirt and mud but blood. We are like lambs being led to slaughter, following one another because we know of nothing else to do. Despite the sweet-sour smell of stale blood and scratchiness of the wool against my nipples, I modestly pull my shirt across my chest. What will be next?

In the last room there is a pile of wood slabs with leather straps across the top. These are supposed to be shoes. Again, we try to help each other find a matching pair, but they were not made in pairs. They're not even made for human beings to wear. Scuffling out of the block onto the camp road, I move into position. We stand in neat rows of five, bald, practically barefoot, and wearing dead men's uniforms. It begins to drizzle.

"Line up!" The drill is repetitive, mundane. We are capable of nothing but obeying orders. "March!" With one hand clutching the stench of my shirt close around me and the other hoisting up the pants that sag below my hips, still possessed by a false sense of modesty, I march.

We stamp our feet awkwardly, trying not to trip or lose our sandals.

We pass the first four blocks before turning into Block Five.

We are so busy trying not to lose our clothing that we do not notice the room we are led into, until the door slams shut and a bolt falls on the other side. Trapped. We stand almost on top of one another in bloody straw. Bedbugs jump, making our bodies black.

We hold our clothes up over our faces; they jump on our bare heads, our hands, all over any exposed patch of skin. In the straw, lice crawl hungrily between our toes.

We have gone quietly for too long. Suddenly there is a surge of dissension. Running to the door, we pound and pound. "Let us out! Let us out!" With both hands we beat the walls imprisoning us. "This can't be!" the voices around me scream. "Please, let us out. We did nothing wrong. There's got to be a mistake. Help us!"

There is nothing but anguish around us. We have revolted too late. It is no mistake. Joining the mass of betrayed girl-women, I pound against the oak of injustice. It beats thinking. Anything is better than facing the facts on the floor and under our feet.

I am tired of being vigilant. I am tired of watching the sun rise on despair. The girl-women around me mirror my thoughts; my face must look as doomed as theirs. The filth, the smell, the sounds of guard dogs barking in the distance—it is too much. The whole night I crouch on the floor, exhausted yet alert. There has been no water for days, no food, not a drop of anything. I don't fall asleep, but quite a few do. Dropping off into unconsciousness, they collapse on the floor, no longer able to feel the gnawing bites of these terrible bugs.

The door to Block Five opens at four a.m. I am still where they left me, wide-eyed and awake. All but one of us scrambles into line and marches out for roll call. She does not move when the guard kicks her. She will never move again.[3]

We stand silently, being counted, unable to move from our neat and orderly rows of five. I do not turn my head. I do not shift my feet. I want to scratch at the bites and the irritating wool

---

3. While it is not certain that twenty-five-year-old Johana Grunwaldova died in Block Five, she *was* the first girl to die. The next day, on March 28, 1942, Marta Kornova was the second girl to die. She was twenty years old.

against my bare skin. My thumb twitches against my leg; it is the only movement I allow myself to indulge in.

They divide us evenly into two different groups. We are given a bowl for our tea, but there aren't enough to go around; some people share theirs, but right away there are arguments and some of the bowls disappear. It is late morning when we are finally given a little of something like tea, a piece of bread, and a pat of margarine, which they slap onto the open palm of our hands. I notice that everyone gobbles their food quickly, too quickly for their shrunken stomachs. Some get in line again, expecting more, but there are no seconds. They are beaten for being so presumptuous. I chew my bread, slowly spreading my margarine as if I were at a proper dinner. My tea tastes strange, but I do not care. I sip it slowly, forcing myself to make it last, telling my body that it is full and this is plenty to eat.

The first day we clean the inside of Block Ten. Moving in a daze, I hold my shirt closed and try to keep my pants up while dusting, sweeping, washing. We carry out our duties quietly. I am simply grateful to be let out of the block, with all its lice and bugs. There is little else to do but watch and learn. The Germans are disorganized. I notice this immediately, but it means nothing— organized or not, we are at their mercy.

Standing by the fence, I am torn between praying that I won't see Danka here and praying that we find each other if this is where she ends up. I wonder if she will recognize me. I wonder if I will recognize her. Lost in an ever-increasing tide of despair, my heart has one last hope that Danka will hide in Slovakia.

My bones tell me she will be here all too soon.

Across the compound, I see my lovely white boots with their red trim on an SS woman. I want to say something, take them from her and put them on my own feet. Trying to control this impulse to take back what is mine, I force myself to return to the block.

"Line up! Line up!" We move into neat rows of five. The sun sinks in the west as one thousand of us are counted.

A CONCRETE WALL DIVIDES CAMP. The men's blocks are on the other side of this wall, but from the second story of the blocks we can see each other through the barbed wire. In the approaching darkness I stand before the upstairs window looking at the same men I had seen the day before. At least they look the same. Each of the blocks in Auschwitz has windows in the front, and from the second floor we can open them and speak to the men on the other side of the wall. They are half-starved, eager to hear news of the outside world and to make friends with us.

I go to the window and spit on my hand. The reflection is dark and obscured, but I stand rubbing the dirt from my face, smearing the tearstains into my skin so they will not know they've made me cry. I rub my scalp as if I had hair to comb. It is a futile but comforting gesture, reminding me of Mama's hand brushing back my hair. I shut out these thoughts quickly; there is only one thing to remember—don't reminisce. My reflection in the window blinks back her tears. I want to rant and rave, but I can only stare at the picture before my eyes. What have they done to us? Who is this person staring back at me? The men in camp no longer look insane. They look like me.

"Is anyone over there Polish?" a man asks from the other side of the wall.

"I am," I answer.

"Can I help you?" he asks.

"I could use a rope to hold up my pants, and a nail." This is called organizing. Really it is scrounging, but organizing is more appropriate when you consider our circumstances and how dangerous having anything extra is.

"Run downstairs. I'll throw something over." This is my first care package, and with grateful admiration I retrieve a rope with a nail, wrapped tightly around a stone.

I spend the rest of the evening fraying the rope into four pieces, so Erna and Dina can hold up their pants too.

It does not take me long to figure out that resourcefulness is as precious as food in this place, and nothing passes under my feet unnoticed or unassessed for its potential. By taking a stone, I am able to hammer the nail through the metal rim of my bowl, then I thread one of the pieces of rope—my new belt—through the hole.

To keep my shirt closed, I tuck it in my pants and tie the belt tightly around my waist. This is how it is. My life depends on this precious bowl that I can drink from and wash in. I will work with it.

I sleep with it. I always keep it by my side. It is red.

There are no showers, but there are three toilets in Block Ten and a place to wash our hands. For toilet paper there are scraps of newspaper, but these disappear quickly. There's always a line, so we don't have a chance very often to use the toilet or wash our hands, but at least it is possible. There are bunk beds that have straw mattresses on them and thin blankets. The first night we have two people per bunk, but there are empty bunks waiting for more girl-women just like us.

My bed is next to a wall with a window that is boarded up, but through the slats in the boards I can look into the yard of Block Eleven. The struggle for sleep is not hard after so many nights of sleeplessness, but somewhere in the middle of the dreamless night there are gunshots. Awake and alert, I lie on my pallet of straw pulling the blanket closer around me, but it cannot warm the chill in my spine; my cup attached firmly to my waist is no comfort either. Somewhere someone is dying.

ROLL CALL ON the second morning comes just as early, just as rudely. Four a.m. Frantically we jostle one another, trying to get in line; anyone not in place is beaten. We seem to always be marching from one place to another and standing for a long time doing nothing. The whisper comes down the line. They are tattooing us.

How can they do this? We came here to work, not be slaves. I am standing with Dina and Erna, just in front of them when the line moves forward. There are two sisters in the front of the line; I believe they are numbered 1001 and 1002, but the order has no meaning. We are—all of us—the first Jewish women in Auschwitz. My number is 1716. Dina is 1528. Erna is 1718 . . .

The tattooing is painful. The men prisoners do not delight in sticking the needle, like a shot, in our left forearms over and over. They know how much it hurts. Still, the SS force them to hurry, so there is no time to be gentle or concerned. It is as if each stab will burst any shred of ego left. Branded and numbered like cattle, we rub our arms as we had rubbed our naked heads, trying to make the pain go away.

The Nazis are starting to arrange things now. The *kapos*, who are German prisoners, are put in charge of us when we are outside of our blocks. We learn how to distinguish the kapos by the color triangle they wear: green signifies that she is in for murder; red means she is a political prisoner; black represents a prostitute or asocial prisoner.

A young Slovakian Jew called Elza is chosen to be our *block-owa*, our block elder, and is in charge of us when we are inside the block. Her duties include getting us out to roll call and dividing the bread loaves that are assigned to each room. There are also *sztubowas*, room elders, who divide the loaves between everyone in the room and hand out our portions. Between them, the block elders and room elders steal bread for themselves. It is easy to see that they are doing this, and I realize almost immediately that I have to be frugal with what I get. Sometimes there might be half the portion allotted for me, and sometimes there might be the whole portion; it all depends on luck and whether the room elders and block elder are honest people.

From the window I hear a man outside and across the wall asking, "Where are you from?"

"Tylicz, near Krynica," I answer.

"Go downstairs," he instructs, leaning his head sideways to see which way the watchtower guard is facing before tossing a piece of bread over the barbed wire for me to eat. I run out the door and grab this morsel just as a stone wrapped with paper also lands at my feet. I grab the note and run back in the door before the watchtower guard swings back toward the camp road. Panting inside the doorway, I put the bread in my pocket and crumple the note in my hand before walking nonchalantly past Elza's room. In the corner upstairs, I unfold his note and read: *Destroy this note the moment you read it, in tiny pieces. 12,000 Russian soldiers were here when we came. 5,000 are left, 7,000 have been shot. Your clothes are their uniforms. I am from Warsaw.* Shredding the paper into tiny pieces, I return to the lower floor to stand in line for the toilet, where I dispose of the confetti.

This map was drawn according to Rena's recollection of the women's camp and details have been corroborated by the director of the Women's Museum, Oświęcim, Poland. The wall dividing the men's and women's camps was torn down in 1942 after the women were moved to Birkenau (see B Ia in Birkenau map) (Wyman). The asterisk marks the execution wall, where prisoners were shot.

We seasoned prisoners of two days eat our bread slowly and sip our tea as the precious rarity it is. We have bowls tied to our waists and spoons in our pockets. We get up in time for roll call because late sleepers get beaten. We are fast learners.

Outside, I see the man who gave me his bread earlier. He nods.

I have organized a scrap of paper and scratched on it, *Thank you for your note. Where are they killing the Russians?* I try to throw the stone over the wall but miss. It takes three tries before I am finally able to arch it past the electric fence, where it lands at his feet.

Turning my head, I try to pretend that I am doing nothing, breathing a heavy sigh of relief that no one has seen my poor attempt at communication.

Along Block One there is a new line of well-dressed women who have just gotten off the trains. On the other side of the barrack, a line of newly dehumanized girl-women wearing Russian uniforms exits. My heart beats faster. Narrowing my eyes, I squint against the sun, scanning for a face in the crowd that my heart distinguishes long before my eyes.[4]

"Danka!" Her beautiful chestnut-red hair is gone, but they cannot remove her brown doe-like eyes or touch her pretty face.

My arms itch to grab her. If I can just touch her, I know I will never let her go, but there is nothing I can do because there is a man with a machine gun and a dog standing guard over the new prisoners.

My feet hold their ground, forcing me to wait, but I see her and in that instant of recognition I find my reason and will to live.

There is a moment of general confusion as the new girl-women mill about, and I take that chance to merge with their ranks.

"Danka!" I grab her frail shoulders. For a moment she looks into my eyes terrified and threatened by this stranger. The stone in my stomach hardens—she does not recognize my face. Then she throws her arms around my neck, sobbing. "Rena!" She falters.

"Fall in! Get moving!" the SS start yelling.

I loop my arm under Danka's shoulders, preventing her from swooning.

"When did you eat last?"

"I can't remember. Oh, Rena, it was horrible. There were so many people on the train. We were sitting on top of one another. It was unbelievable."

Her face scares me. There is no focus to her eyes.

"How did it happen that you came here?"

"Because you are." Her voice is so naive, so young.

"What do you mean?"

"Our friends were going to hide me on a farm, but I had your letter and I told them I wanted to go work with my sister. You are all I have, Rena."

---

4. "March 28 [1942] . . . 798 Jewish women from Brunn [Slovakia] . . . receive Nos. 1999–2796" (Czech, 150). This was the second mass registered Jewish transport. Danka was numbered 2779.

"Danka, you shouldn't have come. We should have stayed in Slovakia and hidden. This is bad . . . real bad."

"March! Get in line!" The block elders push us into line so they can march the new prisoners into Block Five.

"Follow me." I push her past the others and march over to Elza.

"My sister has just arrived and she is so hungry and tired," I beg. "She has had no food since Bratislava. Please, Elza, let her be in our block! I am afraid for her."

"Okay, your sister can share your bunk." We are lucky; Elza has a heart. "You can help me with dealing out the bread and take an extra portion for yourselves."

I do not ask what will happen to the girl who was sleeping next to me; I know already that one does not ask. This is a selfish act, perhaps, but I have a sister who I have to keep alive and she is all that matters.

I know this is going to be a tough assignment for Danka. I can see in her face a look of bewilderment and shock. I will have to try to be by her side every moment. As if I have the power to shield her from the SS. But I actually believe I can; I have to believe I can.

We are in Block Ten for the night. We stare at our surroundings with frozen faces. The man I have been corresponding with calls my name from the windows, tossing over a bit of bread and another note. I go downstairs and retrieve it with more expertise and less hesitation this time.

"Here, Danka, a little extra bread from a fellow Pole." I am grateful for the extra portions from Elza and any Polish friend, and split the bread with Erna and Dina.

The note says: *They are being shot in the Block Eleven, next to you. Tear this up immediately.*

Taking Danka's hand in mine, I look into her face for an undisturbed moment. She is so tired she can barely keep her eyes open, but she tells us all that has happened to her.

"What about Zosia and the children?"

"I heard nothing."

"Maybe they will be okay."

It is a dim prospect, but we cling to whatever hope we can muster. There are tears streaming down our faces as the magnitude of what is happening around us begins to sink in. I am frightened. We are in prison. Our only crime is that we were born.

"We can't cry very much here," I say, dabbing her tears and mine with my sleeve. "We can't let them know they've gotten to us. You see here—this is the enemy and we're going to have to be real clever to outsmart them. Are you listening to me, Danka ?" She nods as I wipe the tears from her cheek.

"Then listen good to what I'm going to tell you. We're farmers' daughters. We're going to work, but that is what we do already.

"The work here will be nothing to us. And this is my dream, Danka—I am going to bring you home. We're going to walk through our farmhouse door, and Mama and Papa will be there waiting for us. Mama will hug and kiss us, and I'm going to say, 'Mama, I got you the baby back.'"

"Yes, Rena." Danka lays her head on my chest, falling asleep in my arms.

I stare into the darkness, cradling my sister until her breath lengthens and deepens and I am sure she will not wake. Gunshots crack open the night. Through the slats of the boarded-up window I watch Russian soldiers collapsing to the ground. There is so much I want to ask God for, but my lips are numb and my mouth is frozen open in disbelief.

I am wearing the uniform of these dead soldiers' comrades. Tomorrow more girl-women will march through the iron gates; they will be handed the uniforms of the men I have just witnessed die. My throat swells shut. I cannot tell anyone what I have seen.

Only my whispers can be heard, but I do not believe that anyone is listening. "God help us."

FOUR A.M.

"Raus! Raus!"

The room elders beat the bunks, poking the girls who are not early risers. It is Danka's first morning and she wakens with a start. I wish there had been time to prepare her for the ordeal of rising and roll call, but there has been no time to prepare her for anything.

"Rena?" In a daze she looks at me. How I hoped it was all a dream, a nightmare.

Today we will work. I have been eager to get busy and finish this prison life, and I wonder if they will release us sooner if we work harder. Anxious to wash my face, I am in line for the toilet immediately.

Danka moves slower, and as the line of women desperate to go to the bathroom lengthens she gets pushed back.

The kettle sits outside the door of the block. We hold out our bowls as the block elder scoops a ladle of tea into our bowls. We step into the dark. Our breath, the steam rising from our tea looks like specters and phantoms floating in our midst. We sip our tea quickly, hoping it will warm our insides, but the chill sweeps through our muscles.

The mist traces halos in the searchlight beams above our heads. Harsh light. I am not sure if it is the actual coldness of the morning, the lack of sleep and food, or abject fear that is making my knees and teeth knock together uncontrollably.

The SS walk up and down our rows counting our heads. They seem to take a long time as they compare notes and lists, unsure of what they are doing.

"Rena, I have to go to the bathroom," Danka whispers.

"That's not allowed. You should have gone before roll call."

"I can't help it."

"You have to wait until roll call is over." Reality is cruel. She holds her legs together.

"Pick your *kommandos*!"[5] an SS man orders. The kapos come toward us, sizing us up and down. I take Danka's hand, leading her back to our block where Elza is standing on the steps.

"Elza, will you please let my sister inside? She has to go to the bathroom; she has diarrhea."

"I can't do that. You know nobody goes into the block after roll call. There are rules! Besides, the room elders have already cleaned the bathrooms."

"Please, Elza. You know they will beat her if she messes herself."

---

5. *Kommando* is a German term implying a work detail under the command of a superior.

"I don't care." Her eyes glare at me, defying me to argue with her. "I gave you bread. What more do you want?"

"She has got to go!" I grab Elza's shoulders, shaking her. "How can you be that way?" I nod at Danka to run inside while I distract our block elder. "Don't you have a mother?" I yell. "A sister? Were you born from a stone? Who do you—arghh!" The words catch in my throat as the breath is slammed out of me and my collar is pulled back, choking me. Hurled through space, I fall roughly to the ground, seeing only the reddening face of an SS woman before her boot finds my ribs.

"You! *Scheiss-Jude!*" My arms fly across my face, my most precious possession. She pummels my thighs and my back, but I do not scream or cry. I have seen enough abuse in the past few days not to encourage it through pleas to stop. I bear her assault like a stoic as she steps on me again and again and again. When she finally stops, I crawl to my knees looking for someone to help me up. Danka has returned from the toilet and is crying without any noise. My legs are bruised, my ribs hurt. I can barely breathe, but I have my face, and after a few moments I can walk.

We join the ranks of still unchosen girls. A kapo points at us. "You there! Line up here!"

I grab Danka's hand, pulling her with me. The kapo must have seen me get beaten and I wonder why she's chosen us. I have never been hit before and hide my eyes, ashamed to look into our kapo's face. I feel so small and insignificant. I feel completely worthless.

"March out!"

The fog is rising. We follow the other groups out the gate, toward the fields, to work. Shuffling our feet so as to keep these so-called shoes on our feet, we try to march. Some girls are still holding their pants up; some, like myself, must hold our shirts shut. The wind pierces the bullet holes in our uniforms.

There is a draft at my knee and one by my heart. I wish I were not so sore. After two days of doing little else but cleaning and worrying, work will be a welcome relief. I want to show them what a hard worker I am and how proud a farmer's daughter can be of her strength. I ache all over.

"How are you feeling?" I manage to ask Danka. Worrying about her will take my mind off my throbbing bruises.

She nods, afraid to answer. An SS man passes us. They are the monsters hidden in the mist, our nemeses dressed in gray. They are everywhere.

"Halt!" There is a pile of sand and dirt and stones before us.

Our kapo orders, "You will sift this sand through these nets and load it onto those lorries. *Schnell!*"

We take shovels from a shed before beginning to dig the rocky soil and toss it through the net. It does not take long for our hands to ache and our shoulders to grow sore. Blisters appear almost immediately on our palms, and just as quickly they pop and make the shovel handles slippery. A young girl leans against her shovel to breathe for a moment. A whip cracks across the air, striking her on the cheek. Her cry is spontaneous. Shocked, she returns to her task with renewed vigor as a welt of blood forms on her cheek. I catch Danka's eye for a split second. Do not stop.

Once the lorry is full we are ordered to push it up the hill, where we must unload the sand into a separate pile. We line up, four on each side of the lorry. The wheels are steel and made for railroad tracks. Forging forward, we hold onto the cold metal sides, heaving with all of our might. Movement is slow, but once the momentum is built we manage to complete our task. After unloading the carts, we push the lorries back down the hill with relative ease and start all over again. By noon we have completed many trips.

A huge cast-iron kettle is carried into the fields by male prisoners.

Other kommandos arrive at the kettle and we line up for the noonday meal. Hungry and eager to have time to eat, Danka and I push our way into line. The kapos serve us. The servings are pitiful. We can see a few vegetables hiding deep in the murky depths of the water, but the ladle does not even graze them. It does not deserve to be called soup; it is barely turnip broth.

"Tomorrow we'll get in the back of the line," I tell Danka.

"Why?"

"Because the less water there is on top, the more likely we are to get a piece of meat or turnip."

We sip our noonday meal slowly, hoping to savor what little there is, hoping it will give us the energy we need to continue.

My mind tastes these circumstances like strange food. For a moment I allow myself to brood. This is slave labor we are doing. I cannot accept this thought, though. It will get better. I am just hungry.

Maybe they will give us more food tonight after a hard day at work. We are working toward a goal: freedom. We are helping the Germans build something. These justifications, no matter how small and insignificant, help me get up, get in line, help me continue working.

The weather is not encouraging as the afternoon labors on, and a steady drizzle turns to sleet. The mud becomes like cement, grabbing at the wheels of our carts, and as the temperature drops, the metal we cling to freezes to our skin. Whips snap above our heads, sometimes landing against our backs like stinging wasps.

At least we have wool shirts on to protect us from the elements and the rawhide. Like a team of plow horses we are prodded. A girl pushing the lorry loses her shoe. Our kapo pulls her out of line quickly, before the cart can lose its momentum. The girl looks in the mud for her shoe and then I do not notice what happens to her.

We have our own shoes to worry about.

Somewhere in the late afternoon, as the gray sky above us darkens, we hear the blessed order to "Halt! Line up!" We stand in line, muddy and worn out. We are not the same girls who marched to work this morning; our heads hang lower, our eyes do not dart as quickly and alertly. Danka's cheeks are sunken, her eyes almost vacant. We march defeated to the blocks.

Evening roll call lasts forever. We stand in our neat rows watching the other details enter camp. Some of the girls are carrying a body. I want to shield my sister's eyes from this sight, but I cannot move. An SS guard orders that the body be dropped next to us. I am counted. Danka is counted. The living are tallied in a separate column from the dead. I think it is dark but cannot be sure; the lights from the watchtowers are a constant brutal sun that does not warm.

We hurry into Block Ten, our new home, in silent shock. The room elders dole out our crusts of bread. There is no extra food for the hard day of work; there is not a slice of meat or cheese, just a smear of margarine on our dirty hands. Sitting on our beds, we stare at this meal. How did it come to be called dinner? Slowly, gently, we begin to lick our palms.

"I can't take this." "Look at my hands." "I have blisters." "I'm starving. Why won't they feed us more?" The voices timidly emerge along the rows of bunks. Others are already curled up on their mattresses, weeping in their sleep. A few voices can be heard talking to the air and I wonder if I was right about the men I saw on our first day here. Maybe this is a place for the insane, maybe it will not be long before we are all talking to the air. It seems so long ago that I thought the men in camp looked like lunatics. It has not even been one week.

I go downstairs after eating to wash myself. My nipples are raw and red from the scratchy wool shirt and the cold that corrodes my skin as viciously as the bugs I am infested with. Why didn't they let me keep my bra and underwear? I feel as if someone has taken sandpaper across my breasts until there is no skin left. Closing my shirt, I return to our bunk upstairs. Danka is already fast asleep. I try to lie down next to her but my side is too tender.

Pulling my knees under me, I crouch over my legs, allowing my shoulders to fall forward. My head rests on the mattress.

I wonder how I will ever fall asleep, but I am too tired not to. Like a small boulder I slumber.

∞

FOUR A.M.

"*Raus! Raus!*"

We roll out of bed and race to the bathroom before the line is too long. We get our tea and drink it quickly while we wait for the SS to count our heads. The tea is not warm enough to warm our hands or our bellies. We line up behind Emma, our kapo. Somehow we have learned her name in the past few days. She has a black triangle. She is a prostitute. We march behind her in rows of five in the dark to the field where we will sift rocks and sand all day.

The mud is so deep now that it is almost impossible to push the lorries. Still we haul our loads through the muck. Like

Sisyphus, in the Greek myth, we are punished, forced to push that eternal rock up a hill.

Again at noon we are allowed a few moments of rest and some turnip stock. Even waiting at the end of the line does not assure any pieces of vegetable or meat, but the broth is a little thicker or maybe we just think it is.

On Saturday, our Sabbath, we work. It is just another way that they undermine our faith and challenge our fortitude. We toil in the mud, forgetting that it is against Hebrew law to lift a hand in labor on this holy day. We shovel and push, sift and haul, from sun up to sundown.

On Sunday there is no roll call. It is the Christian Sabbath and they honor this day of rest, though not out of Christian charity.

It is a free day, if anything can be called free in Auschwitz. We sit on our beds, speaking to one another for the first time. "Where are you from? How old are you?" Meaningless chatter that has no place in memory. We do not discuss our circumstances. Bashfully, we try to rid ourselves of the lice embedded in our uniforms and every crevice of our bodies, scratching our heads, brushing out our underarms. I take off my pants and run my fingers along the seams and pockets, pulling the bloodsuckers off and squeezing them between my fingernails until they pop or squish with my blood.

Within an hour my fingernails are black and blue from killing the parasites, so I toss them on the floor, squishing them with my shoes or just ignoring their squirming white bodies. If I think about what I'm doing, if I look at them for too long, I will vomit.

It takes all day, this ritual cleansing. I wash my face and hands three or four times, hoping to feel clean again. It is futile. Finally, I must lie down and rest. Sleep is not forthcoming, though, for there is the gnawing of the lice I have missed, the voices of Slovakian girls around us, my sister's heavy breath. She slumbers. I must keep watch. I lie on my bunk staring at the ceiling, waiting for sleep to take me away. Some nights it comes swiftly. Some nights it lingers just on the fringes, out of reach. Sometimes I hear the rifles firing at the wall in Block Eleven. Other nights I hear nothing, but this does not mean there are not Russians being shot.

It only means I don't have the energy to hear or think about the dying next door.

In the morning, before anyone else has even opened their eyes, I wake knowing that something has changed in my body. I stare up at the bunk above me for a few minutes, wondering what I have sensed about myself; then it comes. The slow moistness on the wool against my legs. The cramp in my stomach. I sit up with a start and pull down my trousers to check. The stains on my thigh are unmistakable. I have my period.

Slipping downstairs to the toilet, I look for something to use, but there are no rags or sanitary napkins, only small squares of newspaper. The flow has increased since I stood up. As I check the searchlights before stepping outside, blood trickles down my leg. I remember Mama handing me a soft piece of cloth and saying, "Go put this on and bring me the other one. Don't look at it!"

"Yes, Mama." I obeyed her words. She didn't want me to be frightened by my own blood.

I scour the ground looking for anything that might help me hinder the flow. There is nothing. The kettles are being brought to our door, and I know Danka is up by now, wondering where I am.

Returning to the block toilet, I take a few squares of newsprint. Wiping them against my trousers to make sure they're clean, I shudder. Then, without thinking any further about it, I crumble them up and place the newspaper between my legs. I spend the day completely self-conscious, afraid of what getting my period means in this place. I cannot speak to Danka about it. Dealing with this curse means praying that it will go away quickly and never return.

There are more girls in our ranks today; a transport must have come in.[6]

Emma collects us for work and we march out to a large, open field. I am grateful that there are no lorries and sand for us to cart today. My back is still sore, though the bruises on my leg are almost gone.

---

6. April 2–3, 1942: Passover had just begun as two more transports of women arrived from Slovakia bringing another 1,962 girl-women into camp. It would be another ten days before another transport arrived, and this time it would have men on it, as well. The only other transport to arrive in March was the first transport from France. It had 1,112 men on it, numbered 27,533–28,644 (Czech, 150–53).

There is a large pile of bricks. "You will carry these to the other side of the field. You must carry ten bricks apiece!" Emma tells us.

We pick them up one by one, balancing them in our arms until we have a full load.

Arms throbbing, pulled almost out of their sockets by the weight, we walk carefully so as not to trip. The shoes impede us, slipping side-to-side underneath our feet. It's hard enough to keep the shoes on in the mud; now we cannot even see where we are going with so many bricks in our arms. The rocks and brambles grab at our feet as if we are making our way through a maze. We cannot drop one brick and pick it up without losing the whole load. Emma follows behind us, whipping us to work harder.

"Halt!" Emma stands by the kettle serving our noontime snack. We sip the broth hungrily. It is hard to slow the gulping tendency because the stomach craves more. We carry bricks for the rest of the day until we hear "Halt!"

We take our bread at the door. Am I imagining it or have the portions gotten smaller for Danka and me? The block elder's sister has arrived in camp, and Elza has seen to it that she is in our block. I believe she's eating our bread.

"I'm going to go to the window to see what I can organize," I tell Danka, walking to the front of the block. It is a newly born bartering system, and what I trade with the men on the other side of the fence is simply being Polish. They long to speak with their countrywomen, and Danka and I are two of just a few Poles in the women's camp; we have this one advantage over the Slovakian girls, who do not speak Polish.

"What's your name?" I hear a man's voice from the other window.

He sounds sympathetic.

"Rena. My sister and I are here, and we are both very hungry."

"Go downstairs. I'll throw you something."

I wait and wait by the door; nothing falls by the steps, though. Elza's door is a crack open. I worry that she will punish me for being downstairs after yelling at her the other morning. Something falls in the dirt. I check the guard tower. He is looking the other way. I dash out the door, grabbing my parcel, and lean against the wall, breathless. It is hard to comprehend that such a mundane task means risking my life—I could die for something as insignificant as a piece of bread the size of my hand.

Danka looks at me in horror when I hand her half of the bread. "It's Passover, Rena. We shouldn't be eating leavened bread."

"It's a *mikvah*, Danka. A gift. I am sure God will understand."

FOUR A.M.

"*Raus! Raus!*"

We roll off our bunk, slipping the sandals onto our feet. We divide the extra portion of bread and quickly eat.

"March!"

Even though we are tired we try to march proudly, just as we are instructed to.

"March!"

Heads forward, we step in unison, playing the part of dutiful servants to the Third Reich, but there is nothing to be proud of. We organized an extra piece of bread. It means a lot to us; it is nothing to them.

"Line up across the field!" The pile of bricks has not gotten any smaller overnight. We line up, wondering what this chore will mean.

"You go on the right side of me," I tell Danka.

"Face me!" We shuffle into position, standing about ten feet apart, and wait. Orders are barked in German. The girl in front of the line picks up a brick and throws it to the girl next to her, who throws it to the next girl. The whip cracks as the girl in the front shakes the cobwebs from her brain and grabs another brick.

The girl to the left of me tosses the first brick into my hands. I toss it easily to Danka, turning back just in time to receive the next brick. At the front of the line we can hear the SS yelling, "*Schnell! Schnell!*" The tempo increases so that there is barely a moment between tossing the brick to our neighbor and receiving the next brick. Within twenty passes, blood begins to ooze from cuts on my hands. The rough edges of the baked clay slice into our palms, repeating the injuries over and over. Danka is slow at this chore and doesn't always turn in time for me to throw my bricks, but the girl by my side is not waiting for anything. She throws them anyway.

I want to scream at the pain in my foot when the bricks land on my arches or toes, but I do not. I do not do anything to call attention to myself. I throw the bricks as I have been instructed, but I do not throw them at my sister's feet; I do not inflict the torture on her that is being inflicted on me. I grab these bricks quickly from my feet and hold them until Danka can catch up; sometimes I am holding two or three bricks at once, sometimes I have four. Danka sees that I am in trouble and speeds up, but she is like me, unwilling to throw bricks at her neighbor's feet. We are lucky in one thing only: the SS do not see the bricks falling on our feet. Others are beaten for the same offense. Last week our backs hurt from the strain of pushing and shoveling; today our sides hurt as we twist and sway with the weight of the bricks. Every muscle throbs.

Lunch comes hours after the sun has risen, hours after the first welt raised its angry head on our hands. Each a mass of rough cuts and torn skin, our hands hurt just carrying our red bowls full of gray-white soup. We sit for about twenty minutes before marching back to the line, to the bricks. Our stomachs and the pain in our hands gnaw like persistent rats at the last vestige of our humanity.

The afternoon drags on.

At sundown we march back to camp. We stand at roll call. We are counted. There are a couple of bodies piled next to us. They look so alive, as if you could reach out and wake them. If they don't look dead, I speculate, could we all be dead? Maybe this is all there is, maybe there is no world beyond us. One can't think like this without going insane. I stop pondering any thoughts that might lead to insanity. Focus again on the present. The girl-women who carry bodies into camp at the end of the day are in work details under the kapos with the green triangles that signify they are convicted murderers. At least our kapo is not one of those.

FOUR A.M.

"Raus! Raus!"

We stand for inspection. We can barely keep our eyelids open but for the crisp German orders cracking around us in the night that is really morning. We line up behind Emma. There are a few missing and a few added to our kommando.

My heart sinks as we near the field where we worked the day before. The SS orders are derisive; if they could laugh at us they would. "Move this pile of bricks back to the other side of the field." We stand, unable to move, unable to comprehend.

"*Schnell!*" The whip snaps; we slaves scatter.

Danka stands next to me, away from the pile we must move. I pray that the girl next to me doesn't throw bricks on my feet. The first brick slices into my hand as the sun breaks through the clouds. Pain and light. I toss it to Danka, willing it to land gently in her hand, pleading with the brick not to hurt my sister. This is useless! It hurts a lot more knowing that this work is futile, knowing that they see our labor as worthless. How long can this go on?

Our hands will be stumps if it continues. This is not work. It is meant to destroy us. Like a thunderhead obscuring the sun, I blot out this thought.

After evening roll call, for some reason I linger outside, unwilling to run into the block for the night. Maybe it is the faint smell of spring in the air; maybe I am too tired to run behind the others and wait in line. Danka has gone ahead.

"Rena? Rena!" I look through the wire of the men's camp at a skeleton who seems to know who I am. I cannot move. Squinting my eyes, I stare and stare.

"It's me. Tolek." The bones of his skull seem to stand up out of his skin. His eyes bug out above his cheekbones. He checks the guard tower to make sure no one sees him.

"Tolek! What are you doing here? How long have you been here?"

"I was arrested a few days ago for smuggling people across the border."

"Did they hurt you?"

His mouth does not speak, but his eyes answer my question.

"You look hungry," I say. "Wait here. I'll get you my bread. Lucky for you I haven't eaten yet!"

"I can't eat your bread, Rena!" He turns slightly so no one can tell we are having a conversation.

I turn away from him. "You and Andrzej saved our lives, Tolek. Danka and I would be dead or worse if you hadn't taken us to Slovakia. You have been arrested for saving people like us!"

"And look where it got you."

"We are alive and that is enough. You never took money for that trip; now you must at least accept my miserable bread." I start to walk away against his protests. "I won't take no."

My feet have hope in them again as I run to find Danka. I have seen someone from our past; we are not dead. I can help someone.

I no longer feel helpless or at the whim of a fate governed by German SS. I run breathless and tired up the stairs to the bunk Danka and I share. "Danka! Tolek is in the men's camp!"

"Tolek?" Life flickers in her eyes. "Where?"

"Outside. Come on. He's very hungry. We will have to share your bread tonight." I stop, looking directly into her eyes. "He looks terrible, like he might drop of starvation. We must help him."

"Yes, of course." Her eyes are full of tears. We run downstairs and out to the camp road, throwing our meager meal high over the barbed wire. There are no second tries tonight; it lands at his feet.

"*Bög zapłać* [May God reward you]." Tears get caught in his throat.

"May God reward you, Tolek," we answer, moving away from the fence, unable to risk speaking further.

Danka squeezes my hand. "He'll be okay, won't he?"

"I hope so."

The next few days we hoard our bread jealously so that whenever we see Tolek we can throw him an extra portion. . . . Then he stops coming to the fence.

LIKE ME, ERNA keeps a look out for Fela among the new arrivals, but we work so hard each day that it is not easy to know when there are new transports. I don't know how she knows, but somehow Erna finds Fela amid a group of newly shaved girl-women.

We take Fela into our block and hold her as she tells us news too grim to hold in our hearts, and we weep for the girls from Tylicz.[7]

On our fourth Sunday in camp they shave us again. We had secretly hoped they would let us grow our hair back, but after the weeks of itching stubble it is shaved off again. Between the lice, the bedbugs, and the hair, there is always a nagging prickle somewhere on our bodies. I long for order and neatness, any way to feel better and not so filthy.

Our kapo, Emma, is brunette. She pulls her hair back tight against her head and wears a babushka. She is taller than most of us. Her friend Erika—also a kapo—has curly blonde hair and a pretty round face. She is slim and of medium height. Our blocks go from Five to Ten. Emma, Erika, all of the kapos live in a different block, but they are in camp with us. Only the SS live outside the electric fences.

I haven't seen Tolek in quite a while and am worried about him. It is dusk, time to be going into the blocks, time to be getting to sleep soon so we have energy for tomorrow, but I scan the men's camp for our friend's face.

Erika walks by and then turns back. "You want to come and see our block?" she asks me. I am startled but do not show surprise. This seems like a strange offer.

"I'm not allowed. I'm Jewish." I tell her.

"Yah, of course you're Jewish or you'd be living in my block, but come see it anyway. I'll take the responsibility."

Sure, I think, you'll take the responsibility, but I'll take the beating if we get caught. The sun glows red on our faces as I follow her lengthening shadow.

She opens the door for me and I step into a world of neatly made beds and rooms where there are sheets and pillows. There

---

7. Fela Dranger arrived on the eighth mass registered transport to Auschwitz on April 3, 1942, and was numbered 6,030. There were 543 men and 457 women on that transport with her. By August 15, 1942, "only 41 of [the men] are still alive; i.e. within 16 weeks, 502 men die"; death records of the number of women who died within the same period of time were either destroyed by the SS or never accurately recorded (Czech, 158).

is a blanket that looks thick and warm. How I'd love to have a blanket like Erika's.

"Have you ever loved a woman?" she asks me.

I come out of my reverie. "Of course. I love my mama and my sister, who is here with me."

Erika smiles benignly. "Would you like to sleep here tonight?"

"Oh, no. I'd be terrified! My sister would worry, too. It's not fair that I should get to sleep on cotton sheets while she has straw."

Then, fearing that I have been rude, I quickly apologize. "Thanks for asking, anyway. I can't leave my sister, even if staying here meant having a good night's sleep and being warm."

Erika laughs. "You go back to your block. You're not ready for this." She leads me toward the door. "Here." She slips me an extra portion of bread. I take it quickly, not understanding why she would offer me such a nicety, not comprehending anything that has just happened. The light from the kapos' block illuminates the ground and then is severed as Erika shuts the door. I disappear into the closing night.

In our block I split the extra piece of bread with Danka. The crisp, clean whiteness of the sheets in the kapos' block haunts me. I cannot bear to think about the filth I wear, the conditions in which we are kept. Where our hands were once blistered we have grown huge calluses. My chest and legs are always red from bites and the wool rubbing against my skin. I want to scratch and scratch at the dirt on my body until there is nothing left for the bugs to gnaw on. Suddenly I am struck by an idea and take off my pants.

"Rena, what are you doing?" Danka sounds concerned.

"I'm going to fold these horrible trousers and put them under our mattress at night so they have a crease down the leg."

"Don't, Rena. It's cold."

"I want to look neat, and there is no place to wash and iron these clothes." I spit on the fold and begin running my fingers down the material, squeezing it together. "If I can't be clean, at least I can be neat." My glance falls to the floor. My shoes are filthy.

Our poor feet are too miserable to look at for long. They are no longer pink with health but pale and dyed with reddish brown stripes left by the leather straps. Soon it will be summer and at least our feet will not be cold, but now it is spring, and the weather is the worst it's been in years. I spit on the leather strap, using the inside of my pant hem to polish the leather. "I can clean my shoes first without dirtying my pants too badly!" I hold the first strap out for Danka to admire.

"You're crazy."

I return to pressing the crease into my uniform before motioning for her to move. Lifting the mattress up, I lay my trousers lengthwise, smoothing them until there is not a wrinkle. I place the mattress back in its place and let Danka get back in bed. She shakes her head but doesn't say another word.

In the morning we roll off our straw pallets. I lift up the mattress, retrieving my neatly pressed pants. Shivering a little, I pull them on, tuck in my shirt, and tie them with my rope. Smoothing my trousers down my leg, I smile; the leather strap has a sheen even in the dark. What I wouldn't do for socks.

"You look nice, Rena," Danka observes.

We rarely have to use the bathroom more than once a day because of dehydration, although I try to wash both morning and night. It is more to my liking to use the facilities in the evening than to wait in the morning line and chance a beating at roll call.

WE TURN OVER the dirt in a field. Shovel after shovel, we lift the damp dirt and rocks into the air, dropping them back to the ground. Sprigs of spring-grass shoots stick up from the earth.

When no one is looking we sneak these little blades into our mouths. The white portions of the grass are sweet and succulent. However small, they comfort our dry throats.

The SS woman over our detail today is gorgeous. Her raven-black hair gleams in the sun. She must have had a perm. I had a perm before I came to Auschwitz. She is dressed in gray. Her skirt is tailored to her waist and her boots are polished to an obsidian gloss. Her skin is alabaster, radiant against her rosy cheeks, and her lips shine with health despite the wind.

The wind nips at us between the holes in our clothes. The SS woman's black cape keeps snapping in the wind as if teasing us,

saying, Look at me! Look at me! Aren't I gorgeous? Look how far
superior I am to you.

She stays far away from us. We have lice. We are poison to her
sophisticated senses. I cannot help but steal a few precious glances.
Her beauty holds my gaze. I am in awe. We are so wretched in
comparison.

She is *Reichdeutsche.* Her German shepherd has fine blood-
lines too; his head is not too pointed and his ears are upright,
attentive to her voice, her commands. He is gray and black. He
matches her outfit. Together they strut outside of the *postenkette,*
the work boundary that separates her from us slaves. Her whip
cracks against her boot. The wind cracks her cape. We shovel.[8]

Out of the corner of my eye, I see her take her army cap off
her head. Her hair dances in the wind, against her cheeks. Her
eyes are defiant as she looks at Emma, who is not, who will never
be, her equal. She throws her cap outside of the boundary that we
are restricted to work within. I quickly drop my gaze to my work.
The wind stills.

"You there!" the SS woman barks. "Get my cap."

A girl looks up from her work, glancing at the rest of us, but
we are busy. We are invisible. She is not. She puts her shovel down
and runs quickly across the field to obey the order. She does not
think about it. She does not question it. She is a slave just as we all
are. Hesitating before crossing the boundary to retrieve the wardress's cap, she casts a glance back at the SS woman.

"*Schnell!*" The wardress cracks her whip. Stooping to retrieve
the cap, the girl moves tentatively toward the Aryan. Her frail and
skinny arm holds out the cap timidly.

"Attack!" The wind grabs the order with a hiss.

The girl freezes, paralyzed between fear and confusion.

The dog rushes past us, snarling. The girl's hands fly to her
face.

I move in front of Danka. "Don't look."

---

8. This SS woman was most likely Juana Bormann. She was transferred from Ravensbrück to Auschwitz in March 1942, and was known as "the woman with dogs"
(Clark).

He lands on the girl's chest, driving her into the ground. Her screams lacerate the sky, rending the breath from our mouths, splitting our hearts apart. We cannot cover our ears. We cannot breathe.

The screams, oh God, those screams. There is no sound on earth as horrible.

I glance, just once. Her bloodied arms flail the air. The dog reaches her throat. Cemented before my eyes, never to rest, is her spirit as it departs, separated from her body by a dog's jaws on her neck.

There is no silence like this silence . . . empty . . . silent.

The reverberation of death. I turn over the earth. Danka follows my lead. The girls next to us lift their shovels. Nobody breathes.

We work harder than before. As fast as possible we shovel, almost hysterical, faster and faster. Our muscles ache. Our ears weep with the echo of her screams. Only the sounds of the dying are immortal in Auschwitz.

The dog pants. The wardress pats his head. He licks his paw. "Good boy." The wind whips her cape. It begins to rain. We shovel faster and faster.

"Halt!" Jarred, Emma motions for two of us to carry the body into camp. The girl looks like a little spider somebody squashed underfoot—so thin, so fragile. I take her arms. They are not cold. They are sticky.

We march. With every step I take her head flops against my back. With every tap of her head, every step I take, her cries tear my soul. I tighten my grip, afraid that I may drop her, afraid that I might damage her further, afraid . . .

There is no silence in my head. There is only screaming.

FOUR A.M.

"Raus! Raus!"

We roll off our bunk. My period has arrived again, even though everyone else's has stopped. I rush to the toilet. Today I am lucky; there are newspaper scraps. I stash extra in my pocket before hurrying outside to get my tea. We get counted.

More and more prisoners keep arriving.

There are French women now and more Polish women. Those who are Gentiles are put in a separate block from us Jews. They are better than us. Some of the Jews are from the ghettos in Krakow. There is one young girl called Janka who we all cherish. She is just fourteen but had the guts to lie about her age on the train platform. For one so young and pretty, it is hard to believe she is also so streetwise. Her young life has been war and the ghetto, and I think she can be ruthless, but then Auschwitz is a good place to learn to be ruthless. Janka is a rare bird. She loves to flirt with the men, and they give up many portions of bread for her smile and because she has news of home, and perhaps because she reminds them of their own daughters.[9]

FOUR A.M.

"Raus! Raus!"

It is Sunday. How many Sundays have we been through? We do not talk about it. Danka and I pick lice off ourselves. It is disgusting, but it is worse to have lice than to pick them off. We go outside for a look around. Summer is here, but I am never warm.

I wonder if the chill will ever go away or if it is like the permafrost in Finland, always just below the surface of our skin.

"Danka! Rena!" We can barely believe our ears. Scanning the fence, we see Tolek. He is looking much better, more like the boy we used to know.

"Tolek! Where have you been? We have been so worried."

"Are you hungry?" Danka asks.

"No, no bread. I have gotten a good work detail emptying the latrines. We take the filth to the fields, where the local farmers

---

9. July 4, 1942: "For the first time, the camp administration carries out a selection among the Jews sent to camp." The selection takes place on the unloading platform and "old people, children, mothers with children and pregnant women are told they will be driven to the camp. Then they are taken to the bunker in Birkenau and killed in the gas chambers." While the total number of people on the transport was not recorded, 264 men were given numbers 44727–44990 and 108 women were given numbers 8389–8496 (Czech, 191–92). Janka would have arrived on July 4 or after. Her number is not known.

take it to use on their crops for fertilizer. There is a kind farmer who sneaks me food from his kitchen whenever he can."

"That's wonderful."

"If you had not shared your bread with me, I would never have been given such a good job. You gave me the strength to go on."

"You gave us hope, too, Tolek."

"I'm going to throw something over." That is the cue to keep our eyes peeled for danger and to be ready to hide the thing coming over the wires. The guard in the watchtower is looking in the other direction. The coast is clear. A large chunk of real bread falls at our feet.

It is manna from heaven.

"Thank you, Tolek." Danka flashes her beautiful smile.

"It smells like home." I slip the loaf under my shirt.

"Thank you both. I must go." We watch our friend disappear into the men's camp.

The smell of the yeast-risen dough drives our nostrils to distraction.

"Come on, Danka, let's go back to the block and have a feast."

Huddled on our bunk with the Dranger girls, we divide the bread. This is not the sawdust-and-water biscuit-shit we get from the Germans, this is heavy Polish bread that comes from the earth and has been kneaded by a farm woman's hands. Our taste buds cannot cease watering. I imagine that the whole block can smell it. Our teeth tear at the dough and our jaws hurt after not chewing anything substantial for so long.

There is a memory that surfaces just behind my eyes, something about bread and Mama. I push it back, unable to think about anything dear or sweet right now. Tucking the thought back where it belongs, I continue the meal Tolek has shared with us, but there is a pain in my chest and something dampening my cheeks. I chew tenderly, wondering where my sniffles came from and if I've caught a cold, while wiping my nose with the back of my woolen sleeve.

∽

FOUR A.M.

"Raus! Raus!"

Roll off the bunk. Stand in line to pee. Get a splash of tea. Step into the dark. Wait on the camp road. Stand for roll call. Get counted.

The sun rises. Get counted. Step in line behind Emma. March out to the fields. Work until they say "Halt!" Get soup. Sit down for a moment. Get up. Get in line behind Emma. March back to the fields. Work until they say "Halt!" March in neat rows of five back through the gates, under the words ARBEIT MACHT FREI—the sign means nothing anymore. Stand in neat rows of five. Get counted. The sun sets. Stand in the dark. Get counted. Go to the block. Get a piece of bread. Stand in line to wash. Nibble at dinner. Make it last. Lick your hand. Lie down. Wake up.

FOUR A.M.

"Raus! Raus!"

At roll call a man called Himmler appears in camp. He must be important. He watches the order in which we line up. The kapos are counted. They are prisoners too. He looks at his list. "One in the ranks has finished her prison sentence today!" he announces.[10]

Silence. He reads her name. There are a few shouts and hugs of congratulations among the kapos. We watch, stricken. No one will read our names at roll call, pronouncing freedom. We know this now. They are prisoners. We are slaves. They are human. We are not.

It is finally hot. We crave water. We work in the hot sun until we are burnt and blistered by its rays. We now wear striped dresses, which are no more comfortable than the Russian uniforms. At least the dresses do not have bullet holes in them.

---

10. "July 17–18 [1942] . . . Himmler inspects the Auschwitz camp complex, takes part in the killing of a transport of Jews, attends roll call in the women's camp, and approves the flogging of female prisoners. He also orders Rudolf Hoss, the commandant of Auschwitz, to proceed faster with construction of the Birkenau camp" (Rittner and Roth, 29). The Kapo, Luise Maurer, is not released until late 1943 (Czech, 199).

There is a rumor that Auschwitz is going to be used just for men again. We are going to be moved to Birkenau.[11] There are other rumors of a gas chamber and a crematorium.

"What is Birkenau?" We do not believe the other rumors; they were started by the Germans to dishearten us.

FOUR A.M.

"Raus! Raus!"

Roll off the bunk. Stand in line to pee. Get a splash of tea. Step into the dark. Wait on the camp road. Stand for roll call. Get counted. The sun rises. Get counted. Get in line behind Emma. March out to the fields. Work until they say "Halt!" Get soup. Sit down for a moment. Get up. Get in line behind Emma. March back to the fields. Work until they say "Halt!" March in neat rows of five back toward. . . . Wait! We've turned. We are moving away from Auschwitz.[12]

Voices murmur through our ranks. We march. This is a change to our routine. The unknown is dangerous. Eyes vigilant, senses alert, we march away from Auschwitz, away from the walls and watchtowers. The sun sets. There are fences and more barbed wire towering before us. We march under a different gate with the same sign, ARBEIT MACHT FREI. We are not fooled. We stand in neat rows of five. Get counted. Emma and Erika and the other kapos go to their new blocks. They have moved with us to this new camp.

We stand in the dark getting counted. We are assigned to Block Twenty, or is it Twenty-Two? Erna, Fela, and Dina are assigned to a different block. It is dark when we step inside.

---

11. Auschwitz (Auschwitz I) is approximately two kilometers from Auschwitz II, often referred to as Birkenau; they were both a part of the same camp complex known as Auschwitz-Birkenau.

12. "August 5–10 [1942] . . . The women's section at Auschwitz I is moved to Section B- Birkenau" (Rittner and Roth, 29). "Birkenau was a swamp fenced off by electrified wire. No roads whatsoever, no paths in between the blocks. . . . March to mid-August 1942 . . . about 17,000 women prisoners, most of them Jews, arrived at Auschwitz. A large number of them (probably about 5,000) perished before the transfer of women to the camp at Birkenau" (Strzelecka, 401, 394).

The floor is dirt. There are no bunk beds here; there are shelves, wood planks, three tiers high. We are supposed to sleep here? Where are the mattresses? Our beds look like horse stalls. There is a sour smell of human odor. There are rags for blankets. We stand, squeezing our bread in our hands, unable to cope, unable to move.

A girl begins to cry. Her fear grabs us, and like dried straw we burn inside. Tears cannot quench these flames of disaster. We are lost. This is Birkenau.

BIRKENAU

(Auschwitz II)

HOW WILL WE SURVIVE THIS PLACE? What do we have to do to in order to live? What does this life mean? These are not questions that abuse our thoughts every waking moment of every day; they are simply undercurrents, concerns that cannot be answered. What is there to know? We did not receive a ticket when we entered Auschwitz-Birkenau saying, You will leave on such and such a day; you will leave alive. There are no guarantees. Birkenau is a cruel awakening. In Auschwitz there was a lot of death, but it was not such a daily fact of life. Now we see death every day. It is a constant, like our meals. And there are not just one or two girls dying, like before, but tens and twenties and losing count.[1]

I know that I must be with my sister. I know that I must make sure she lives; without her I cannot survive. I do not admit that to myself, but I know she is a part of my truth, my being. We cannot be separated; there is danger in separation.

It is colder than it was yesterday, but lately it is always cold. Even in the heat of summer I did not feel warm. We are wet for days after it rains; damp penetrates everything. How does one measure temperature when there is but one temperature? It is a

---

1. "The girls' camp suffered the most, as it was not fitted with sanitary installations, and the poor wretches were covered with lice. . . . Suicides were frequent and were mostly committed by throwing one's self against the high tension wires of the inner fence. This went on until they had dwindled to 5 percent of their original number" (Wyman, 32).

dull chill, like the numbness in my mind—always there, taken for granted, eventually ignored.

I used to love the warm, sparkling days of summer, but this year it seems to have disappeared. Can it be fall already? How long have we been here? What month is it? There must be trees somewhere in the world that are changing color, preparing to welcome winter with their fiery reds, oranges, and golds, but I do not see any changes here. It is always gray. I myself am gray.

We have a calendar in Birkenau. It is hunger.[2]

The emptiness in our stomachs never ceases, just as the chill never leaves. It is our only clock, our only way to discern what time of day it is. Morning is hunger. Afternoon is hunger. Evening is hunger. Slowly we starve until we cannot make out anything beyond the gnawing of our intestines grinding against each other.

A block elder asks me if I want to be a room elder. "No, thank you," I tell her, but in my head I think, I can't take bread from others who are as hungry as me; I can't hit people suffering just like I am. I repeat my private chant: be invisible. That is one of the rules I live by. Those who are too visible eventually get struck down, so I stay in the background and try simply to get by.

There is only one thing that exists beyond the gates of Auschwitz-Birkenau. It lies in wait for me like a beacon of light shining through the fog. I hold it before me constantly, every second of every day. It is the only thing that keeps me going: Mama and Papa. They beckon to Danka and me from the fringes of my mind. Their hands wave against a backdrop of snow and winter sky. *We're here!* they cry. *We're waiting for you to come home.*

We're coming, Mama, I remind them. *Don't leave us here alone.* And they don't. I hear Mama's voice comforting my troubled mind, soothing the worries of our existence. The only thing she cannot help is the hunger, but even that dulls in comparison to the knowledge that Mama and Papa are waiting for Danka and me to

---

2. Polish Jews and Russians were referred to as "useless eaters" by Herbert Backe, Hitler's minister of Food and Agriculture, who was the mastermind behind the "Hunger Plan," which posited that food was a major factor in winning the war; therefore, making sure the *Wehrmacht* had enough food meant others had to starve (Collingham).

return to Tylicz. I frame this picture in my mind and hang it on a mental wall where I can gaze at it constantly. I know they are there. I work because they need me. I eat because they are waiting. I live because they are alive.

Mama, I brought you the baby back. I repeat it over and over in my head. It is the refrain to the song that keeps me strong and healthy and spirited: Mama, I brought you the baby back. My one great feat in life, my fate, is to survive this thing and return triumphant with my sister to our parents' house. My dream cannot be marred by German whips or chains or rules. I will succeed because I have no other choice. Failure does not even occur to me. We may die in the interim—death cannot be avoided here—but even that will not dissuade me from my sole purpose in life. Nothing else matters but these four things: be with Danka, be invisible, be alert, be numb.

I wonder if I will ever wake up to turn over in a real bed again. Will I ever open my eyes without German commands and decide to sleep in because it is raining out and I don't have to get up yet? Will I ever dream again? The days are long and hard but the nights are devoid of even the relief of dreams, the pain of nightmares. I crawl onto my shelf and pull a woolen rag around my collarbones. I pretend that it will warm me. Falling into unconsciousness, I am woken by barking, by gunshots, by nothing at all . . . by four a.m.

. . ."*Raus! Raus!*"

The room elders hit the girls who are still sleeping and those who aren't quick enough to scramble off the shelves we lie on. Is this place so different than Auschwitz? The room elders, the block elders, all have an edge in their voices that I haven't heard before.

For all their privileges, the extra food they pilfer from us less fortunate slaves, they also have a dirt floor beneath their feet. They have cots rather than wood to sleep on, but they are in a converted stable just as we all are.

"Come on, Danka." I shake her gently. "We have to get up and find the bathroom." There is no toilet in the block, as we had in Auschwitz; there is a bucket. The pot-bellied stove sits at the end of the rows of stalls and toward one end of the block, close to the block elder's room. There is a curtain dividing the block and room elders from the rest of us.

"Where's the toilet?" I ask, ducking as the stick strikes for my head. This is not a place for questions. We run outside. The kettle of tea is sitting in its customary place by the door. We hold out our bowls; the ladle splashes lukewarm tea across our hands.

Standing in neat rows of five in the dark, we eat our remaining piece of bread and wait for the SS to arrive. We have noticed that the day goes better if we can eat something before we work, so Danka and I always eat only half our portion at night, saving the rest until morning.

SS men Stiewitz and Taube march up and down the rows counting our heads. Wardress Drexler, the head of the women's camp, watches; her buck teeth stick out even when her mouth is closed. Roll call takes at least two hours this first day in Birkenau. We are not used to standing for so long at attention; fighting the urge to shift our feet, we must not even yawn. Every few minutes Taube hits someone for not looking attentive enough, for shifting her body, for no reason at all.

"Dismissed!" The orders crackle through the dawn light. I take Danka's hand, stepping quickly toward Emma. I have had her in my sight ever since she came out for roll call. With all the changes in the past twenty-four hours, I'm determined to keep one thing constant, and getting on Emma's work team is the only thing I have the slightest control over. She spares us a brief smile as we line up behind her. It is a small comfort to see a familiar face in such terrible surroundings. Emma's is that face.

We work all day and march back to the stables. "We should try to sleep here." I point to an area far enough away from the block elder's room to give us time to get up in the morning without getting struck by her stick. We crawl onto the shelving cradling our bread and clutching our blanket between us. Silently we chew half of our bread, hiding the remainder in our pockets. During the afternoon I have learned that Birkenau is where the Russian prisoners of war were kept. With a shudder I recall the bodies falling into the mud between Block Ten and Block Eleven. They must all be dead now.

These first few weeks we are barely surviving. The food is less than it was, which means it has gone from a crust to half a crust. The soup is so thin there is no use to wait at the end of the line for a piece of turnip or meat, and the tea is practically clear. Every morning that we wake up at least one girl has died in our block. There are no exceptions. We are dropping like flies.[3]

You have to have a brain to figure out all that is going on, the tricks to being camp smart: where it's the warmest, who's the most dangerous, who doles out a bit more soup. The new arrivals barely have time to figure out how to survive before they die.

After roll call you don't know about anything else that's happening. You can't keep brooding about what is befalling you and everyone else because then you won't have the energy to go on, and you have to keep going. The work you do may kill you, but if you don't do it, you will be killed.

No matter what the detail, we work, we dig, we carry, we sift, we push, we die. But Emma does not kill prisoners; this one thing I know. Every morning Danka and I run to Emma to get in her detail. Birkenau is bad, but Emma does not make it worse.

IT IS SUNDAY. We stand at roll call, but then, rather than being dismissed, we are ordered into a block where tables are set up. As we step inside we are handed a postcard and a pencil.

"You will write your family and tell them that you are fine and like working here," we are ordered.

I stare at them incredulously, unable to believe that I must write lies to my loved ones.

"Dear Zosia," I scribble at the top of my card.

"You will write exactly as you are told: 'We are being treated very well,'" they dictate to us. "'We have plenty to eat and the work is not hard. I hope to see you soon. Love, . . .' Sign your name."

I remember Zosia's cries when she said Nathan's card meant he was in Siberia, and on the bottom of my card I jot quickly in Polish,

---

3. "As the history of Nazi Germany so emphatically shows, racism's 'logic' ultimately entails genocide. . . . Any consistent Nazi plan had to target Jewish women specifically as women, for they were the only ones who would finally be able to ensure the continuity of Jewish life. Indeed, although the statistical data about the Holocaust will never be exact, there is sound evidence that the odds for surviving the Holocaust were worse for Jewish women than for Jewish men" (Rittner and Roth, 2).

It's cold here, just the same as Nathan told you. I pray Zosia sees the truth behind my words. I pray she and her children will not follow us to Auschwitz. We turn our cards in and are excused. I feel weak, shaky from the ordeal. As hard as we toil every day, writing those few words to Zosia has taken more out of me. Danka and I do not discuss the cards we have written. We do not discuss family at all.

My monthly curse wakes me. In the confusion of moving from one camp to another I didn't even think of sneaking newspaper squares with me. I didn't think the latrine in Birkenau would be any different than the toilet in Auschwitz. How naive I am; newspaper is a luxury that we no longer deserve.

Once a month my period still arrives without any prior warning. It is something I dread and wait for, never knowing when it will make its appearance. Will I be working? Will I be in the shaving line on a Sunday, embarrassed in front of the men? Will today be the day I cannot find anything to stop the flow and the SS decide to beat me to death for being unclean? Will today be the day the scrap I find gives me an infection?

I hate the smell. I hate not being able to take a bath. The sink in Auschwitz was a relief, but in Birkenau there are no sinks, just faucets. It is impossible to remove the dirt and grime from my body without soap. On Sunday, if there's time, I use my red bowl for a sponge bath, although there is no sponge and the water is nothing but cold. No matter how hard, nor how often I scrub, it always feels as if something is left on my flesh. I worry that the smell of blood will attract the dogs to me. Of all camp horrors, the dogs scare me the most. I pray that if I must die, I do not die screaming.

The routine has changed slightly in Birkenau. It is easier to use the latrine in the morning because at night, after the door is shut, no one can go outside. So I try to get up before the room elders and sneak outside before the line gets too long. If that doesn't work, I use the bucket under the cover of darkness and then slip back into the bunk next to Danka for a few more precious moments of rest.

As bad as Auschwitz was, I miss it. I miss being able to wash my face and hands, I miss the straw mattress and the little blanket Danka and I both had. Now we must fight for just one blanket, and that barely covers us. In Auschwitz, the bunk beds we slept on were spacious in comparison; now there are six women per shelf. We are crowded so close that we almost have to touch.

As if that isn't bad enough, almost every day there's another transport, and more and more girl-women are filling the camp. The girls coming in from Holland still have polish on their nails.[4]

There are so many more of us in this new camp than there ever were in Auschwitz, roll call takes twice as long as it used to. At the end of the day, when we're finally dismissed to our blocks, we run as fast as our weary legs can carry us to make sure we have a blanket and the best place to sleep. I have decided that we will always try to sleep on the middle tier of the shelves. The top is too high to climb up to after a hard day of work, and the bottom is too cold.

We take our bread, stepping into the dank block. Together we crawl onto the shelving, nibbling on half of our bread before collapsing into the despair of dreamlessness, crushing the other piece of bread in our hands for morning's breakfast. It is not safe in our pockets anymore. There are those who will try to pry open our hands while we sleep, to steal our food. There are those who will grab our blanket off our bodies while we sleep if we do not hold tight onto it. Some nights we come in from work and someone has taken our blanket already; some nights we wake up shivering because someone has ripped it from our hands. I cannot get up and do the same thing, though; taking someone's blanket while she sleeps is too heartless, so Danka and I huddle closer for warmth and wait until the next evening, when I will take a blanket off a bunk that has not been claimed yet. I have that right; someone has stolen ours.

In line for bread. The block elder calls out my name. "1716! You look sturdy. We're going to perform gymnastics on Saturday night. Can you do a cartwheel?" I nod my head gingerly. "Good! You want to earn an extra portion of bread?" I nod again, afraid to say no. "Then you and a few others will come with me and practice a gymnastic routine to perform for the SS this Saturday

---

4. Jews from Holland had begun to arrive in mid-July 1942, just before moving to Birkenau (Czech, 198).

night." I hand my portion of bread to Danka and follow the block elder and about ten other girls outside.

"We'll start with some tumbling," the block elder instructs us.

"Who here can do a flip?" Two girls raise their hands. "Somersaults? Handsprings?" I raise my hand with a few others. We line up according to our talents and proceed to work through our paces.

"Smile when you finish that round-off!" she shouts. "Hold that pose after you finish the cartwheels! Thrust your chest out! Chin up!" It is beyond strange to be tumbling across the floor of a vacant block on a little stage. It is even stranger to try to pretend we're having fun doing these antics.

We work for about an hour before we are excused. "Okay, get some sleep. Tomorrow we'll practice a pyramid." We trudge back to the block sore and tired from the physical exertion. I can't believe they're going to force us to perform for the SS. We continue to practice our routines for two more nights.

Saturday night as we receive our evening's ration the block elder tells us, "I have gymnastic uniforms for you to wear for the show. After you eat, come to my room and I'll give you the clothes." In her room, we each get a sweatshirt and pair of shorts to change into. "You will get your extra portion of bread after the show." She reminds us of the reason we're doing this charade.

"Now go change and meet me at the door in two minutes!"

A selected group of prisoners are allowed to watch. Danka is among them. The SS sit down in the back of the empty block to be as far away from the stage as possible. It was bad enough doing these tricks with no one watching, but now that the SS are watching the humiliation is ten times worse. A bulb hangs over our performing area, lighting the plywood stage. The SS sit in chairs at the other end, eager to watch their monkeys perform. They chat merrily, enjoying their Saturday night out, as if this entertainment were the circus coming to town.

We march into the center of the lights and bow to the officers.

They clap halfheartedly. The block elder beats on a drum she has organized from someplace, trying to give us a sense of rhythm. I do three cartwheels in a row. Applause. A girl does a flip. Applause. Somersault. Applause. I cartwheel in a circle. There is no smile on my face when I stand upright. Applause. The lips won't go upward no matter what I do. I can work ten hours a day, I can be starved to death and watch people die, but I cannot smile—that is impossible.

The wood under our bare feet is hard and unforgiving. I complete a round-off. Applause. A girl does a split. Applause. The bottom of the pyramid lines up. The second level gets on top of their backs, then the third. I vault on top of all of them, praying they don't collapse beneath me from fatigue. Then I stand up, raising my hands over my head, opening my mouth slightly. It is not a happy face I wear, it is a questioning face, a mouth hanging like a question mark. Why am I doing this? Is it really worth a piece of bread?

The applause is mediocre. I leap to the ground. We line up holding hands, bowing to our superiors, then turn around and march, chests out, chins up, back to our block.

In the block elder's room we return the gym clothes and take our extra piece of bread, like dogs getting a bone. "Good work," she praises. "Next time, we should try some more difficult flips." Eyes lowered, I scan the ground for some relief while splitting my portion of bread exactly in half to share with my sister.

There is not going to be a next time—can't she see how sick and tired we are? Just these few days of practice have taken their toll on our bodies. I'm afraid I have lost more weight; I know some of the other girls have. All for a piece of bread? We should have an entire meal for the work we did. I never want to do anything like it ever again. Crawling into our space on the shelf, Danka whispers, "You were good, Rena." Her voice is so sweet, so loving. My head droops. My eyelids fall. I disappear.

❦

MY FAVORITE JEWISH holiday is Yom Kippur because on that day we fast, and afterward everyone forgives each other and hugs and makes up. I love the whole idea of wiping the slate clean and beginning new and fresh. Fasting is an act of strength and spirit. And through fasting, I learned that being hungry was all in my mind. I even would dawdle on the way home from temple, just to stretch out my fast as long as possible. After sundown when we could finally eat, I would savor each morsel and eat slowly, so I could think about how my hunger was already gone. There was a sense of accomplishment in fasting all day, a sense of peace.

Somehow we figure out how many Sundays we have been in camp and this tells us it is Yom Kippur.[5] So Danka and I fast from sundown to sundown. In my heart I pray: Oh, Lord, my Lord, please help my parents and protect them until we can return home. Tell them we are alive and that we love them. Tell Mama that I know she is watching over us through your eyes. Strengthen our faith and our bodies. Let us not falter from hunger. In your name, Lord, who is my Lord.

There is power in my prayer; it strengthens my arms and my back as we sift the sand all day. The knowledge that our God is near us lifts our spirits and we work with renewed hope in our hearts, ignoring the bread deep in our pockets and refusing the soup at lunch. In the evening, after sundown, we eat yesterday's bread for supper and save today's for morning. It is something to fast, but we are so hungry already that fasting makes little difference to our stomachs. We simply do as we have done every year of our lives since we were old enough to fast on this holy day.

∞

DANKA IS BEHIND me, waiting for her soup, when the kapo accuses her of coming back for seconds and hits her on the head with the steel ladle.

"I'm never going for soup ever again." She stands in front of me crying, her bowl empty.

"Danka, you have to get soup. They don't feed us enough for you to skip a meal."

"I'm never getting in that line again."

"Here, share mine."

"No, you don't have to do that."

---

5. Yom Kippur was on September 21, 1942; Tishri 10 in the Hebrew calendar.

"Why not? It could've been me who got hit. She just chose you because she's cruel and selfish and she wants your meal, too."

"I'm not taking yours."

"Well, you better, because I'm not taking any until you do, so you're going to let the whole thing go to waste. Come on, take some." We take our spoons, scooping together out of the same bowl. She sips it hesitantly.

"You didn't fill your spoon up as much as mine. Take some more."

She takes a little more, smiling vaguely. There is a little tidbit of turnip floating around. I push it toward Danka. She pushes it back. And so we eat my portion of soup, two spoonfuls at a time, splitting the turnip evenly between us.

The next day she refuses to get in line at lunch, and I have to convince her all over again to take some of mine, and so it goes; we count our spoonfuls and share my soup. I wish she would return to the soup line but keep my mouth shut.

It is Sunday. It is fall. We get off our shelves. Get our tea. Eat our half piece of bread. There is a rumor that there is going to be a selection.

"What's a selection?" we ask among ourselves.

We groom ourselves all day, pulling lice from our armpits and clothes. There is no fighting these creatures; they are everywhere.

I spit on my shoes and wet the crease on my pants. It is important to look good if there is going to be a selection—whatever that means. I want to look right. Sunday fades with the light of a pale sun.

FOUR A.M.

"Raus! Raus!"

We grab our tea as we step outside. I notice that something is different immediately. The guards do not count us at once. Instead they stand at one end of camp, ignoring our neat lines and perfect rows. We wait and wait. Well after the sun is up, we wait. The row at one end begins to move forward slowly. We strain our eyes to see what is happening but they are too far away. "They are selecting us." The whisper scurries down the rows, informing those of us who are not yet moving toward the SS.

"What's it mean?" Danka asks.

"I don't know," I lie. I have an idea, but it is not something I will share with anyone I care about. We stand in our lines, forced to contemplate what new Nazi trick this is.

"They're deciding who will live and who will die," the whispers confirm. Our ranks grow silent and still. How can this be true?

How can they do that? We have seen how they step on us like cockroaches—why does this next thing comes as such a surprise? We move forward. I take Danka's hand, squeezing it reassuringly. "I will go in front of you," I whisper.

There are two sisters at the head of the line. I recognize them from the first transport. Like me, they've been here since the beginning. They step up to the table of SS officers. An SS points for one to go left and the other right.

"No! Please!" the one who has been chosen for life cries, falling on her knees. "Let me go with my sister," she begs the officer, careful not to touch him. She huddles at his glossy obsidian boots weeping for mercy.

He points. She follows her sister. Hand in hand they step toward the flatbed trucks.

I squeeze Danka's hand one last time before stepping in front of those who will judge me fit or unfit. Tomorrow may have no meaning for us if we do not pass this selection—and if we do pass? Tomorrow may have no meaning for us.

I hold my breath. The thumb points for me to live. Stepping forward hesitantly, cautiously, I wait for my sister . . .

The thumb points for Danka to follow me. I breathe.

SQUINTING FOR A LAST glimpse of the sisters, I suddenly wish I had gotten to know them, their names, anything about them. All I know is that they were in line before me when we got tattooed the second day in camp. I think they were the girls who were numbered 1001 and 1002. I look at my left elbow. The gray-blue ink blazes up at me. 1716. I haven't seen many numbers lower than

The Hartmann siblings (left to right): Bianca and Andrew
(survived), Valika and Olga (did not survive). There are no
known photos of Magda. Photo courtesy of Avi Mizrachi,
Holocaust Education Projects.

mine since we came to Birkenau. I wonder how many of us are left from the first transport.[6]

They push and heave the girls who have gone the opposite direction as we have onto the flatbed trucks. I haven't seen the dreaded trucks since my first day of arrival. Danka's face pales as the blood drains from her cheeks. Frozen with fright, she watches the girls scramble against one another as SS beat them with riding crops. Cattle and sheep are treated with more respect. I take her hand, trying to pull her away from the scene across the compound, but recoil at the touch of her clammy flesh.

"Come on, Danka. There's nothing we can do for them now."

"Where are they taking them?"

"I don't know, but it can't be good. Her eyes glaze over. The sun has sunk below the horizon. I cannot believe we've spent an entire day waiting for self-proclaimed gods to decide if we are fit enough to deserve life. That night there are fewer girl-women in our block. We do not ask where they've gone.

---

6. Although the data from the first transport list may never be completely analyzed accurately, it appears that close to five hundred of the girls were sisters or cousins. The dates of death for women from the first transport who died is incomplete as well. We do know that Olga (age seventeen) and Magda (age eighteen) Hartmannova died early on, and we provide their family photo here, as it is possible that they were the girls Rena remembers.

The following morning we line up for roll call, but we are not counted. In neat rows of five we wait. In the dark. In the morning light. In the noonday sun. We wait. The line moves forward. There is no pause for lunch, there is no break from standing and waiting.

We are "selected" again.

∞

FOUR A.M.

"*Raus! Raus!*"

There is another selection.[7]

∞

ONE NIGHT AFTER roll call the block elder gives Danka and me and quite a few others packages from the Red Cross. We stare at these packages, puzzled by their presence in this place. They even have our names on the brown paper: *Rena Kornreich* and *Danka Kornreich*. The stamp is from Switzerland. I stare at it for the longest time. It's colorful and ornate and confirms that there is a world beyond the electric fences and barbed wire that surround us. It is proof that somewhere someone cares whether we live or die.

We tear open the brown paper, ripping open the boxes as if we are opening presents from family. There is a can of sardines, a package of crackers, and a sweet tea biscuit. Slowly we unscrew the top from the sardines. They are so salty. After not tasting anything with flavor in six months, they are a smorgasbord to our mouths. We stick our fingers into the oil and lick slowly, trying

---

7. "October 1 [1942] . . . A selection is carried out in the women's camp, Section B-Ia, in Birkenau. 2,000 prisoners are selected and killed in the gas chamber the same day . . . October 2 [1942]. . . . A selection is carried out in the women's camp. 2,012 prisoners are chosen and killed in the gas chambers . . . October 3 [1942]. At another selection in the women's camp in Birkenau, 1,800 female prisoners are selected. They are killed in the gas chambers" (Czech, 247–48). This is the first time a selection is mentioned of female prisoners outside of the infirmary or transport.

to make it last, but even if we could lick it all night it would never be enough. The crackers and biscuits we stick in our pockets to save until tomorrow.

I feel stronger that day, savoring the crackers with our soup at lunch and saving the biscuit for dinner. The sweet cake serves as an actual dessert after our meager supper. It plunges our senses into another realm, melting in our mouths, leaving them yearning for more. We've craved sugar since the day we arrived in camp; it rushes through our bodies, but then it is gone. We are grateful for these three semi-meals, but the next day our stomachs yawn and ache for more and there is nothing left to eat except bread, tea, and soup.

"Are you going to get the soup today?" I ask, hoping the care package will have encouraged Danka's appetite. She shakes her head. I treat her as gently as possible, but if she doesn't start eating more and getting her own soup again she will turn into a *muselmann*, and from that there is no way back.[8] If we become emaciated, we're goners. I try and try to get her to get her own bowl of soup, but her spirit is dwindling before my eyes. How do I get my sister to want to live? Without that desire there is no way we can survive, and I need her just as badly as she needs me.

When we march out to work and return at night, now, there is a band playing and we're supposed to step in time to the music.[9] It is a paradox to everything else we do, a slap in the face to what dignity we have left. I think the Germans like the fact that it degrades us just one more rung down the ladder of life. The musicians have it better than we do, but we do not begrudge anyone who has the luck to find inside work. Besides, they're forced to play no matter what the weather, and they can be selected, just like anyone else, if they get ill or look poorly. They do not have it so much better. We are all slaves. One slave may have an easier

---

8. *Muselmann* is camp slang for those who have lost not only body weight from starvation but the will to live, becoming living skeletons.

9. Wardress Maria Mandel, former supervisor of Ravensbrück, became head supervisor on October 8, 1942, and organized the female orchestra in Birkenau (Rittner and Roth, 29). Mandel's sister, Wardress Elisabeth Hasse, is also in camp.

job, but we are all still slaves. The only way to avoid sure death is to work inside, but even that doesn't mean you can escape death completely.

FOUR A.M.

"Raus! Raus! Schnell!"

We rise off our beds of icy, hard wood. It is difficult to move. We are stiff and worn out. Every joint and ligament cracks with fatigue. It is freezing. The tea has lost its steam in these sub-zero temperatures. Even the SS, who are so punctual in everything, take their time entering the gates, counting our shivering bodies. It is the first frost of the season and our bodies are not yet used to the chill in the air.

My mind moves as sluggishly as the blood in my veins. A temporary lapse of conscious alertness, being at the end of the rows, and a brief pause crossing the yard to our detail, and Danka and I are late for Emma's detail.

"I'm full," she tells us. An SS signals for her to march out. She shrugs her shoulders; there's nothing she can do. We stand there looking forlornly at the kapo we have adopted as our own guardian, but her kommando—our kommando—marches out, leaving us behind. With a shiver I turn away, my sister in tow, hoping that Erika's detail is still open.

"Fall in!" A whip crosses my shoulder blades as our course for Erika is redirected and we're herded into the rows of another kommando. Snatched up by a kapo eager to fill her numbers, we line up behind this stranger and set off to work. Her eyes are bright and cruel. Her face is grim. She is all we have been trying to avoid. Her triangle is green. This kapo is a murderess. The tension in our ranks is palpable. We march in perfect unison.

"We have to be careful," I warn Danka, daring only the briefest of whispers. "Very careful."

It is a day without end. This kapo delights in finding fault and brutalizing us for it. She has a nose for the weak, and these she tortures unmercifully until they collapse and she can finish them off with one quick kick. By lunch she has killed three prisoners. She is as deft at killing. At lunch she merely splashes our bowls with broth; it lasts for barely a few sips. There are no regulations on food. No one cares whether she hoards it for herself or deprives us out of cruelty. She is evil embodied, relishing every moment she can impose pain, a sadist at home in a world of victims. We are her personal peons.

Won't she tire of her abuses? No, she continues throughout the afternoon, beating, destroying, demolishing us like little dolls. One girl is crippled beyond belief, and then, as an added measure of spite, the kapo leaves her broken and suffering on the ground next to the dead, knowing her turn will not come until she is dragged to the gas. There are no mercy killings here.

When the order comes to stop working, the crippled girl is forced to walk with only the aid of one other girl. Her whimpers and moans accompany us as we carry the dead and the wounded back into camp: three bodies in twelve hours.

Like all kapos, Emma hits us, but she does not do it out of enjoyment; she does it for show. If the SS are around she has to act tough, but she never beats anyone to bleed, and she never beats anyone to death. She hits you if you're lazy or do something stupid, and she'll smack you so the SS won't think you're favored, but the only dead we ever carry in from working under Emma's eye are killed by the SS or have collapsed from starvation or illness.

No matter what work atrocities they give us, Emma rarely adds to it. There are very few constants in camp, but Danka and I are a constant to Emma, just as she is to us. The three of us are there day after day. Maybe Emma isn't mean to us because she recognizes us. There are so many prisoners now that there are always new faces, new numbers, but we're the old-timers, standing in front of her every morning, doing our best to survive.

Not until we suffer the kommando under the murderess's command do we realize how lucky we are to have this secret ally in Emma. It is not that we are friends, or that she will do anything out of the ordinary for us—we are Jews, after all—but I think there is a place in her heart for my sister and me. I am counting on it—what else is there to depend on? There is so much uncertainty. Emma simply gives us one less thing to worry about.

∞

FOUR A.M.

"Raus! Raus!"

We crawl off the planks. Our shoes are already on our feet because they are never taken off. We step into the neat rows of five, sipping our piss-warm tea. The sky above us has not changed in the two hours of roll call; as winter nears the days are so short we march out to work and return in the dark.

Trampling through the mud toward Emma, I look across the masses of girl-women getting into their lines for work and recognize my cousin Gizzy. She is looking at me as well. Neither of us smiles.

"Gizzy's here," I whisper to Danka. "I'm going to find her after work tonight." Danka nods silently. It's too wet to speak.

Bread in hand, I find Gizzy's block without too much difficulty. She is already lying down when I arrive and half asleep. Her breathing is hoarse and vague. She is ill. I dig what is left of my fingernails into my hands, mustering the courage I need to continue.

"Gizzy? It's Rena . . . your cousin." Her eyes flicker in recognition.

"Rena?"

"How are you?"

"Not so good."

"How long have you been here? Where is Cili?"

"We were in hiding. She escaped . . . I got caught . . ." She pulls her blanket up around her shoulders. "It's so cold." I cannot respond. From beneath the blanket her feet hang out like two huge blue balloons. There is a smell emanating from the flesh. I try not to breathe. "Rena, I have bad news for you . . ." She seems unaware of her legs.

"What?"

"Schani is dead." She falters. "I'm sorry to be the bearer of such sad news, but I thought you should know. He jumped off the transport train on the way here, and they shot him."

I feel the pit swallowing me whole. What a waste of human life. Such a sweet man, Schani Gottlobb. My fiancé. Gizzy introduced me to Schani at one of the Zionist organization dances. So long ago.

She takes my hand in hers. Her eyes close, heavy with fatigue, and my gaze drops once more to her gangrenous legs.

"You need medicine," I tell her. "I brought you some of my bread. Here, share it with me." I divide my portion, handing half to her. "Would you like me to get you some water?" She shakes her head. "Everything will be okay, Gizzy, you'll see. I'm going to get you something for your ankles, and we'll get you some shoes so the cuts on your feet won't get infected, or be so cold. . . . We should get you working inside." I stroke her hand comfortingly. "I have to get back. It's getting late. I'll see you tomorrow after roll call."

"Thank you for the bread, Rena. Give my love to Danka."

"You'll feel better tomorrow, you'll see," I tell her before stepping outside into the winter night.

My eyes smart in the cruel wind, making my eyes water. Tears stream unwelcome down my cheeks. I do not know how long it has been since I cried, and I am not even sure that this can be called crying. Noiseless, like two rivers.

There are so many things to mourn that I'm not sure which one I'm weeping for. Walking back to our block, I cry for Schani's death. I cry because there's not going to be a wedding, and I remember how when I first came here I thought there would be. I cry for myself and my sisters. I cry for my cousins and friends. I cry because it is dark and no one can see me. I cry because there is no reason not to.

FOUR A.M.

"*Raus! Raus!*"

My face feels raw from the tears I shed secretly last night. I wish I had some lotion to smooth on my cheeks to protect them from the elements. Danka and I take our tea and step into the lines already forming for roll call. It has grown warmer during the night, but the wind seems to be pushing the clouds away, and I hope that means an end of the rain. The SS trudge up and down our tidy rows, counting, hitting, counting. The hours drag by. The sky does not change. I scan our ranks hoping for a glimpse of Gizzy, knowing that the chance of finding her face among so many thousands is slim. Roll call ends.

"I'm going to find Gizzy and bring her to Emma's detail," I whisper to Danka, wheeling away, anxious to conduct my search.

Gizzy is nowhere to be seen, though. I retrace last night's footsteps to her block and find her leaning against the wall outside. This is where they put people who are dying or dead, so they can be removed from camp.

"Gizzy. It's Rena." I collapse in the snow, pulling her into my arms, trying to hold back the cold. Her breathing sounds like castanets. Squeezing her tightly, I try to warm her, try to protect her from the rain. "Come on, Gizzy, hang on. . . . Fight it." Swaying her limp body back and forth as if I am rocking a newborn babe, I tell her over and over, "Live. You have to live. . . ." Her bones dig into mine. "You will see, Gizzy, everything is going to be fine."

There is one more rattle. A final gasp. Her breathing stops.

I cannot let go of her body. As if I were falling upon the Wailing Wall in Jerusalem, I rock and weep. My heart howls. *Lamentations.*

It is time to go to work, my internal clock warns me.

Laying Gizzy's cold body gently on the ground, I kiss my hand and place it upon my cousin's brow. "Good-bye," I whisper before stumbling away. The tears stick to my cheeks; they are bitter, tasting like the day we left Mama and Papa behind. I stare at the fences, the wires, the towers. Mama is there, waving to me from beyond this prison. "Help us, Mama. Please. Gizzy's dead."

The wind confiscates my words, abandoning them to the growing darkness in my heart. Pain and light. But her lantern's golden glow bobs across the roads and hills of Poland, and I know she's waiting for us to come safely home.

Danka stands before me. Her eyes reach deep into my soul, shaking it back from its silent sorrow. She knows. I say nothing. She leads me toward Emma. I cannot stop trembling, but her hand squeezing mine feeds me the courage to continue.

"March out!" We tramp through the mud, out of the gates of hell, to work.[10]

FOUR A.M.

"*Raus! Raus!*"

Birkenau is so huge I haven't spoken to Erna and Fela Dranger in ages, but one evening I find them in the latrine and we hug.

"Where's Danka?" Erna asks.

"She's holding our space in the block and making sure no one steals our blanket. How are you both?"

"As well as can be expected. This is some hell."

"Is Dina still with you?"

Erna nods.

"I'm going to try to get Danka into the White Hats sewing detail. You want me to organize kerchiefs for you too?"

"Yah, sure. Winter will be terrible if we have to work outside and in these shoes."

"You'll have to give up a portion of bread."

"Whatever we have to do . . ."

"I'll see you tomorrow or in a few days." I tell them which block we're in so they can find us and then depart back into the night.

Finding friendly faces amid so many strangers is a comfort. I realize this immediately after I leave the latrine. Now I have three more people to worry about though—how will we manage? Danka is the most important, of course, but we grew up with these girls. If we don't help each other, who will?

It takes me a few days to organize the kerchiefs, but finally a girl who is working in Canada[11] agrees to bring me four white

---

10. Gisela Schützer died on October 23, 1942. (Source: Pánstwowe Muzeum Auschwitz, Digital Repository of Prisoner Archives, based on the partially preserved *Death Books of Auschwitz Concentration Camp Prisoners*, 1941–1943).

11. The place where personal effects were stored after having been removed from prisoners and those who were condemned to die was referred to as Canada because that country symbolized abundance and a place far from the war. "Canada" grew from five barracks initially to thirty (Rittner and Roth, 427).

kerchiefs. In exchange I trade her two portions of bread, one from Erna and one from me. I hand the kerchiefs to Erna and explain the plan to her. "In the morning, stand as close as you can to the sewing kommando kapo. As soon as roll call's over, give them to your sister, Dina, and Danka; then get into the line as quickly as you can."

"What about you, Rena?"

"I'll keep working with Emma to keep the door open in her detail in case the inside work doesn't pan out. It's okay. Even though the work's outside, I'll be safe."

FOUR A.M.

"Raus! Raus!"

Danka stands next to Erna and Fela. We are counted. I stand farther away, separated for the first time from my sister during roll call. I do not like her being out of my reach. Roll call dismissed, I dash over to Emma's detail before it's full. Everything in Birkenau is first-come, first-served. I stand behind Emma, keeping one eye on the sewing detail. Erna and Fela have their kerchiefs on; Dina is wearing hers. Danka looks lost; she doesn't have a kerchief on. My eyes sear into the back of Erna's head. Where's Danka's kerchief? My mind screams. It's no use. Danka is thrown out of line. She looks across the camp for me, but it's too late; another kapo has signaled for her to get in line and march out. I watch helpless as my sister goes to the fields to work without me. What have I done? Oh Lord, what have I done?

All morning I work, wondering if my sister is dead yet. I can barely finish my soup at lunch. And my stomach is so tied up in knots of worry that I don't appreciate the extra broth. I simply miss my sister and wish she were here to share it with me; I know she won't eat lunch today. Through the afternoon I try not to think about whether I will ever see Danka's smile or her beautiful eyes again. I cannot stand the time it takes for the sun to cross the sky. Finally Emma orders "Halt!"

We put the tools in the shed and march into camp. We're the first back. Usually it is a relief to be in early, but today it is torture. Every kommando marching in seems full of dead or injured workers, and they all look like Danka. My eyes play tricks on me and my mind follows. In one kommando she is being carried between two girls, her body bruised and battered; in another, she limps, leaning heavily on someone's shoulder. Weak from hunger, mad with worry, I believe that my sister has died a hundred times over. Then I really see her. She has been beaten, but she is alive. I cannot run and hug her; I cannot move until we have all been counted, but I see her and she is alive. Roll call ends and we reach each other through the throng of milling girls heading for their blocks. I hold her fiercely, unable to let go. "What happened?"

"I lost my kerchief."

"Erna had one for you."

"I lost it."

"I gave her four!"

"She gave me mine."

I yell at Erna. "What did you do that to Danka for?"

"I gave it to Danka last night and only had three in my pocket, Rena!"

"Erna, this is no joke here." I grab her collar and try to shake good sense into her. "Danka was almost beaten to death today."

"It's not my fault!" She weeps.

"Rena, it's not her fault!" Danka grabs me away from Erna.

My fury betrays me and I refuse to listen to my sister. Erna is the source of my anxiety. Erna has betrayed us. "What is sorry? I gave up my bread so my sister can have a safe place to work that won't exhaust her and you almost murder her by your negligence." I struggle to quiet my voice. "Erna, this is serious. It isn't like going to school or Krynica. We can die!" I point up at the watchtowers and whisper hoarsely, "See that! If they say so, we are dead. There are no second chances. You have got to use your head."

"I'm sorry, Rena."

"Erna did nothing wrong." Danka takes a kerchief out of her pocket and hands it to me. "I couldn't find it at the right time and then it was too late."

I am too overwrought to understand, but I cannot blame Danka; she is my little sister.

I hand Danka's kerchief to Erna. "Tomorrow she will be in the sewing room with you. You will see to that—understand?"

"Yes, Rena. I promise."

"Mistakes here are fatal."

"I know, Rena."

Danka shadows me back to our block; I barely sleep that night for worry. Please Lord, let Danka be safe. Watch over her, if I cannot.

The next day Danka gets into the sewing room. Now I march out alone with Emma. I miss my sister terribly, but at night as I wait for her at roll call I can relax a little, knowing she has not been beaten. She is not dead. The sewing detail doesn't last long, though; because the work is easier, everyone in camp starts organizing white kerchiefs and sneaking into that detail. We're getting too smart for them. So they cut down on the workers they need, and Danka is one of the first to go. This time I'm watching closely, though, and take her hand, swooping her into Emma's detail. I'm not letting her out of my sight for another day of outside work; my nerves couldn't stand it.

Erna manages to get Fela and herself into the detail in Canada. "This is good work, Rena," she tells me in the latrine one night. "It's so easy. All we do is fold clothes, and when the SS aren't looking we can check the pockets and find all sorts of food left in them. We ate all day today. There were cookies and oranges—I even found a chocolate bar! The best thing, though, is it's under a roof."

"There's a roof?" Chocolate is beyond my realm of imagination, but a roof is something I can connect with. Finally a work detail that can protect us from the elements. It is our only way to survive, I know this; outside work is hard, but next to the SS, weather is our worst enemy, and winter is coming.

"I've organized two red kerchiefs for you and Danka." Erna checks the area before taking my hand in hers. "Tomorrow, march out with us. Only twenty-five can come, so be early."

I squeeze her hand warmly, retrieving the kerchiefs in a deft and invisible moment. I know she is returning the favor and that she stills feel guilty about the mix-up over the sewing detail and Danka getting beaten. I enter our block feeling slightly relieved. Tomorrow we work inside.

∞

FOUR A.M.

"*Raus! Raus!*"

We march out to Canada. There are mounds and mounds of clothes; I have not seen so many garments since Uncles Jacob's dress shop. There's a long table in the middle of the room, where we fold the clothes, pile them into bundles, and bind them with string.

"Where are these clothes going?" I whisper to Erna.

"Germany," she answers.

"What are you doing?" an SS man hollers.

"Nothing," a girl at the other end of the table whimpers.

His whip raises into the air, falling on her hands with a smack. "You were eating! You are here to work, not fill your filthy faces!" He strikes her again and again. A girl closer to me sneaks a morsel of food while his attention is diverted. Danka folds the clothes in front of her, staring into space. She is far away.

The whole day this SS man beats us to fold faster and work harder. There is not a minute when we can look for crumbs or candy in the pockets of the clothes.

I fold a Persian lamb coat. Touching its silky smooth fur, I lovingly reminisce about the last time I touched Persian lamb. Schani had promised me that someday I should have a coat as fine as my aunt's. I fold the sleeves behind the back, remembering how lovely Aunt Regina looked in her fur coat. I fold the front of it slowly over the arms, pulling out the shoulders so it won't wrinkle. The tailor's tag gleams up at me, white satin against the curly black fur. The words *Jacob Schützer, Bardejov* leap off the tag.

"No. Oh no," I gasp before I am able to quiet myself.

"What is it, Rena?" Danka comes out of her daze just in time to see that I am folding Aunt Regina's coat.

Where is the justice in it? Where are they? Where is Cili now? Where is Aunt Regina? . . . Where is Uncle Jacob? . . . I cannot bear to stay in this place any longer. Looking outside, across the compound, searching for some relief from the horror in my heart, I see an SS man standing on a ladder. He opens a can and pours something into a hole, then ducks down quickly as if he's avoiding something that doesn't smell good coming from the can.

"What's that man doing?" I ask, incredulous.

"Pouring the gas in," Erna hisses. "Don't watch."

I can't believe it, but I cannot avert my eyes. The rumors of gas chambers and crematoriums are true? I stare and stare at the proof before my eyes. My aunt and uncle could be in there right now. Dying.

I can see it, but I cannot accept it. What does this mean? That my parents could be in there, too, right now?

No, they are safe. They are waiting for me to come home. I can see Mama waving to me. Her babushka still draped across her shoulders. She is far away, but I know she is waiting for us. *I'm coming, Mama. Don't leave without me. I have Danka with me. We're all right.*

Blinking hard, I force myself back to the present. Bundling up my aunt's coat, I wish I could bury my head in it and sob, but I fight back the tears in my eyes. The mounds of clothes glare at me. These coats and dresses and suits and hats have been taken from my people. Where are these people now? Are they in camp wearing the same uniform that I wear? Are they dead or are they dying?

"You know what we have to pray for, Rena?" Erna's voice slices through my thoughts.

"What?"

Smoke billows out of the chimneys.

"Not that we don't get in there, but that when we do end up there they have enough gas so we die and don't go into the ovens alive."

"Oh, my God, Erna, we don't want to work here anymore." I imagine the screams of mothers and children and grandparents as they wither into nothingness just a few hundred meters away from where we fold their clothes to be shipped to Germany for *Reichdeutsche* to wear. "I don't know how you do it," I tell my friend.

We are from the same village. How is it she can take this barbarism in stride while I must turn and flee from it? I respect her nerve, but I'm not as strong as Erna. I cannot fold the clothes of my mother's brother's wife, watch the gas go down the chimney, and not die a little more inside. If my sister and I are to live, we will have to find another way; this detail will destroy our spirits if it doesn't destroy our minds first.

The next day Emma is waiting for us. She doesn't say a word about where we were the day before. We just get in her line and nod to her. She doesn't ask questions. And we pretend that nothing ever happened.

∞

"RENA." ERNA JERKS her head toward the latrine. I lift my chin slightly upward, letting her know I'll meet her there. A few moments later we stand together next to the boards with holes in them that are supposed to act as toilets. She pulls a gift out from under her jacket, shoving it into my hand.

"Erna, you shouldn't have." But she is already slipping something else from out of her pocket. In my hands is something I have been dreaming of for months—a bra. I put it on hastily before anyone can notice, but cannot withhold my sighs. My poor nipples, scabbed and blistered from the constant rubbing of wool, are immediately relieved.

"Here, take these, too." Erna hands me a pair of underwear.

"That's not all. We're getting shoes for you and Danka, too."

How? I want to ask, but knowing better I simply nod my thanks and whisper, "I am indebted to you." We exit the latrine separately.

I cannot believe the difference these tiny luxuries make in my outlook, my mood. To have one less thing to be in pain about gives me less to worry over. Such a small comfort, but my focus is more clear, and I feel more alert. I think this bra helps save my sanity.

It is much harder to get shoes. But Erna thinks of a way, and in each shoe is a sock to prevent blisters and keep our toes even warmer. These shoes make all the difference in the world. They cover our feet completely, protecting them from the elements and the rats; they lend support, keep our toes warmer, and don't fall off in the mud. The only shortcoming is they do not dry easily. We can use the potbellied stove, but it would take the whole night guarding them to dry them completely. After a short time by the fire, we put them back on our feet and go to bed. The leather grows hard and inflexible, but that is a small price to pay for keeping one's toes. No one who is still wearing sandals will survive the winter. Except to dry them, the shoes never leave our feet; to leave them unattended for even a second would be to go barefoot. Shoes are a precious commodity here. Danka and I are lucky to have friends as dear as Erna and Fela, who have brought them to us without even asking for a piece of bread.

I AM CONCERNED about Danka's depression. She doesn't seem to care about ever getting her own bowl of soup again. This is something beyond her fear of the kapos serving the food. She seems so downtrodden, as if she's giving up on any hope of survival, and this depression is eating away at her soul. She is absent; her eyes are glazed over most of our waking hours. I don't think that she's too far away, but I know I must try to do something before she goes beyond my grasp. Struggling with what to do about my sister's failing faith, I finally decide that there is no other course but to confront her.

It is late. The rest of the block is sleeping fitfully. "Danka," I whisper into the dark, "are you asleep yet?"

"No."

"What's bothering you? Something's wrong, I know it. Why're you so sad?"

"I don't know."

"Please talk to me. How can I help you if I don't know what's going on in your head? I feel you shrinking away from me. You have to tell me what's wrong."

"What sense is there to this?"

"To Auschwitz?" I'm puzzled.

"To everything." She pauses. "What if there's a selection and I'm selected to die?"

"What makes you say that?"

"You look better than me. You aren't losing so much weight, and you're still strong. What if I can't make it?"

Slowly it dawns on me. "Remember those two sisters?" I take her hand. "And how the one begged to go with the other one?"

She nods in the shadows.

"I will do the same, if it comes to that."

"They don't allow it all the time, though. That was the first selection. They were soft. Now if someone begs to go with their mama or sister or daughter, they laugh and push them away."

"I will do whatever it takes, even if I must strike the SS."

"Then they will kill you immediately—that's no good."

There is something else lurking behind her eyes. It isn't dying alone she's afraid of, but I'm not sure which fear is possessing her.

"What is it you're really afraid of?"

"Being thrown in the truck," she confesses. "They treat us like rotten meat. . . . I don't want to be discarded like that, thrown onto the flatbeds . . . I'm afraid of what Erna said. Maybe there won't be enough gas, and I'll go into the crematorium still alive. . . . What if they're trying to conserve the gas?"

I cannot answer that question. How can I assure her that there will be enough gas to kill us when we arrive at the ultimate destination of all prisoners in Auschwitz-Birkenau? I cannot lie to my sister, but I can promise one thing.

Everyone is sleeping around us, but with everyone talking out of their heads all the time anyway, no one pays us any attention—it's too commonplace to hear voices and screams in the night.

"Sit up, Danka. Come on, sit up." I hold out my hand. "You see my hand here." I put her hand on mine and look into her eyes. "Our parents are standing here in front of us and my hand is our Talmud, and on this holy book and before our parents I make this oath to you: that from this day on, if you are selected I will join you no matter what. I swear that you will not go onto the trucks alone."

It is pitch-black in the blocks, but I can almost see the light flicker back on in my sister's eyes as I make this promise. Exhausted, I release her hand, and we fall back against the cold wood, pulling our blanket close around our bodies. Sleep comes swiftly, carrying us away to a land where there are no shadows.

At lunch the next day, Danka stands in line and receives her first full helping of soup in months.

∞

I SHIVER UNDER the thin blanket protecting us from the elements. There is something like ice touching my body. Recoiling, I struggle to return to the solace of sleep. I hate the rats that wander in between our bodies, chewing on whatever does not fight back. I jerk my feet; it is an automatic response to the varmints that cross our feet at night. Again I feel the pressure and push back against it. My jaw clenches shut as I fight to squeeze in a few more moments of unconsciousness. The ice brands me. Involuntarily my hand reaches out to shove away the weight lying against me, then recoils, recognizing the touch of human flesh. She is solid, devoid of all warmth, absent of life.

The room elders begin the morning ritual, banging on the sides of the shelves with their sticks, yelling and beating anyone within their reach.

"Go outside and get your tea." I move Danka toward the door. "I'll fold the blanket this morning."

"Why?" she asks innocently.

"Just go, Danka. Let me do this for you. We should start taking turns tidying our beds. This morning it's my turn. Go on, I'll catch up with you." I wait until she is outside.

"Somebody help me carry this body out?" No one wants to assist me. I understand their fear, but I don't want to be beaten for not removing the body. Tapping a neighboring bony shoulder, I ask, "Can you please grab her feet?" The woman nods reluctantly, helping me shift the corpse off the shelving. "I'm going to stop at the door. I don't want my sister to see."

Danka has her back toward me, so we take the body out, placing her at the end of the lines for roll call, where she will be tallied along with the rest of us. I am dying to wash my hands, but there is no time for that now; I must grab my tea and get into line next to Danka before roll call begins. Wiping my hands against my trousers repeatedly, I try to scrape the feeling of cold flesh from my body's memory.

All day we work, and periodically I scrub my hands with dirt and then against my woolen pants, trying to get rid of the aura of death still lingering on them. The afternoon soup does not warm them; cupping them and blowing my hot breath into them does not thaw death's chill. Wringing my hands together until they ache, I cannot dislodge the obsession in my mind. I hesitate to take the evening bread before washing my hands but am too hungry to avoid the food. In the latrine I finally get a moment to rinse my hands and face, but there isn't enough water in the world to wash her frozen body from my mind. How I long for a hot bath, how I long for a cup of cocoa to sweeten my mind and sweep away the frigid fears devouring me.

"You should always sleep on the outside, next to the stall divider," I tell Danka as we crawl into our place on the shelf-beds. I never want her to be touched by death.

She blinks in wonderment at my statement. "Are you okay?" she asks.

"Of course." I pull the blanket up over our shoulders, snuggling as close to my sister as I possibly can, trying to avoid the touch of the girl already asleep next to me.

You cannot count on anything here. You cannot even count on the ground beneath your feet.

∞

THERE IS A new layer of snow that glimmers across the compound creating an illusion that it is clean. That fantasy will not last long, though; as soon as the SS begin counting us and we step out of our ranks and into our work details, the ground will once more become the frozen, grayish-brown slush that it usually is. The ice breaks beneath SS boots as they walk up and down our rows counting, counting. Our breath mingles in the air without prejudice; the last few flakes dropping from the clouds fall upon our eyelashes without discrepancy. I stomp my feet to wake up my still-sleeping toes, making sure they don't freeze in the stupor of standing, waiting. The stars glisten above our heads like bright icicles hanging indifferently in the heavens. I stomp my feet.[12]

∞

WE STAND IN line for selection. It is a long day; no food, no water. I haven't seen Adela Gross except for a few times in camp.

---

12. The first snows began in early November; the mean temperature in November and December 1942 was 4.1 Celsius (39 Fahrenheit).

We didn't know each other well, but I recognize her as the rabbi's daughter from Hummene and remember her from the first transport.

The line moves, and I catch a glimpse of Adela stepping forward. For a moment I am struck by her beauty and remember how gorgeous her beautiful red curls were before her head was shaved. I am astounded that despite the hardships of camp she still looks pretty.

She steps up to the death squad. The SS stare at her. Her chin is tilted slightly, bravely upward.

The thumb points away. She moves toward the ranks of the doomed.

I am confused. How can she be selected? She looks better than me. Adela should stay alive. It must be a mistake.

The next girl steps up to the death squad.

Furious at the self-proclaimed gods who rule our lives, I wish I could yell at them, make them see their error. But I must prepare myself for the thumb. Squeezing Danka's hand one final time before letting go, I march toward my fate. We are hot or cold, there is no in-between. We are hungry and miserable. In a few moments we may be dead. Not sick, not hungry, not hot, not cold—dead.

I step up to the death squad, chin up. The thumb points.

Danka follows my lead, stepping up to the death squad. The thumb allows us both to live for another day. The girl behind us steps up to the death squad.[13]

The trucks begin loading the girls, the women, my friends. Normally I don't watch, but this time I must. Running the selection over and over in my mind, I search for the reason in their decision. Why? Why? There is nothing wrong with Adela. She is a lovely young woman. She is beautiful. We are nothing but pieces of scrap wood.

---

13. "May 31 [1943] . . . Nos. 123205–123234 are given to 30 men prisoners and Nos. 45681–45698 to 18 female prisoners. . . . The occupancy level of the women's camp in Birkenau is 20,542" (Czech, 409–10). By the author's calculations, if there were 20,000 women in camp and a selection lasted fifteen hours, then 1,333.3 women were selected per hour, 22.2 women per minute, or one woman every 2.7 seconds.

Adela Gross—from Gross family archive

The reality strikes me squarely between the eyes, as if Taube himself has hit me. Their purpose is not only to destroy and defile us; it is to make a mockery of every positive value we have: beauty, grace, love. Adela is thrown onto the flatbeds with the rest of the women, but she turns to help those behind her. Her chin still tilts with courage and dignity. She is not afraid. Her arm encircles a weaker girl whose knees are failing her. The trucks spew their exhaust as they head for the gas chambers. I cannot wrench my eyes away from her departing form. There is a tearing inside of me, as if a cord is being severed in my heart. As the trucks drive away, part of me dies with Adela.[14]

∞

14. The date of Adela's death is unknown, but on December 5, 1942—St. Nicholas Day—"the SS carries out a large-scale selection that lasts the entire day. Afterward, approximately 2,000 young, healthy, and able-bodied women are brought to the gas chambers in the bunkers" (Czech, 279).

DANKA HAS GOTTEN SCABIES. Many have contracted this disease from living in such close quarters, and it's quite dangerous if it's on an area of the body that's visible. Fortunately, they're not on her face or hands and her legs are so covered by mud that no one notices anything beyond the dirt. But at the drop of a hat the SS can deem us unworthy to live, and the selections seem to be occurring on a more regular basis. I search my memory for a remedy, allowing just enough of the past to return to my present so that Danka can get well and I remember. . . .

> *We had gotten scabies at school and been sent home along with the other children who had contracted it.*
> *"Rena! Danka! Come into the kitchen and let me rub this sulphur onto your poor bodies." Mama opened up the door of the stove, rubbing the lotion into our skin. "There you go. Now I'm going to wrap you up and let you sleep by the stove tonight so the salve can soak into the sores and make them disappear." We wore our one-piece pajamas, the type with the trapdoor in the back. Then Mama wrapped us up in old blankets and slid the bench out of the szlufbank so it would make a small sleeping space for us. Fluffing the down in our pillows, tucking us in, she hugged and kissed us good night. "Sweet sleep." The next morning she heated water and used the big washtub to bathe us in, scrubbing us hard with sulphur soap.*
> *"Mama! You're treating us like laundry," we giggled. "That's because I don't want a spot on you!" She snuggled us, wrapping our little bodies up in towels and rubbing us dry. "Now you look like two healthy young ladies again!" She unwrapped the towels, revealing our creamy skin as fresh as a newborn's. "It's still itchy," Danka complained, hugging Mama's leg. "It's okay. I'll wash you one more time and then you'll be all ready to go back to school."*

I hold out my bread to the block elder. "I need some sulphur."
"What for?"
"Scabies."
"Humph, better get rid of them soon." She disappears into her room. As always, I must wait until she sees fit to come out again and crouch against the wall, dozing. Surprisingly, she does not take hours to return with the lotion.

"Here. You know how to use it?"

"Yah." I take the salve. *"Děkuji,"* I say thank you in Slovakian.

Danka and I stand next to the potbellied stove in the middle of the block. "Do you remember when Mama wrapped us in warm blankets and had us sleep by the stove, when we were little?" I ask, rubbing the sulphur into her skin.

"We had scabies then, too," she answers quietly.

Our stomachs growl as we split Danka's portion of bread between us, speaking quietly or not at all. I wait with her, knowing she'll leave the fire too soon if she's tired, and I want to make sure the heat makes the ointment penetrate her skin. I feel like Mama as I go through the motions of mothering my sister, only this time there are no blankets to wrap her in, or flannel pajamas. The smell of the sulphur is strong, but it is not so noticeable above the other body odors we constantly live with. I determine that it will be safe for her to leave the salve on throughout the work day before we wash it off.

"How are you going to wash it off?" Danka asks.

"I'm going to have to use our bowls to rinse you, Danka."

"I can't eat from mine if you do that." She looks terrified by the thought.

Why not? I want to ask. What's the big deal? But I keep my mouth shut. I don't want to risk her refusing to eat again. "We'll use my bowl," I suggest. "And I'll share yours until Sunday, when I can clean mine out real good."

The next evening I get some water and rinse my sister's body of the salve. They're gone.

Danka checks her skin, relieved. Mama's angelic face floats on the periphery of my vision; I am grateful that there's no sign of infection from the sores.

∞

WE STAND AT ROLL call waiting to be counted. They walk up and down the rows counting, hitting, shouting. Danka shifts on her feet, so I quickly cast my glance sideways. She's fine, just sore and hungry as I am. My fingers reach out and touch her hand, reassuringly. Her fingers touch mine. This is our check-in. Every morning, if it's possible, we send this silent message to each other—I'm okay.

We are in the front row today. This is unusual; normally we try to be in the back or the middle, hidden and anonymous. It's harder to watch or be prepared when we're among the first to receive whatever they have in mind.

In the distance I can see a column coming toward us. I have never seen anyone on this road before. My mind churns. Who is arriving in hell today? Their feet try to march, but they're not doing a very good job of it. There is a whisper through our ranks: "They've emptied a Jewish orphanage."[15]

The SS have their rifles up on their shoulders. "March!" Their orders snap through the stale morning air. My heart stops. My eyes focus on the column. Hundreds of pairs of tiny children's feet file past me and my sister and every woman in camp. Some of their little faces are buried in their toys, choking the stuffing out of these inanimate objects of comfort. The younger ones hold the older children's hands. Their eyes stare at us big as saucers, lost as lambs. There is a tearful gasp somewhere deep inside our row. Is it a mother reminded of her own dear baby?

Their innocent faces look around in wonderment at the fences, the buildings, the grownups. Do they think we are insane, as I did when I first arrived? Are they wondering why so many grownups looking like their mamas and papas do nothing to protect them? Are they afraid?

My mouth drops open. I cannot bear to look at this. I cannot turn away. They can't be serious. Why would anyone want to kill babies? How long will it take them to suffocate? Will they cry out in fear with no one to comfort them?

The SS march them toward the gas chamber. Clutching dolls and stuffed animals close to their hearts, they shuffle past in rows of five guarded by SS men with their dogs and rifles. What do they think these children are going to do—escape? Revolt? But

---

15. "January 30 [1943] . . . 518 children are killed in the gas chambers. . . . [And the next day, on] January 31 . . . 457 children are killed in the gas chambers" (Czech, 319).

it is a rule, always to the gas chamber the SS are posted every fifth row on each side of the column, and they always follow rules. They don't want anyone around; they don't want the truth getting out. We know the truth. It has taken a long time for it to sink in, but there is no mistaking it anymore—the evidence is in the smoke-filled air and the empty compound after a selection. Still, they want no one disturbing their plans. The Germans have a saying, "Order is order." They stick to their rules like glue.

I am standing there just like a ghost. Their little angelic faces, the white knuckles of their tiny hands haunt me. I fight back my tears, my rage. My heart screams, Stop! Stop this madness! They are babies! Clenching my jaw, I shut my eyes.

God? I rarely say *God* anymore, but seeing their faces reflected in my heart I must try to pray one last time: God, you are my God, and I believe in you. Won't you strike just one of these monsters down? Smite just one SS for these children, your children. You, who I obey and believe in so much with all my heart? I have never held so much as a penny in my hand on the Sabbath, and since I was old enough to fast I have always fasted on Yom Kippur. Don't allow this to happen. Give us a sign that you have not forsaken these children, the children of Israel. Never mind my suffering. It does not matter the time I have been in this place. Never mind all the things I've heard about people being burned and gassed, all the things I've seen for myself, not wanting to believe any of it is true. Never mind about me. What about these sweet children? For them, show them you are our God and kill just one of these Nazis.

My hands are fists of fury tight against my thighs. My eyes squeeze shut, holding a vision of lightning striking the guards in their neat and orderly tracks. Not one adult can move to save these toddlers, only divine intervention can supersede now: Please, God . . .

They fade in the distance, nearing the gas chambers. My heart screams. Stop! Someone passes by me. Halts. Her feet crunch against the gravel road as she steps back to look at our stricken faces. Her hot breath hits my cheek. I open my eyes warily into the cool cruelty of Hasse's stare. Her clean boots, her polished and shiny skin, stand before us in full Aryan superiority.

She has seen our agony; she has read my mind.

I know from the moment I hear her voice that religion will never be the same for me. I will still pray; I will try to believe and have faith, but it will never be as pure and sincere as it once was. Her lips pull back into a grimace that I am sure is meant to be a smile. Her words are harsh and staccato, like machine-gun fire; they shoot us down.

"Where is your God now?"

There is no answer.

ROLL CALL IS ENDLESS. To work would be a relief, anything to take our minds off of the children, but there is no respite in this place. Smoke comes out of the chimneys. My nose quivers at the reek of burning flesh, the smell of little children being incinerated. The sun disappears behind a cloud of gray.

If children cannot be saved, what is the use of praying for anything anymore? Hasse's voice plagues my wavering faith, dogging every breath I take.

"Where is your God now?"

I do not know.

⚬

"WHAT'S WRONG, RENA?" I have been staring at nothing for days, going through the motions of survival, unable to shake the cherubic faces haunting me.

"Did you see them?" I ask Erna.

"Who?"

"The children"—my voice cracks—"hundreds of them." I cannot let myself feel this much pain and still survive, but it is a fresh wound, not yet disguised by the calluses I have learned to develop.

She nods and places her hand on my shoulder. "Fela and I will be moving to a different section soon. We won't be able to talk anymore."

I will miss my friend, but I do not want a job in her new work detail. She does not talk about it, and I do not ask, but I know it is not a job that I could do.

"We will miss you."

"You must get out of Birkenau, or get in a kommando that is inside, at least."

"We will."

She moves away. "I will see you before we go."

I try to manage to smile. Be brave—another rule of survival.

A few days later, Erna signals me to meet her in the latrine. "I have something for you." She reaches into her hem.

"Erna, you have to stop risking your life bringing me things."

"Yah, but we are moving tomorrow, so these will be the last gifts I can bring you." She takes my hand, slipping something long and smooth, and something else very small into my palm. "I know how clean and neat you are."

I glance quickly into my hand. There is a nail file and a small silver elephant. "They're beautiful." I am overwhelmed by her generosity.

"The charm looked as if it belonged to a child, and I thought of you," she whispers. "Elephants are supposed to be good luck. I don't want it to go to the Germans."

"Thank you, Erna. I will treasure them always." Tears spring to my eyes before I can quench them. We embrace quickly, but we do not say good-bye. Good-bye is not something one says in Auschwitz-Birkenau.

I slip the trinkets into the hem of my skirt before departing from the latrine. The silver elephant is a reminder of the children I watched walk to their deaths. The only mark of their passing, a tiny gravestone in my hand. I place it under my tongue during selections so it can be spit into the dirt if I go to the gas or if I am beaten to death. My commitment to this small child's charm is that it should never get into Nazi hands, that even if I do not survive, it shall.

On Sunday, sitting on our bunk, I take out the nail file. It is mother-of-pearl, and under an etching of a cathedral it says *Buda-pest*. Hiding it in my palm, keeping the file covered so that it looks as if I am wringing my hands, I begin to clean my nails. It is an

*The elephant and nail file Erna organized, the wedding ring,
and the watch Marek gave Rena before the Death March. (Photo K. Abato)*

elevated feeling, to have one's nails clean after being dirty for so
long. This simple manicure becomes a part of my weekly ritual.
My thin thread to sanity grows longer: be with Danka, be invisible, be alert, be numb, be clean.

I CRAWL OFF THE BUNK, leaving a still-sleeping Danka behind,
and head for the latrine. My period does not last as long as it used
to, and the flow is not nearly as heavy as it was in Auschwitz, or
even a few months ago; for this I am grateful. Danka hasn't had
her period since the beginning. She, as well as most of the girls
and women in camp, lost hers almost immediately. Breasts and the
cycle disappear as quickly as our fellow prisoners. It is something
in the tea; I think they call it bromide. I don't know why the bromide doesn't work on me, but the starvation does. My period is
slowly slacking off as the weight drops from my body.

Taking a cloth that Erna also organized for me out of my
sleeve, I thank her in my heart again as I leave the latrine with a
semi-clean kerchief securely in place.

EVERY THREE WEEKS, on Sunday, the only day we have even a
moment's rest, we are lined up and marched outside to another
part of Birkenau to be shaved.

"Strip! *Schnell! Schnell!*" The SS shout at us as if we were deaf. Undressing, we place our clothes in a pile. Sometimes we stand for hours without a stitch on, outside in the elements or inside in the drafts. Our own Jewish men, prisoners obeying orders, wait for us, clippers in hand. The line to the shaving is long, but I think compared to all the other horrors this is not so horrible.

This is not the worst thing that happens to us in Auschwitz-Birkenau. It is not nightmare-making. But it is consistent, like everything the Germans do. Every three weeks like clockwork. Our own boys, our own men are forced to see our nakedness, forced to shave our heads, our arms, our legs, our pubis. Sometimes the men shaving the women are friends, sometimes they are relatives; mothers get shaved by their own sons, sisters get shaved by brothers—everyone suffers embarrassment. Danka and I are lucky. We meet no one we know.

Why can't they let the women shave each other? We are young women, virgins; it is not in our religion to bare ourselves even in front of our husbands. This is not life-threatening, but it is degrading. One more degrading thing they make us do.

The German officers parade back and forth, looking at us as if we are interesting specimens in their insect collection. If there is a beautiful girl, they stare unrelentingly. How anger-defying it is to stand and be visually defiled by these murderers. What I wouldn't do for a tap with hot water and a scrub brush, to wash the Nazis' eyes from my flesh. We are silent in our shame. . . .

There is no discussion and little whispering. The clippers are heavy, like shears for sheep, and they nick our flesh easily. Our boys, our men try not to hurt us, try to be careful, but they must cut quickly so they don't see our eyes, see our bodies, get beaten for being too slow, too prudent, too kind.

"*Schnell! Schnell!*" Little streams of blood trickle down our legs and necks as the SS men hurry them on. We hurt on both sides.

It is so demeaning. I can't bear it. I become a piece of flesh staring through the body of the man shaving me, staring at the other side of the room. I turn off the emotions inside of me until I see nothing and feel nothing. It is quite conscious. I hear only the command to move when it is over, and then it is only the flesh moving.

I am gone.

It is the body that finds its clothes. The body that shivers un-controllably from cold and fear and anger, quaking from unshed tears of shame. It is the body that waits for its sister. The feet stand in line until they are told to march. The hand takes her hand and together they return to the women's camp. The body enters the block. The arm takes the bread from the room elder. The mouth opens and closes, chewing bread—or is it sawdust? Everything tastes the same. Everything feels the same. I know at some point I will return to the body, but it takes time, and time is measured by tea, soup, bread, tea, soup, bread. Whenever it gets too much for me and I am about to burst, I turn my emotions off like a faucet and let the body take over. Sometimes it is the body that wants to survive, more than the spirit. There are days when the spirit has been sucked out and only time will tell if it will come back to feel again, come back to life.

No, shaving isn't the worst thing. It isn't life-threatening. But it *is* bad.

IT IS SUNDAY. I walk around camp looking for any tidbits or any-thing that might be useful lying in the mud.

"Rena!" Someone calls my name. Looking around, I see no one and start to move away, thinking perhaps the wind is playing tricks on me.

"Rena." This time it is a hoarse whisper. I stare and stare at a skeleton leaning out of the iron bars. Barely recognizing the face, I search through my memory for the name that fits the chiseled features before me. It is Erna and Fela's older sister.

"Pepka? Is that you?" I try not to look dismayed.

"What are you doing in Block Twenty-Five?" I shudder. Block Twenty-Five is the place we avoid no matter what the cost. No one who goes inside those doors comes out alive. The women inside this block are ill and put there to be starved to death or carted to the gas and then the crematorium.

She cannot speak easily but manages to whisper, "Water."

I run to get her something to drink, trying to shake her image away from my eyes. Her face has fallen inward, collapsing into her soul. She is a shade of the Pepka I once knew. I wish Erna were still in camp; she should know about her sister, but there is nothing anyone can do.

I place my bowl, brimming full of water, into her skeletal hands. She drinks greedily, barely able to contain her gulp at life, before handing it back to me. Her hands tremble. Retreating into the darkness, her eyes plead for me to save her. Her voice is silent.

I am helpless against the walls, the bars. I have no food to share with her, no medicine to heal her ills, no way to get enough water that she will never thirst again, no way to get her out of the Block of Death. She is doomed and I am helpless. Pepka's eyes become those of my own sister, Zosia. What if Zosia were in Block Twenty-Five? Would someone take her water for me? Would someone tell me she were there? What about the children? If Zosia was in this hell would they already be dead? I wish for someone to share this burden with but must blot these thoughts out quickly before they find a home in my mind and drive me mad. Maybe the children are in an orphanage. Maybe Zosia sent us the packages from Switzerland and she is safe. Zosia and Mama and Papa will be in Tylicz, and when it's all over we will be reunited again. My mind slows its whirling descent into despair. Fragile hope replaces doom—this is all that matters.

∞

SELECTIONS ARE SPORADIC. There is no telling how often they occur or when we are going to march out to roll call and instead of working stand all day, in neat lines and rows of five, and wait to be selected. There is usually one SS man who stands in judgment while the rest of them watch, but sometimes there are two making the decisions. When there are two, they both must give you the thumb toward life, otherwise you go to your death. No questions are asked; there is no appeal process, just a thumb. Usually there's a physical test, so that if you do get the thumb toward life you must then jump across a ditch to prove you are worthy of their decision. With shaking knees and no room for the take-off, we try to vault across this last obstacle between us and supper tonight. Sometimes I think the only thing that saves me is the fact that

I don't want to get dirty before I die, and somehow that resolve levitates me beyond the filth and mud in the ditch. Very few do not make the jump.

Depending on the number of girl-women in camp, selections take anywhere from ten to fifteen hours. We stand without food or drink all day and sometimes into the night, waiting to discover if we will wake up tomorrow, if we will ever eat again. There are no last meals, like criminals get before they are executed; we are not as good as criminals. We are nothing in their eyes—we are merely pests to be exterminated.

When we first came to Birkenau there were six women per shelf; now, except after a selection, we sleep twelve or more. If we want to turn over in the middle of the night we have to pull ourselves up with our hands and twist our bodies around like a screw. Danka and I always wake each other when we want to turn; it's easier if we both change positions.

There is no way not to touch the girl next to you. My prayer has become that no one dies next to me—this is a selfish prayer based on a desire to stay warm. I don't want to be frozen by a cold body in the middle of the night, but it happens, over and over again.

When a selection is over, there is plenty of room on the tiers to sleep, but the barrenness of the blocks is haunting, and rest is kept away by sleep demons and the souls dying in the gas chambers. In the morning we wake exhausted, watching the new arrivals come in from the transports. We see their faces, stricken and in denial, their uncertain fates written across their brows. They're lost and scared. Uncertain about this hell they've come to, they still wish they had hair, they wonder where their loved ones have disappeared to. They think we look insane.

There is nothing we can do to prepare them—no orientation, no list of things to be wary of, no rules for survival. There is only tea, soup, bread—they have no bowls yet. The first night they can't find blankets and search for a place to sleep not realizing that they must cram themselves in among the bodies already sleeping, where once again we're wedged in tighter than herrings, twelve to a tier.

∾

FOUR A.M.

"Raus! Raus!"

We maneuver our bodies out of the group sleeping on our shelf. Slip outside with our tea and get into line for roll call. Last night there was no moon, and on nights when the sky is dark, those with suicide wishes use the blanket of blackness to dodge the searchlights and run for the fence. This is freedom.

Their figures look like dancers frozen against the shadows of abruptly awakened ghosts. Mouths gape open like question marks, as if committing us to bear witness that we heard their screams in the night. They hang, charred, on the electric wires of humanity.

Spellbound, I cannot tear my eyes from their grotesque forms. How I envy them. What is it that has driven them to grab the wire? What is it that drives me to stay among the ranks of the semi-living?

∞

TAUBE MARCHES ALONG our rows, but he is not counting us today. He seems excited, as if he has something else on his mind. "What we need are calisthenics! Yah, exercise is the key. Healthy body. Healthy mind." He turns to our row. "Do knee bends!" he orders.

"Down! Up! Down! Up!" We bend our creaking joints and stand upright, again and again, exactly as he demands. "Ten, and down! Eleven, and down!" We count in our heads, trying to focus on something besides our weakening legs and trembling thigh muscles, twenty, twenty-one. . . . "Twenty-nine, and down! Thirty, and down! Knees to the ground." We falter, not understanding his request. "Kneel!" He cracks his whip across a girl's shoulder blade. She sinks into the mud. "Lie down! Heads down!"

I grab Danka's hand, pulling her with me. "Put your face in it, Danka. Don't move. Don't look up," I manage to whisper before my mouth is in the mud.

Taube stomps towards our row. Noses touching dirt, eyes staring into the ground. His black boots pass us. His boots stop. Trying not to breathe. A girl nearby raises her head. I can see from the corner of my eye her upturned face gasping for breath.

The boot falling onto her face, pushing it deep into the earth. The crunching of skull bones sickens the air. I want to vomit. He moves on. I cannot help but listen for the sound. A few rows away it rises from our ranks—the crunch, the silence. I blink. I am leaving my body, fleeing the horror around us. But I cannot get far enough away. I cannot allow myself to leave Danka behind.

Finally the word "Dismissed!" releases us from our hold to the ground. Roll call is over. Timidly, those of us doing Taube's version of calisthenics get on our hands and knees, turning our faces in horror at the smashed skulls of the girls who will never rise again.

"Don't look, Danka." I move my sister away from the girl next to me. Hand in hand, we find Emma, line up behind her, and march to work.

WEEKS JUST . . . are years here.

IF THE WAR is going well for the Germans, once in a while we get a slice of meat in the soup or with our bread. And sometimes the very Orthodox girls will trade their meat for bread because they won't touch unkosher meat. I don't know how they can survive without meat for long. They have something that I don't, though; they have their faith. I do not know where my God is.

They slap the portions on our hands. We lick our open palms slowly, savoring the smear of margarine or mustard; occasionally there is a bit of smelly Limburger cheese. I despise the taste of mustard after the first few months; still, I lick it up as the precious morsel it is. When there is margarine we rub the residue into our hands for moisturizer. The skin on our hands and faces cracks in the cold.

Sausage is never more than bite-size, but we eat hungrily, unable to pause or slow down. Danka never wants to eat it. "We have to," I tell her. "Food is food, and this is all we have to depend on." And there is never enough of it. Our stomachs ache constantly. Every moment of every day, awake or asleep, we are hungry. The constant gnawing caused by this starvation is exhausting. Between working ten and twelve hours a day and avoiding the SS, there is little energy for any other activity. Thinking is becoming impossible.

When the war is going badly for the Germans, it is worse for us. The bread is little more than water and flour, and the portions are rarely larger than our hand. But lately it looks as if the Germans are going to be occupying the whole world, and like giving a dog a bone, they toss us slightly larger portions. We take the food eagerly but receive it with the knowledge that this piece of cheese means the Nazis are in Holland, this piece of meat means they're in France. I don't know which to long for more—food or freedom.

∞

IT IS SUNDAY. We lie on our shelves delousing ourselves or trying to rest, squeezing in a few extra hours of sleep. I clean my nails deftly, hiding the nail file in my hand while staring into space.

"Attention!" our block elder shouts. "*Raus! Raus!* Get out. Now!"

We can hear Hasse's voice outside shouting, "Get out here, you lazy imbeciles! I have work for you to do!" Confused, we jump to the ground, running for the door. Some girls scramble for their shoes, others grab their bowls; Danka and I forget everything, thinking only of avoiding Hasse's whip. Our minds are buzzing. We arrive outside first, standing at attention as the rest of the block rushes into line.

"Rena, I left my bowl." Danka tugs on my arm. I look quickly around us. Hasse is not there.

"I'll get it." I dash back into the block. My heart racing, I grab Danka's bowl off our sleeping area and run out the back door directly into Hasse's path.

Her eyes glare at me. I freeze. She raises her gun. My heart stops.

A gunshot rips through the air.

I collapse to the ground. Mud splashes onto my clothes and up my nose. I feel no pain. I wish I could see my sister one more time before I die. There are sounds coming from above me, horrible, guttural sounds.

Hasse is laughing. "The miserable *mist biene* thinks she's dead!" Hasse guffaws.[16] Her joviality pummels my ears. "I didn't shoot you!"

I raise my head, looking up at the SS woman's hideous grin.

"Hau ab! Get lost!" She waves me away.

What an idiot I am! Jumping up quickly, I brush myself off hoping Hasse doesn't change her mind and shoot me anyway.

"Hau ab!" she yells again.

We work all afternoon carrying stones, knowing this is worthless work only to keep us busy. We will miss this day sorely in the middle of the week. Next week we will be shaved again, another Sunday with no rest. How will we ever catch up?

∞

WE WORK IN the spring dirt, turning over the soil the same as we did last year. The fresh young sprigs of new grass stick their white tips out of the soil, tempting us to gather them for a midday snack. The succulent, sweet juice of these grasses is a pleasant sensation to our tired taste buds and parched throats. We sneak them into our mouths when Emma and the SS aren't looking.

The girl next to me falters in her digging. I follow her gaze.

Stooping to pick medicinal herbs, a group of broken souls moves slowly past our detail in blue-and-gray-striped dresses with clean, white pressed aprons. Their skeletal forms do not haunt me as badly as their bottomless eyes. We freeze for a moment of shock before returning to our work. Their knees quiver weakly, as if each step they take is their last. I shudder, surprised by the chill racing down my spine despite the warmth of the day.

I have seen many things between Auschwitz and Birkenau, but never have I seen anything comparable to this. I have seen despair and hopelessness; I have seen insanity at first onset, but

---

16. *Mist biene* is German for "manure bee" or "dung bee."

I have never seen any face so devoid of life. Even the dead look more alive than these walking corpses.

"They are experiment victims," the girl next to me whispers. Danka's face pales. My hands tremble. "They torture them until they are dead or vegetables." She turns another shovelful of dirt over. "After they are done experimenting with them, they go to the gas."[17]

Of all the horror we see daily, of all the shattered selves we witness on a regular basis, they are beyond any realm of imagination. They look as if the spirit God breathed into their souls has been utterly sucked out. They're no longer human beings, having long ago ceased to be girls or women. They are a child's nightmare.

∞

"RENA, I HAVE SCABIES and terrible cuts from a beating I got." My cousin's wife begs, "Please, help me." I look at her without pity, without feeling. Still, I must help her. It is not in my heart to turn family away, despite how she treated me when Danka and I first arrived in Bardejov. She invited us to her house and served us a cookie and cup of tea, while still in her bathrobe and her hair in rollers. She kept fidgeting and acting like we were a nuisance, then abruptly told us she had errands to run, indicating it was time for us to leave. She didn't ask us about our parents or how Danka and I were doing in her city. She was so well bred, so wealthy. We were the poor Polish cousins to be swept under the carpet to avoid embarrassment.

I was not fond of her because of this incident in Slovakia. Then I heard she had made trouble in camp. She was caught on her hands and knees inside the soup kettle, licking it out, scraping

---

17. "April 30 [1943] . . . 242 female prisoners are earmarked for experimental purposes . . . housed in the experimental station of Professor Dr. [Carl] Clauberg in Block 10 of the main camp" (Czech, 386). "By the time [Dr. Josef] Mengele arrived in May 1943, Auschwitz was packed with almost 140,000 prisoners and stretched for miles in all directions" (Posner and Ware, 20).

what food was stuck to the bottom with her bare hands and feeding herself like an animal. An SS woman who found her, beat her for behaving so despicably.

I am ashamed to say that I do not trust her now and am afraid to have anything to do with her. She has no self-control, and for all her airs and superiority, people like her are dangerous in camp. I do not doubt she will do anything to save herself and cares nothing for me.

There are scabies on her face though. She will die at the next selection if I don't help her. "If I'm going to get you any salve, you must promise not to tell anyone what I've done for you," I tell her. I do not want to have anything more to do with her.

"I promise. Just this once. If you would help me, I will never bother you again." I am cold-hearted, committed to little else but my sister and our survival. I do not turn away from her, but I am confused that she doesn't hand me her portion of bread to barter with when I go to the block elder, and since she doesn't offer it, I do not ask her for her food.

Taking my portion of bread to the block elder, I trade my only meal to get her the salve she needs. I know that if our roles were reversed she would not give up her bread for me, she will not even give me her bread for her own self, but I am expected to sacrifice mine for her.

She snatches the salve from my hand, hiding it quickly in her dress. "Thank you, Rena."

"You must be more careful in the future," I warn her. She disappears into the night. I do not feel virtuous or good about myself. I feel used and hungry, but I also know that I will never look back and regret trying to help my cousin's wife. There is little we can avoid in Birkenau, but trying to act with a little bit of dignity helps me. It reminds me of home.

Sometimes Jewish beggars came to our door Friday, before Sabbath. Mama had Danka and me stuff burlap sacks with straw for them to sleep on in the kitchen. The day after Sabbath, Mama had to burn the straw, scrub the floors, and boil the sheets and pillowcases to get rid of the lice and fleas they left behind. Danka and I

*didn't like cleaning up after these people, but Mama would remind
us that they had children and were less fortunate than we were.
The same was true for Gypsies and Gentile beggars. No one who
came to our door ever left empty-handed.*

This is Mama's legacy to me—to treat everyone with compassion.

∽

FOUR A.M.

"*Raus! Raus!*"

The horizon grows dark. The wind shifts. My nose twitches
in the breeze. They don't smell like rain clouds.

I feel myself detaching from my body; it happens sometimes
and I am helpless against it. The chimneys are smoking. I watch
myself move away as if I were taking a step to one side, leaving
my body behind. There are footsteps approaching. My eyes shift
toward the sound; my mind remains stationary. Hasse smiles like a
hunter who has captured its prey and is about to skin it alive. That
is how she feels to us, ruthless and capable of snapping our necks
in two without the slightest hesitation.

She flips up her hand at the gray clouds covering the dismal
sky. "Look how the French models are burning!"

It doesn't matter who you are, if you're rich or beautiful or el-
egant—if you're a Jew, you're nothing! She is always ridiculing us,
gloating at us. I cannot fathom her cruelty. She continues down
the line, counting and smiling, a sadist thrusting her verbal knife
into each of our hearts for the fun of it.

∽

WE ARE WORKING on the new blocks, digging sand out of a deep
hole and sifting it through the mesh nets. It's old and familiar to
us now, this digging and sifting. Our hands are hard. They no
longer bleed from the long hours of work, except occasionally
when we throw the bricks and our palms get cut once more. But
that detail has become less frequent as they find real work for us

to do. We load the lorries with the sand, pushing them toward a building that is closer to a men's kommando than our own. There are tracks for the lorries to glide along now, so pushing is not the horrific task it was a year ago. But it's still difficult, and as we heave the sand toward its destination I cannot believe we ever accomplished this task with no tracks, up a hill, and wearing slabs of wood on our feet.

We approach the men digging trenches to bury pipe in. Emma is watching the group sifting sand, and the farther away we move from her, the closer we get to being within earshot of the men. There are no SS nearby or watching. It is a precious moment.

"Is anybody Polish there?" a man asks from within the ranks of working men. We scoop the sand out into a pile next to the building.

"My sister and I are," I whisper back. Stealing words carefully. None of the other girls—who may be Dutch, French, German, or who knows anymore—pay attention to our snippets of conversation.

"Where're you from?" The lorry is empty. Grabbing onto the side of the car, we push it back to the piles of sand and reload. It takes a long time to fill the lorry. I am warm and cannot tell if it's the warm weather or my nerves making me shake. I long to have a conversation with this stranger on the other side of the fence; I long to know his name, his place of birth, his family. . . .

Pushing the thoughts of normal life back where they belong, I gouge the dirt and rocks that must be sifted. Danka has slowed and quickly I double my effort by taking a scoop from her section every few minutes.

"Take this lorry," Emma instructs. I grab the side, making sure there is room for my sister to hold on. We push it back toward the men's detail and begin relieving the car of its cargo. My eyes check the area for SS.

"Tylicz, near Krynica," I finally get to answer. We dig. The sound of shovels grating against dirt and pebbles seems louder than before. They dig. Our silence magnifies the noises around us.

"Krakow." We dig. They dig. An SS man appears.

∽

FOUR A.M.

"*Raus! Raus!*"

Anxious to get to work this morning, I have already been to the latrine by the time the room elders are hitting and yelling. Under a blushing sky we eat our snippet of bread and drink our tea. The days are growing longer, as do our hearts; not only do the seasons pass us by, but the longer the sun is in our sky the longer they work us. Sleep is just something slipped in between roll calls. Danka crosses her arms across her chest, holding her elbows. "I'm cold, Rena."

"The sun will be up soon."

"No, I mean I have a chill." There is a thick crust on her swollen lips.

"What is that on your lips?"

"I don't know." She touches her mouth. "I'm so thirsty." I hold her forehead in my hand.

"You're hot," I say, trying to quench the worry and alarm surfacing in my mind.

She nods. "You have a crust on your lips, too." I touch my lips, feeling the flakes brush off from beneath my fingertips. Placing my hand to my forehead, I tell myself I feel fine.

"Are you hot?" she asks.

"No, Danka. We work so hard and eat so little that the body must try extra hard to warm itself." I lie to my sister as I lie to myself.

She is warm, too warm for the temperature outside this morning. She is ill.

I do not say anything about this knowledge; I just make a mental note to myself. I can be alert for SS and green triangles, selections and dogs, but disease, this is something I cannot foresee. It comes upon us despite everything else we do to survive. This is our second spring. I can remember almost nothing of last year, nor do I want to. Still, I run through what memories surface about the first camp to see if any illness was common then, at this time of year. All that comes to mind is the biting bugs and the itching bites; the clouds of mosquitoes that infested camp last summer. So much has changed since last year that I cannot pick one change that stands out from the rest and fear that there are no answers in the past.

We march out with Emma toward the sand. Suddenly I am overcome with the fear that it was all a trick. The kind Pole from Krakow speaking to me yesterday will not be there today. A million things could've happened over the night. He could be dead, they could've moved his kommando to another area. My friend is gone. My fingers twitch against the burlap dress I wear. Agitated, these thoughts race through my mind without reason or logic. We're going to die. The pit yawns before me. Fear chases me toward its jaws. We will die not of selection or gas but in the hospital. Which is worse? The hope that has given me strength and energy to endure seems to run out of my fingers and toes and ears as all the fluids in my body drain away. We march toward the sand. My eyes glaze over.

Then I see them. The men are working in the same area they were yesterday. The pit disappears. We are safe once more—or are we? Danka is hot. The fever is gaining.

We push a lorry toward the building. I see the tall, skinny one and his shorter friend as we start unloading our cargo. The sun beats against our bare heads, keeping at bay the chill that sends shivers between Danka's scapula and spine. She is sweating too profusely. A stone falls to the ground a few feet away. I mark the place with my eyes without stopping my work. The lorry will be unloaded shortly. There are no SS. I focus on my work. I move a step towards the stone, digging, digging. In a few moments we'll be done. Digging, digging. I stoop quickly, my hand landing directly on the note. Firmly grasping the paper around the rock, I let the stone slip from my hand. We stand along the sides of the lorry getting ready to push. There is a moment, a second, in which to move, and I quickly adjust my shoe in that split of time and stillness, slipping the note under my foot. We push.

The afternoon wears on. Danka sweats. There has to be something I can do. The fears of the morning are gone. There is not time to fret over death. We are alive; all I can do is try to keep us that way.

"Halt!" We quickly put our shovels in the tool shed and line up. "March!" We march toward camp. "Heads up!" We raise our chins, lift our feet as if we are proud to be slaves of the Third

Reich. The only thing we have to be proud of is that there is no one to carry in today. Today we have all survived the Nazis' whips and boots, but a secret enemy is among us.

Tomorrow, if nothing happens tonight, Danka and I will return to Emma as we have done every day for weeks, months—over a year, now. We will not recognize anyone in our detail tomorrow, just as we did not recognize anyone today. We pay no attention to faces. We survive by ignoring the temporal and have stopped looking for repeaters, those who work in our detail day after day; it is useless, in vain, depressing. They don't exist.

After roll call Danka and I get our bread and excitedly read the note from the man on the work team: *I'm Heniek. My friend is Bolek. Your names?*

"Which one do you think likes me?" Danka asks.

"Look at you, all flushed by the thought of flirting with a boy in camp," I tease her gently, afraid that she is flushed because of her illness, not love. "I'm going to get a scrap of paper from the block elder to send them a note. You wait here."

I had typhus when I was twelve and remember the symptoms for that disease. Although it's the most common illness in camp besides scabies, Danka doesn't have typhus. I do not know what this enemy is. I have three missions as I leave Danka behind: one is to get a scrap of paper, one is to find out if there is an epidemic in camp, the last is to check outside for a morsel of anything edible. Whenever I have any extra energy I scour the grounds, organizing what tidbits I can.

Sneaking among the shadows, I pass the kitchen, all of my senses on alert. Finally, just as my eyes and legs are about to give out from weariness, I spy a peel of potato in the mud. Grabbing it, I dart back to the wall. It is a small morsel of food, barely big enough for one bite. I stare at it, looking for the proper place to mark it in half. Finally, I dig my fingernail into the pulp so I know exactly how much I must save for Danka. My mouth waters but I do not risk even a nibble before I can share it with my sister.

Back in the block, I go to the block elder's door. She seems in a good mood tonight, handing me a scrap of paper and a bit of pencil. "Don't get caught with it."

"Can I ask you something?" I figure it's worth a try. If anyone would know about what's going around camp it would be a block elder.

"What?" She doesn't seem to mind my intrusion into her time.

"Is there any illness in camp that causes fever and crusting on the lips?"

She peers at me closely, warily. "Swamp fever—malaria," she says, shutting the door in my face.[18]

I ponder her words while I scratch our names out in our note to Heniek and Bolek. Then wrap the note firmly around a stone and secure it in my hem for tomorrow. Back in our bunk, I hand Danka the pitiful piece of potato and we nibble on it, trying to make it larger and more savory than it can ever be. "Thank you, Rena."

How I wish it could be more. I long to take care of her properly, feed her chicken soup, lots of water, bed rest, all the things we're not allowed to have. Her eyes glisten like glass in the dark. I am worried. The conclusion the block elder has stated is not an optimistic diagnosis. I say nothing to Danka, but I have heard of this happening in the whispers around camp. The mosquitoes are terrible this spring, and the swamp we live in makes our bodies their banquet tables as they suck us dry. There is no defense; between them and the lice infesting us, we are too weak from starvation to fight their gorging. I fall asleep feeling a wave of chills wash across my own muscles in quiet spasm.

THE STONE LANDS close to Heniek. He retrieves it easily, bravely glancing at the note. He taps his friend. We dig. There are no SS nearby, so we slow the progress of unloading the lorry just a little bit in order to steal what bits of conversation that we can.

They dig. I am so concerned about Danka that for a moment I wonder if anyone can help us.

---

18. "June 3 [1943] . . . 302 female prisoners who are ill with malaria are transferred to Lublin (Majdanek) C. C." (Czech, 411).

As if reading my mind, Heniek asks, "Can we help you in any way?"

"I think my sister has malaria." I'm not sure if I should continue.

Quickly I glance across the work area; no one can overhear us. My shovel never falters from its movement. "Maybe if we had some tomato juice and a slice of lemon, we could wash the crust from her lips. It might break the fever." I have managed the impossible, communicated one entire sentence without interruption.

Rocks against metal scrape abrasively against one another. I can continue these movements for hours without aching muscles or fatigue—digging, digging. We work without faltering. We go back for another load. I work twice as fast, hoping to get one more load in before the men leave, before nightfall. I am shaking with nervousness. Emma signals for us to take the lorry.

"Be quick!" she orders. We push the lorry along the tracks. Our heads down, we unload the cart without looking at the men.

"You need quinine." He sounds hopeful.

"Yah, sure . . ." It has been a long time since I felt any hope. He digs. We dig. The sun nears the horizon. The lorry is almost empty. We disembark from our task, preparing to push the cart toward the sifters and Emma, away from the men.

"Don't worry, Rena." I hear his voice fall across the fence and cling to it as if it is a life raft on an angry sea. For some reason I believe Heniek can help us; I do not know how, but for a moment I breathe easier.

THE CRUST ON Danka's lips is worse, but she does not feel as hot today. I wonder if the volatility of this fever is one of its dangers. We dig and sift all morning until lunch and never load the lorries. I want to scream at Emma to let us take the lorries, but all we do is sift and sift and sift. At least there will be plenty to move tomorrow, but that means they will patrol us closer if more groups are moving the lorry loads. Lunch comes and goes. There is a portion of meat in my bowl. I bite it in half, handing the remainder to Danka.

"Is it pork?"

"Eat it." I refuse to answer her question. It is meat; that is all that matters. The war must be going well.

All afternoon we dig and sift. The lorries are not moved.

FOUR A.M.

"*Raus! Raus!*"

We line up at roll call finishing our tea, eating last night's bread.

"How are you feeling today, Danka?"

"Better." She sips her tea quietly. Her eyes gape open at the scene around us. Thousands of girl-women are also holding cups of semi-tea and chewing last night's bread slowly, carefully, trying to make it last. The camp is overflowing. I have never seen so many women at one time; I cannot even comprehend the numbers. Roll call takes ages.

Finally we march out with Emma.

"Take the lorries," she orders us first thing. The sun is just breaching the horizon. There is a golden glow about us as shadows appear where night has been. Danka and I quickly take our place on the side of the carts, pushing the lorry toward the men's kommando. An SS walks by. No sooner is his back to us than a stone falls at my feet. I stoop nonchalantly down to the ground, checking my shoe, and then swing up my shovel quickly, helping remove the sand we sifted yesterday. The hand with the note holds tightly to the shovel. It is a larger piece of paper than the scrap I sent them, and it's so early that I must think of what to do with the note for the rest of the day. In my dress or in my hand? The shoes aren't safe enough for a whole day of work, so the debate continues. In my hem or in my hand? I wonder where to hide the note. My hands are too warm and the shovel slips in my grasp as I scoop the sand over the edge into the growing pile. The lorry is empty. Quickly I hide the note in the hem of my dress with no chance to read it.

It's a long day, a long roll call, but at last we enter the block, more eager to read the note than to eat our bread. It looks as if it was written in great haste. *You saw pipes coming close to your detail. In ground—five steps from pipes—tomorrow.* I cannot believe the words before my eyes.

ALL DAY WE EYE THE PIPES. I can see that five steps from the pipe there is a little rise in the ground, but we must wait patiently. I watch the sky closely as the afternoon wanes. Our timing must be perfect. I nod to Danka. Slowly we dig, little by little, away from the group toward the pipes. We gouge the land, carrying large shovelfuls of dirt to the sifting net, each time returning one step closer to the pipes. There are no SS nearby. I wink, and Danka busily digs around me, loosening the dirt while blocking me with her body so no one can see what I'm doing. Working diligently, she puts on a good show, giving me the cover I need to retrieve our treasure. Quickly I tie a bottle of tomato juice underneath my dress, to the other end of the string, which also holds my bowl. In a bit of cloth there is a lemon and, to my great surprise, tablets. There is a note, too, and these I hide in my hem with the lemon.

"They've gotten us quinine," I whisper to Danka. She digs deeper into the dirt, throwing her back into the work. I was not expecting so much and only have the hem of my dress to hide things in.

"Hurry," Danka whispers, digging, digging. It is very complicated, smoothing the tablets out in my hem so the SS won't notice any lumps. I pray none will fall out.

"Done." We dig around the area, quickly obscuring the hiding place.

"Halt!" Emma yells. Our skin bristles in fear. We stop what we're doing, trying to erase any traces of anxiety on our faces. We look up at Emma.

"Line up!" she announces.

I cast a glance at Danka as we carry our last shovelful of dirt toward the sifting net before carrying the shovels into the tool shed.

My heart smiles proudly at my sister's glistening face. She does everything to the best of her ability, and despite her illness she has been more than stalwart today.

"Here, take one now." I slip a tablet into her hand.

"March!" Our hearts are pounding so loudly that I am sure the band must hear the timing within our chests. Our luck is holding out; for five days there has not been a selection. We go to the blocks, grab our bread, and take our place in the shelves. Holding onto our blanket, I give Danka the tomato juice and lemon.

"You have some," she offers. "You have a crust on your lips, too."

"No, Danka. You're the one who's sick."

"Rena, I can't take it all. You must share it with me."

"You're going to waste it if you leave it for me. I'm not going to take it." She sips from the bottle and sucks on the lemon quietly.

"Wash your lips with the lemon, Danka." I show her what I mean. The crust dissolves under the vitamin juices of real fruit.

Her lips change dramatically as the brown crust that has encased them for days washes away.

"Use the rind." She hands me the lemon rind. I use it to scrub my lips as well. The flavor of the rind is bitter and sharp. It makes my taste buds leap.

"I bet it took twenty people to organize this package," I whisper.

"Read the note," Danka reminds me.

Quinine three times a day, I read softly, out loud. *Watch the pipes—if mound by pipes, something there for you. In few days more juice. Be well. Love, Heniek and Bolek. (Bolek's in love with Danka. I'm in love with you.)*

Danka blushes and giggles slightly. It sounds so strange to hear mirth. "Thank you, Lord, for saving us once more," Danka whispers and squeezes my hand as she falls asleep.

Morning comes, and Danka finishes the tomato juice and eats the lemon rind. I give her a tablet and plan to give her one at each meal until they're gone.

Pushing the lorries toward the men, I check the landscape and quickly toss the note I wrote last night: *Thank you. Danka's already feeling better. Bóg zapłać, may God reward you. Love, Rena and Danka.* We do not have anything else to give Heniek and Bolek but these words. Perhaps, like the tablets to us, love will give them what they need to survive. In this place we cannot be selfish with affection or gratitude. If we don't say it today, there may never be another chance.

Over the next few weeks there is a rise in the dirt by the pipes three times. Each time there is tomato juice, a lemon, and a love note from Heniek and Bolek. One time there are more quinine tablets. Then one day we march toward the piles of sand and there are no men working on the other side of the fence. Our saviors are gone from our view but not from our hearts. We think of them often. We never see them again.

"RENA?" I TURN toward a familiar face from my past. A whirlwind of memory tangles my thoughts. It is someone from home, a Gentile.

"Manka?" I question the face before me.

"Rena. How goes it with you?"

"I am alive. How is it that you're here?" I look at her triangle. It is the color of a political prisoner, but I find that hard to believe. She probably talked out of her head without thinking; she was known for that in Tylicz. I feel myself growing wary—her eyes have that wild look one sees too often behind these fences. She is losing her mind. I remain cautious.

"I saw your parents killed," she says matter-of-factly. "That's right. They came back to Tylicz. They shouldn't have come back. One day the Germans decided to take all the Jews that were left, about eight, and they made them line up in the marketplace. . . ." I cannot believe her callous intonation. "Then they tied their hands up with ropes to a wagon and ran the horses around the circle until every last one of them was dead." She sounds as if she's reciting the alphabet.

"Excuse me . . ." I start to walk away, but her voice follows me.

"They screamed for us to save them, but there was nothing anyone could do. They suffered terribly. They shouldn't have come back, but it wouldn't have mattered, would it? Everyone who isn't dead is here!"

Stumbling through the mud, I try to escape her voice, her hideous voice. I hate you! I want to scream at her face. I hate you.

The vision starts to fracture. The crack is long and deep, scarring my mother's patient and loving face. Mending it quickly, as if I am a bricklayer securing a fortress, I smear concrete across my memory. Mama is waiting for us. They are at the farmhouse waiting. They are safe. Only the rest of the world is in danger. Manka's out of her mind, I tell myself. She wasn't there. She's crazy. She's out of her mind, I repeat to myself over and over again.

The fences of Birkenau stretch before me. I do not get close enough to get shot, but I stand there staring out at the open spaces of my homeland. There are no tears on my face; I'm too dehydrated to cry, but my eyes ache as if tears were falling.

Sometimes I have serious doubts that they are alive, but sometimes I feel as if there's a physical presence next to me. I can smell her. I can feel her touch. I cannot see Mama, but I know she's near. I have moments of common sense and clear thinking when I know this invisible presence means she's gone, but then my cloudy mind obscures that truth. There is less pain living in a cloudy mind, so I don't allow myself to think about things too clearly unless clear thinking means saving our lives.

There is not much time for clear thinking in Auschwitz-Birkenau. When I made the oath to Danka, that was a clear moment. If I'd been cloudy I couldn't have said, "My hand is the Holy Book and Mama and Papa are standing right here in front of us." I'd said it as if they were in a heaven, invisible entities watching over us. That means at that moment I knew they had to be gone, but I rarely allow myself to think that. These two minds have a symbiotic relationship, and as long as no one challenges the logic, each realm can exist.

I shut the door on Manka's account of their deaths. Mama and Papa are alive waiting for us in Tylicz, and Mama is the warm, invisible presence guarding and guiding us. This is how it is. It doesn't have to make sense to anyone but me.

WE ARRIVE AT Emma's kommando in the morning to find fifty middle-aged women going with us to work. We gape at them as if they are aliens from another world. It is strange to see women in their fifties; they usually select any women in their forties or older for the gas. But here they are, these fifty women staring at us, looking like our mothers.[19] Their sweet, wrinkling faces reveal the fear and trepidation this place forces on us all. They are probably thinking about their own daughters and sons and grandchildren. I cannot turn away from their faces. It is terrible to see elder women without kerchiefs on their heads and as bald as we are. For a moment I think how Mama would have felt if she'd been forced out in public without her wig or a babushka.

"Danka, look!" I point to a woman standing in line.

Danka gasps. "She looks like Mama." We squeeze each other's hands, smiling at the stranger. She smiles back at us.

Taking the kerchief from my head, I approach the woman who looks so much like Mama. "You will need this to protect your head from the sun today." I hand it to her.

"I can't take this from you," she stammers.

"You must. I won't wear it." I walk away, blinking hard.

"March out!" We step forward, heading out of the gates. The band plays an out-of-tune polka. There are girls staring at our kommando. Mouths fall open as the mothers pass, marching out to work. The silent wake that follows us is the invisible weeping of each girl remembering and praying that her own mother has escaped this end.

∽

THIS IS THE second year, so there are so many of us that one SS watches one kommando. The kommandos are divided into separate work details, each with a kapo to oversee it. Still, we don't

---

19. "The flow of convoys abruptly ceased at the end of July 1943 and there was a breathing space. The crematoria were thoroughly cleaned, the installations repaired and prepared for further use. On August 3 the killing machine again went into operation" (Wyman, 18). It is likely that the elder women were brought to Birkenau during this time. Historical weather data confirms a heat wave with temperatures in the high 20s to 30 Celsius (low to mid-80s) during that period.

always have an SS standing right over us because they're busy inspecting other work details.

"1716!" Emma says. I lift my head without stopping shoveling to see why Emma has chosen my number out of the ranks. "Come up here." I put down my shovel, moving warily toward the edge of the *postenkette*.

"Stand right here, by the edge of the ditch and keep watch." She looks directly into my eyes. "I'm going to the latrine, and I'm going to be longer than usual." I nod, knowing that she's going to meet a man there. "You stand here looking left and right all the time, and if somebody is coming, jump in and start to work. If they ask where I am, tell them I went to the latrine." I nod.

I stand above my sister and the rest of the kommando looking left and right. My eyes fall on the elder women, and again I look left and again I look right. The sun is hot on our heads. I wipe the sweat from my eyes. The woman wearing my kerchief blinks into the harsh sun as she gazes up at me. I cannot bear to have them working so hard, for hours, without a respite. These women are so much like our mamas, and they have not had a moment to stop and breathe since lunch.

"Why don't you all sit down?" I suggest. "Put your shovels down and rest while I keep watch." Everyone looks up at me. "Go on. I can see if anyone is coming from up here." One by one they sit down, crouching or kneeling in the dirt. The woman who looks particularly like our mother smiles. I look left. The stillness of the girls and women below me allows me a moment of comfort. I look right. The dust settles around their feet and hands. Their heads glisten with beads of sweat, and I can see where sunburn is turning their delicate skin red. I look left. I look right. But I do not look behind me.

"What is going on here?!" The horse gallops up from nowhere. Before I know what is happening, an SS jumps from his steed and throws me to the ground. He kicks me viciously in the back. I cover my face.

"Where's the kapo?" he yells, swinging his steel-tipped boot into my ribs.

"Ahhh!" My hands fly to my stomach. "She's in the latrine!" He kicks my face. Blood gushes out of my mouth.

"And you let them rest?" And again in the stomach and again in the ribs. "You who were supposed to watch? Liar!" And again in the back and again in my face. "Filthy *scheiss-Jude! Mist biene!* You should all be killed!"

I cannot see through the blood in my eyes. He pummels me as if I were a rotten vegetable for compost, but I refuse to cry or beg for mercy.

The girl-women and the elder women busily work, sifting sand, shoveling dirt, trying to ignore my grunts and groans.

"What's happening?!" Emma comes running.

"Where were you?" he yells.

"The latrine, sir!"

"And you let a Jew watch other Jews? You whore! Stupid bitch! I want this prisoner reported for letting your detail rest!"

"*Jawohl,* sir."

"Report her to Commandant Drexler!"

"*Jawohl!*"

"Perhaps next time you will think twice before you go whoring."

Emma takes over whipping me. "You dog! Get back to work!" Her strikes are not as damaging as the vicious kicks of the SS, but that she would beat me injures what feelings I have left for her.

I scuffle away trying to be invisible, hoping he won't start beating me again, hoping he's grown weary of so much physical exertion in this heat. The hooves of his horse pound against the ground as he gallops away. Danka puts a shovel in my hand. Her hand is like ice. I dig blindly at the soil, unable to distinguish earth from sky through the blood and tears.

We work silently, quickly. Everyone is shaking with fear. We do not cease our work; there is not even a pause in the rhythm of our digging.

"1716." I turn toward Emma's voice, unable to see her face.

"Take this." I duck the blow, but instead a rag falls in my hands.

"Clean yourself up." Without another word Emma returns to her post.

I lean for a second on my shovel, wiping the dirt and blood from my eyes and face. The sobs inside my chest rack against my bruised ribs. I am so confused, a miserable "*mist biene,*" just as they call me. I struggle for control. Turbulent emotions well up inside me. My temples throb. My mouth aches. I cannot cry, not only because of work but because of the pain. It will hurt too much to let one sob out. I choose instead to think of Emma. Despite the fact she beat me, it was to save her own skin; the rag says more than any words she will ever speak to me. I focus on digging and Emma, trying to think the pain away.

The woman who looks so much like Mama watches me the whole afternoon. Emma ignores the fact that I cannot work as hard as I usually do. She cracks the whip above our heads and acts tough, but the detail works slowly in the heat and the elder women are not capable of such hard labor. I bear the pain as well as I can, but it hurts to breathe and stand upright. Finally it is time to march back to camp. The two-kilometer march is agony in itself, every inhale catches my ribs like a knife in my lungs.

The marching band is playing, but inside I am dying a hundred deaths, hearing only a dirge; for me it is over. Emma stands to one side of the band as her kommando marches through the gate.

"Wait here." Emma pulls me out. My eyes catch Danka's. It is a silent good-bye. The band plays horror to my ears. I am screaming with pain and still I must stand, knowing in a few hours I will be dead, knowing I have seen my sister for the last time marching through the gates of hell—knowing I have not kept my oath, knowing I have failed her. I dare not shift my tired feet. I dare not turn my head. Staring straight ahead as kommando after kommando marches in, my eyes do not register the faces of any individuals. Some who still have the energy to notice see me there; none has the energy to care. I am doomed in their eyes, another prisoner awaiting her death sentence. They do not need to be reminded about the tenuousness of all our lives.

For the first time in sixteen months of imprisonment I wish I were inside the gates of Birkenau, standing next to my sister waiting to be counted; at least that means I am alive. I watch roll call begin from outside the gates. Floating away from my body, I gaze at the sea of humanity doomed to servitude and wish I were among them.

The sky is dark. I am alone. Even the band has left me behind. The door to the office opens and Emma steps out. The light from inside illuminates her head. Her hair is turning gray.

"Get into camp," she says matter-of-factly. I move away from her uncertainly, afraid she is joking.

"*Hau ab!*" she orders, adding under her breath, "And make sure you're with me after roll call tomorrow."

"Yes, Emma. I will, Emma." To cross through these gates, to disappear into camp to join the ranks of downtrodden girl-womanhood is all I can hope for now, to be counted in that roll call—to be alive.

Danka is outside our block; she waits with tear-stained cheeks.

"Rena?" We grab each other in a fierce hug. "I thought you were dead for sure," she weeps.

"I was. Emma saved me."

"How?"

"I don't know." I have an idea, but Danka is too innocent to hear it, and it is beyond my imagination that a *Reichdeutsche* might have given herself for a Jew like me. . . . But what else does Emma have to trade?

There may not be presents or parties in Birkenau, but the fact that one gets to be with one's loved ones again is a rare gift behind these walls. And this brush with death inspires rather than defeats me.

"We have to see if we can get some kerchiefs for the elder women in our detail."

"Rena, you're hurt. You should lie down."

"I will feel better if I can help these women." We go from one block to another telling the block elders, room elders, and other prisoners about the elder women, begging for kerchiefs so they can at least protect themselves from the sun.

"They can't stand the heat," I tell them. "Look how I got beaten for letting them rest. They are the age of our mothers, and they're not going to survive if we don't do something." Everyone who has a kerchief donates one to our cause. With damp eyes, they give Danka and me a scarf in honor of their own mamas, who are now mere memories in the ashen air. We get ten kerchiefs altogether.

"I have been looking for you." The woman who looks so much like Mama comes up to me as I am gathering the scarves.

"How are you?" I ask.

"I should be asking you that. I want to give you something. Will you please take this?" She holds out her portion of bread.

"No, I can't." I shake my head, retreating from her gesture.

"Please, you are young. I want you to live," she pleads.

"You're going to need it tomorrow. Please, save it and eat it in the morning. It's going to be another hot day. You have your kerchief. You can live. I know you can. Look, my sister and I have gotten more kerchiefs for your friends to wear in the sun. It's going to get better—really it is!"

"You can talk like this after the beating you had?"

"Oh, that. Next time I'm going to look all the way around and be more careful. . . . You'll see, it's not so bad here," I lie to my Mama's face. "Try to eat the bread and drink the tea, for me. Please, try to live. . . . Have you got your tea?"

"Yes, a friend is watching it in the block. I'm going to drink the tea but not the bread. You have it, I don't need it."

"I can't take it from you. That would be like taking bread from my own mama."

"Your mama wants you to have her bread, to live for her."

My eyes sting. "I'm sorry. Thank you, but I cannot take it. Please. Promise me you'll eat it." I hold her hand, folding it firmly around the crust that is so precious many would fight her for it.

"What's your name?"

"Rena."

"You're a good daughter, Rena." She smiles into my eyes. "I know it's unlikely, but I'm going to pray that you meet one of my sons when you are free. Either would be a good husband to you, and if you're not going to meet one of my boys, I'm going to pray to the Lord that you have a husband just as good as my sons and have a good life." Our hands slip apart slowly, and she leaves me standing alone in the night clutching white and red kerchiefs to my breast.

"Rena, are you done?" Danka's voice pulls me back to the present. "We have to get inside."

"She has her bread," I tell my sister. "She'll be okay, won't she?"

"Who, Rena?"

"Mama. We'll see her tomorrow, right?"

∞

FOUR A.M.

"*Raus! Raus!*"

We arrive at Emma's kommando after roll call, but the elder women are not there.

"Where are they, Emma?" I have never asked her a direct question before.

"I don't know."

"Stay here," I tell Danka, hoping to save my place in the kommando. Running across the camp, I look for their stooped and tired bodies in the nearby kommandos lining up for work. Her face is not anywhere. Dashing into their block, I see the block elder. "Where are they?"

"Who?"

"Our mothers," I stammer. "The elder women!"

"Oh." Her voice is quiet. As hard as we have all become, these women have touched our hearts and made us feel again, but the wounds are deep and sore to the touch. "They took them late last night."

Words are stuck in my throat as if someone were strangling me. The block elder and I stare at one another in grief and shock.

"Get out of here before you get caught!" Her voice jerks me back to reality. I leave the block unable to run anymore. My legs are heavy as iron.

Emma's ranks are full. I stare at her, lost, unable to muster my usual gusto of self-assurance. I am slipping into the pit, about to be swallowed up, about to disappear.

Rolling her eyes at me, Emma jerks her head. "Get in!"

Stepping next to Danka, I shake my head and bite my lip. Heads bowed, we march out to another day of work and blistering heat. There are no motherly faces to comfort our losses, but Emma does not crack her whip today unless an SS is riding by. The pain in my back and ribs reawakens, and I am unable to think anything away.

The numbness in my heart expands through my body. The body digs the dirt. The body sifts the sand. The body screams with pain as the lungs expand against bruised, and maybe broken, ribs. But it is the eyes that hurt most. They ache until it feels as if the head will split apart, bleeding across the barren land as we sift more sand to make more bricks and concrete, to make more blocks for more Jews. Despite the sun the sky is black.

We aren't living in Birkenau. We are always almost dead.

∽

SS STIEWITZ IS IN A FOUL MOOD, stamping back and forth, cursing loudly at our hungry faces while we wait for our evening's ration of tea and bread. We don't pay attention to the reason for his tirade; these outbursts of temper are nothing unusual. Even the SS have bad days. He picks the lid up off the teakettle, flinging it like a discus against a wall. It ricochets, flying toward those of us in line.

"Duck, Danka!" She swerves but too late. *Smack!*

The iron lid slices into her head, toppling her under the weight and sudden impact. Blood pours down her face and across the earth. The bone under the wound is visible, but this is a good thing, I tell myself, at least her skull isn't cracked. I pull the cloth I use for my periods out of my sleeve and press it hard against the gash, praying the blood will clot quickly, before any SS notice her lying here. She stirs. "Hold this to your head and press hard." She holds it as I rip off a piece of my slip, another gift from Erna long ago.

"Be still, Danka. Don't move until I tell you to." Her eyes wince with pain. Placing this new strip of fabric against the cut, I wring out the other one before replacing it. The girls in line hide us by moving forward for their bread. Obscured by them, I have a few precious moments to stop the bleeding, check Danka's breathing, examine her eyes. She's in shock; the wound is large and ugly, arching from the center of her forehead down to her eyebrow. My head begins to ache in sympathy with her.

"It's not too bad, Danka. We have to get something on it, though, some salve." I dab the blood gently from her brow. It's oozing more slowly now. "We're going to stand up now and get our tea." I direct her into line to get our tea and bread. We head inside our block.

"I'm nauseous."

"Eat anyway, Danka. You need your strength. It's the cut making you feel sick, not your stomach." She sips her tea slowly, stopping every few moments as if fighting the urge to vomit. I cover her with our blanket before going to wait by the block elder's door.

"Salve for a cut." I hand her my bread.

"Let me see what I have." She takes my bread and disappears. I wait, trying to keep watch on Danka from where I stand. My legs grow tired of standing, so I crouch with my back against the wall and wait. The block is still. My knees begin to ache in this position, so I sit on the dirt floor and wait. The door cracks open. The light from inside falls across the darkness of the now sleeping block. The block elder hands me a smear of salve on a piece of paper and shuts the door in my face.

I wash Danka's wound gently. "Am I going to die from this?"

"No way. It's not so bad, Danka, really. But I know it hurts."

What I'm really worried about is infection, a scar, selection. The wound may not kill her but the effect of it can. I stamp out these worries that divert my attention and resourcefulness. Smearing the antiseptic salve on her forehead, I assure her, "We'll get more tomorrow."

∞

FOUR A.M.

"*Raus! Raus!*"

My stomach growls all day. The soup sloshes in my belly like an ocean of waves with nothing to cling to. Danka is weak, and I can tell her head is hurting, but she manages to work. I trade my bread for more salve to put on her cut and then step outside to go to the latrine. It is in the latrine that information is passed and things can be bartered for. I miss Erna and wish for a moment that I had someone to talk to, someone to share my burdens with. "Have you heard?" a girl whispers next to me. "There's going to be a big selection. They're going to clean out camp." Another voice echoes the information. "There are too many of us."

I walk back to the block in a daze. All I hear, over and over like a child's nursery rhyme chanting in my head, is the rumor:

there's going to be a big selection; there are too many of us. Like an itch I cannot scratch, it eats away at my silence. It's an ominous secret, an unshareable burden. I almost wish they hadn't told me. The worry about Danka's scar eats away at my morale. She'll be selected if they see the cut, and it's healing too slowly. My head churns until I am thinking of everything and nothing at all.

We march out with Emma, but the work worsens with the weather; this is our second fall. There are no days off for snow or rain; I know that now. They will always stand there watching us struggle to move bricks, digging, building. We march in from work, our hands and feet blistered from always being damp and cold; we wait to be counted, wait for our tea, our bread, always working—always waiting.

The SS are more agitated than usual. Swinging their whips and clubs more often, they beat us without any provocation. The work details are stricter and harder. It's as if they're trying to clear out those who won't make the cut when the big selection comes. I scan the rows and rows of women who share my fate. I've never seen the camp this crowded. "There are too many of us." I wonder how it makes the Nazis feel when they can't kill us quickly enough by working us to death. I wonder if they feel at all.

THE SS WALK up and down our rows counting the evening crew, making note of those who collapsed and died during the day. A hush descends through the columns of women. Dr. Mengele has come into camp. We know who he is; there are rumors about him. He stands before us, the glorious angel of doom. It's difficult to believe that anyone so handsome can do the things he's rumored to do.

An SS motions for a portion of our ranks to move away from the main group. Danka and I are in the group separated from the rest of roll call. Dr. Mengele walks slowly among us looking for the healthiest, most able-bodied specimens. It is a moment I have been hoping for; sometimes he chooses prisoners for inside work details, like the one Erna and Fela are now in. This may be our lucky day, the day we find a way to leave Birkenau. He walks by us like a butcher inspecting his meat.

He points at me but passes over Danka. I step out, walking to the front of the line, moving away from my sister. Danka is discarded with the rest of the unfit specimens. Roll call is dismissed. Thousands of women hurry to their respective blocks to grab their bread and a place on the shelves to sleep.

We march away from the regular blocks toward the quarantine block. Turning my head, I catch a glimpse of my sister as the pit in my stomach grows wider and wider. The anxiety of not having her next to me is unbearable. I do not know if this detail is for life or if it is for death. I do know that the only way I can keep my promise to my sister, though, is to keep her with me at all times; too much can happen in a moment. There is no debate in my mind about my duty to my sister; the oath is the driving force behind all of my actions.

Inside the quarantine block we are handed a standard ration of bread. There's no conversation or speculation about the detail we've been assigned. The girls I've been chosen with move to the bunks without conversing, while I dissolve into the background so that no one will notice my exit.

Erika is on watch outside, holding a paper with our numbers on it. This is good fortune, although there is always the chance she won't be nice to me. I don't care about chances. I go straight up to her. "Can you help me? I'll give you my portion of bread if you can get my sister into this detail with me." I thrust my only meal into her hand.

Erika looks at me as if I'm crazy. The decision in my eyes convinces her I'm serious, though. "What's her number?" She takes the bread, slipping it into her pocket in one deft movement.

"2779." I hold my breath. She seems sincere. She seems to care, but one can never be sure. "Can I bring her into quarantine?" I ask timidly.

Erika looks around quickly, assessing the area. There is no one nearby. She crosses a name off the list. "Go get your sister."

"There will be too many, though. What will you do?"

"None of your business," she hisses. "*Hau ab!*"

Obediently I vanish, becoming one with the shadows, weaving my way toward our block. Danka is standing just inside the doorway, waiting for me. Only her eyes betray the absolute terror she is in. I take hold of her hand as I used to when she was little. "I got you into the detail."

"How?"

"Follow me." We step into the dark, sneak back across the camp toward quarantine. The spotlights trace the electric fences, looking for kamikaze prisoners with suicide on their minds. We move like ghosts, avoiding the lights, the guns, the eyes of those in the watchtower.

Erika is waiting outside. We do not step toward her; we wait in the shadows for her signal. She drops her chin slightly in a half nod before turning her back to us. We dart through the door to safety. Careful not to disturb anyone, we tiptoe to a bunk that isn't full and crawl onto the boards. Pulling up the blanket around our shoulders, I put my arms around my sister. I want to chase away the demon dreams that steal sleep from our troubled minds. I want to rest my weary bones and stop the incessant worrying that rattles against the inside of my head.

For the first time in a year and a half we don't stand roll call. In the morning they bring a kettle of tea into the block and the waiting begins.

We're served soup at noon and sit through the afternoon waiting for supper with nothing else to do but listen to our stomachs growl. I'm grateful we don't have to work and try to take advantage of this brief reprieve. We don't feel like speaking with the others, and they do not feel like speaking with us. The first day of quarantine we sleep.

The second day we are not so tired and move about the room asking questions, conversing, asking out loud why we're here and how long they're going to keep us in this place. My hope is that this will be a detail working under a roof. It would be good to be inside on the cold and rainy days. I also hope it's not the kind of detail Erna and Fela have disappeared into, a job that cannot be spoken about.

Danka drifts off into a world of her own. I watch her become oblivious to her surroundings knowing that this is how she survives. Meanwhile, I listen to every bit of information I can gather; this is how I survive—always being aware.

"Maybe we're going to work in the kitchen!" one of the girls says.

"Oh, the food we could eat if we were in the kitchen!"

"I wonder what they'll have us do?"

"It could be anything. Better not to think about it."

Another girl chimes in, but her comment is more to the window than to those of us inside. "At least we're not outside. The weather is terrible today."

Our conversation is sparing. We don't speak to the others for long. We are too exhausted, and we've simply learned it's better not to become close friends with people who may die in a few minutes. There's no sorority of sympathy. We don't discuss our plight or what we're waiting for. If we discuss anything, it is about where we are from, but even that is too painful. We sleep. We drink our tea. We sip our soup. We chew our bread. We wait.

By the third day we're starting to go stir-crazy and get on each other's nerves. The unknown eats away at what little morale we have. There's bickering among bunkmates. The rest has done us good; the little bit of food still leaves us hungry, but at least we do not burn it all off doing hard labor. We do not gain weight, but we do not lose it either.

"*Raus!* Line up!" It's the fourth morning. An attendant from the hospital enters the block. "March out!" We follow her lead, stepping out of quarantine, marching across the length of camp toward another building. The sign over the door reads SAUNA. Inside, the kapo informs us, "Leave your old clothes in a pile here. You no longer need them. There are new uniforms on that table. *Schnell!*"

Stepping naked over to the table, we snatch up the new one-size-fits-all uniforms, pulling them over our bodies. They're exactly like our other blue-and-gray striped dresses, rough as unworn sandpaper.

"Put these aprons on!" We tie clean, white pressed aprons around our waists as we line up again, filing out of the building in twos. We march back across the length of the compound in front of the rest of the women in camp already lined up for morning roll call. The next building we enter is in the middle of the camp; it's a small, one-room building across from our blocks. It's Mengele's office. Inside, the nurse orders us to hold out our arms so the secretary can write down each of our numbers on a list. "1716," she repeats under her breath, "2779." It's strange that we do not have numbers on our uniforms.

Outside, we line up facing the camp roll call, in neat rows of five, ten to each line, forming our new, exclusive work detail. I wonder where Emma is; I wonder if she has even noticed that Danka and I are even gone.

It is strange to watch regular camp roll call and not be a part of it. I have never seen so many people in one place. They look so miserable, so forlorn and dejected. The words *There are too many of us* echo through my mind until I shake my head to free myself of the warning.

Out of the corner of my eye I see a woman with a list in her hand and make a note that her presence is odd. She comes from behind the building, nervously looking this way and that as if she's afraid. She stands for a moment, scratching something out on the list, then cautiously she takes one of the girls by the hand and leads her out the back of the line and behind Mengele's office. They disappear.

My heart races as the realization sinks in. "Danka, this is not a good detail to be in."

Danka's eyes bulge with fright. "Why do you say that?"

"One of the elite just took a friend or relative out of the lineup."

"Who?"

"I don't know who she is, but she's important enough to walk around while the rest of us are standing roll call. She would know if this was a bad kommando. We're not going to work under any roof. This is for death."

"You can't be sure."

"Yes, I can." I look around. My mind runs through every scenario possible. It takes less than a second for me to decide the course of action we must try to take if we are to survive. "Come with me."

Her eyes pop out of her head. "Where?"

"Back to the sauna." I look at the dreaded dresses we're wearing. How could I have missed the signs? No numbers on the breast, new dresses, clean white aprons exactly like the experiment victims were wearing. "Our only chance is to get our old uniforms back before they remove them and we're lost for good."

"We can't do that!"

"We have to." I am fierce.

"How?"

My mind has catapulted beyond the situation we are in, to the particulars that could save our lives. "We're going to pretend that we're just as important as any block elder or kapo. I'm going to take your hand and we're going to march across the compound and I'm not letting go until we're in the sauna."

"In front of everybody?"

"It's a gamble."

"We can't. They'll shoot us for sure."

"Danka! This is something for experiments. Remember the women with the faces?"

"Gathering herbs?"

"You want to be a zombie?" I glare into her face.

"No."

We fall silent as an officer passes.

"You're going to be if you don't come with me now. We have one chance to live and one chance to die. If we cross the compound we might live or die. If we stay here we're dead for sure."

She wants to follow me, I can tell, but fear has her feet rooted into the ground. "I can't," she whispers.

I lean very close to her ear. "I'm going to break my oath to you. I swore I'd die with you, but that was only if you were selected, not if you chose to die. I don't owe that to you anymore!" Our voices are sparse and speculative. The SS are busy counting the prisoners on the other side of the Laggerstrasse. "If you don't want to listen to what I'm saying, then you're deciding to give up your life—but I'm not. I'm going back to the sauna whether you come with me or not." I pray I've scared her enough to come with me.

"What do I do?" Her voice wavers.

"Just walk with me. That's all you have to do. Keep your chin high and believe you're important." Her eyes glaze over. She will do as she's told. "Now give me your hand." Like a cold, clammy fist her fingers wind around mine.

I check the direction the SS are gazing. Taube is beating someone. Their attention is elsewhere. Gathering my self-esteem around me, I imagine the cloud of God descending down upon my sister and me, just as it did on the mount to speak with Moses and take our first step out of line. Past roll call, past the watchful SS, past thousands of other female prisoners, Danka and I walk, hidden in the mists of Zion.

Passing Stiewitz and Taube, we walk with the air that we are doing exactly what we've been told to do. My fingernails dig into her flesh; I'm not letting go of my sister's hand. We walk, convinced that no one will stop us. We are important. We have been ordered to return to the sauna. I repeat this to myself over and over. Chins up, eyes forward, never look back.

The distance seems to remain the same. The sauna gets no closer. The lines and rows of prisoners seem to continue on forever. Through the desert of Birkenau we walk invisible.

Seconds slow to hours as our feet trudge through the mud. Our heads held high, our gaze never veers from our path. Danka's hand turns blue from the tightness of my squeeze. Chins up, eyes forward, never look back.

I open the sauna door without looking behind me. There are no voices behind us ordering us to halt, no gunshots firing at our backs. There's only roll call, the lifeline that we must grab as quickly as we can change our clothes.

We step inside, shutting the door behind us.

"Quick, Danka. We have to hurry!" I whisper urgently. "Undress and give me your clothes. I will do the rest." Tearing the uniform of an experiment victim off my body, I search the pile of discarded uniforms in my underwear. Danka cannot move. She stares at me like a small animal frozen by fear, incapable of helping me, as I fumble through the clothes looking for her number, repeating "2779, 2779" over and over, out loud. My hands tremble uncontrollably as my nerves unravel.

There is no time. Our lives depend on getting back to roll call. We must be counted. We must disappear before anyone notices we're missing from the special detail. Finally, her uniform is on the floor in front of me. I toss it to Danka.

The pile seems to have multiplied since I turned my back. Shaking uncontrollably, I dig through the clothes looking for the one uniform out of fifty that is mine. They are all identical except for the numbers—what if I passed it when I was looking for Danka's?

What if it's not here? Finally I locate the sleeve 1716. Stuffing our new dresses and aprons under the pile of old uniforms, I run to Danka. She has not moved.

"Can you put your arms up?" I ask gently. Her arms float upwards.

I pull the old lice-infested burlap onto her arms and over her head. My fingers quiver as I button her into her old uniform, the number 2779 in its proper place. Then with a shudder I pull the comfort of anonymity over my own head. The number I've hated so much is now my refuge, my only link to survival.

I open the door, carefully peeking outside. The SS are just a row away, coming our way. We have a few minutes to spare. I shut the door—catching my breath, waiting for them to pass.

"Ready?" I don't wait for an answer, pushing Danka out ahead of me and into the neat ranks of five. "Please move up," I whisper to the girl-women around us. "Please move over. Make some room, please." No one pushes back, no one argues. The rows of fated women we depend on move as silently as water, swallowing us into their bosom until we are one with the ranks. The SS move up our row. We hold our breath.

They pass us. We have been counted.

Roll call ends and Emma is waiting. I nod to her as Danka and I take our places in her kommando. She raises an eyebrow at our presence. I think her mouth turns upward slightly, too, but can't be sure; all I know is it feels good to be safe with Emma. We are outside digging, building, rather than in Mengele's and Clauberg's hands. It feels good to work. It feels good to be alive.

∞

DANKA REMAINS IN a daze for a few days. Everything she does is automatic, without thought or contemplation, but sometimes

I believe she looks at me with amazement and maybe gratitude; sometimes I am not sure where she is.

Rumors still haunt the latrines. There are more voices murmuring, "There's going to be a big selection."[20] We are not safe. We are never safe. We just narrowly escaped death for one day—what about tomorrow?

A girl in the latrine asks, "Remember that special work detail they selected last week?"

I watch her warily, wondering what she knows, wondering how much bread she is going to blackmail me for in order to buy her silent allegiance.

"I think so," I lie to her face.

"I heard from someone working in the infirmary that it was for sterilization and shock treatments. He took half of the girls and put hot plates on their stomachs to send electric shock into their bellies over and over again until they fainted. When they came to, they did it again and again until they died."

I feel weak, nauseous.

"The rest he cut open in order to take their female organs out. Some of them are dying from infection now. The lucky ones are already dead." I move away from this stranger's voice; the blood drains from my face.

"Rena, what's wrong?" Danka comes up behind me.

"Nothing, Danka, nothing. I must be hungry." I head back to our block.

"You're not getting sick, are you?" I shake my head. She watches me with concern.

There is a pressure screaming for release against my eyes. I don't cry. It takes time to cry and there is no time. I fight to find a reason, but there is no reason in this place. What did they do when they discovered there were three numbers missing in the experiment detail? Did the woman who snuck her cousin or sister out of line just put somebody else in her place? Why didn't they search us out? They had our numbers written on a list. Why are

---

20. Between 1 and 30 of December 1943 there were 29,513 women registered in Auschwitz II; death records indicate that in that same month 8,931 women died; 4,247 of them were sent to the gas (Czech, 556–57).

we alive and the other girls we were selected with not? Will there ever come a time when we can thank God for being alive today before we have to ask the same privilege tomorrow, and the next day? Is life a privilege or a curse?

Rumors of the big selection increase. One thing after another tumbles across my brain. As if we were never in Mengele's clutches, I go back to worrying about Danka's injury again. The scar's not as angry as it was a few weeks ago, but it is still red enough to attract the bitter eyes of SS selection officers.

"Tomorrow," a voice whispers in front of me. I pass the information down the line. This is how we send news, the same way we toss bricks, from one to another. Usually we're in the soup line or waiting for the evening bread. "Tomorrow."

Taking my bread, I tell Danka, "I'm going outside."

"For what?"

"For anything I can find." I'm irritated. It's not her fault. We're both nervous, weary with the exhaustion living on the edge brings. I need to scour the grounds; I need to do something besides think that tonight may be our last night on earth. Walking past the kitchen, I scan the ground for potato pieces or anything that might be edible. I wish we had some extra food for the selection. Beyond food I don't know what else to look for, and tonight the rats and other prisoners have beaten me to whatever scraps may have been here. Much to my surprise, a light-blue-and-red wrapper with the word *Chickory* on it peeks up out of the mud at me. For a moment I stare at it simply enjoying the familiarity of the logo and the memory it brings with it. Picking it up, I bury my nose in the wrapper, allowing the aroma to carry me back.

"Rena, don't play with that, it will turn your fingers red," Mama scolded sweetly. "Look at your hands! Don't touch anything. Go wash it off quickly. The ink stains."

"What's it for, Mama?"

"It makes the coffee smooth and not so acid on the stomach, just like Papa likes it."

I can smell freshly brewed coffee in the night air.

A familiar redness has left its stain on my fingers. I stare and stare at it, then carefully fold the precious paper into what is left of the hem in my dress. "Thank you, Mama."

I force myself to sleep by telling myself that I need to be fresh for whatever test they give us. Sleep comes fitfully at first and then deeply, until I am no longer conscious of the sounds outside—the screams, the gunshots. Many who hold no hope in tomorrow will risk the moon in the sky trying to reach the fence, and tomorrow morning the SS will have a few less to select for death.

FOUR A.M.

"*Raus! Raus!*"

Morning comes too soon. There is no tea. Fear as thick as fog has descended upon our camp. The dead we carry out each morning have always been pitied by me, but today I feel differently; they have passed away in the bliss of unconsciousness. The bodies on the fence usually make me feel sad, but today I respect them for choosing to rob the Nazis of their secret delight. This is mercy in Auschwitz-Birkenau, to die by your own hand.

It rains, pouring sometimes, sprinkling others, as if heaven cannot make up its mind. But the selection team has no trouble making up their minds. We stand for hours on the Laggerstrasse in rows of five. The line stretches the length of the camp. The morning downpour changes to drizzle. The noonday meal passes without any soup—there's no sense in feeding people who are about to die. In their shiny boots and pressed gray jodhpurs, standing there like gods of the universe, their thumbs jerking this way to death and that way to life, the SS officers stand before their peers, judging our inferiorities.

Taube and Stiewitz walk down the rows.

"Miserable *mist bienes*," Stiewitz yells. "You *scheiss-Judes* get down on your knees!"

My skin bristles. Catching Danka's eye, I warn her in advance. Taube turns to our row. "Kneel down!" I pull her into the mud.

His club swings into the knees of a girl who does not know she's supposed to kneel before him. Her scream pierces the air. He and his cohort walk away smugly. Our knees ache. We do not shift or sway. We kneel without faltering.

Taube's face glowers. He relishes his power. "Lie face down. All the way. Heads down!"

We fall on our stomachs into the mud. Danka needs no warnings for this portion of the exercise; we have seen the results of Taube's version of push-ups many times before.

"Up! Down!" Faces in the mud, we push our frail bodies into the air and drop back to earth for as long as he orders.

"Up! Down!" I have no idea how many push-ups we do; my mind stops as long as my body is in motion.

"Halt!" Taube yells. We collapse in the mud. "Don't move!"

Please don't let the girl next to me raise her head, I pray. Taube moves away from us, heading further down our row. I avoid listening for the sounds I know will follow. They no longer wait for someone to raise her head as an excuse to demolish someone's brains. They simply choose the skull they fancy and crush it before moving on to their next victim.

The waiting is impossible, the terror indescribable.

All we can do is stare into the ground, bore holes into mud and muck, lock our gaze into the earth. We barely breathe.

It is forever.

FINALLY THEY RELEASE us from our "exercises." Helping each other up from the ground, we avoid looking at the bodies that will not rise again.

We move up, edging away from those who've been selected by a foot rather than a thumb. We get closer and closer to the SS gods, trying not to think about what each step means—that someone else has been chosen to live or die.

I look into Danka's face. The mud on it inspires me. First, though, I spit on my sleeve and wipe the dirt and grime off her skin.

"My turn." She washes my face, taking care to wipe away all smudges from the Taube episode. Our faces clean, I stoop to the ground and take a finger full of mud.

"What are you doing?" she asks, alarmed.

"Covering up your scar." I smudge it across her forehead.

"That works, Danka. I can't even see it, and I know it's there."
We edge closer and closer.

"Do you want to go first?" It is time for us to decide in what order we should go before our judges.

"I don't know." Her voice trembles.

"If you go first and they select you, then I can join you more easily."

"How?" We can now see that there is a ditch that we must jump across.

"I can fail the test or look miserable."

"What if you go first and they pass you and then select me? What will you do?"

"I'll run after you pleading with them to let me die with my sister."

"But that doesn't work all the time anymore."

"Then I'll attack a guard and be shot. Then at least you'll know I died too."

"You can't do that! I can't bear the thought of seeing you shot. I want us to be together or not at all."

"Then you go first." I put her in front of me.

She looks at the ground, ashamed. "I'm afraid. I don't look so good as you do."

"I'll go first, then, Danka. I'll go with my head straight up and you go very close behind me. That way they'll be blinded by me and think you don't look so bad at all." She doesn't look bad; she has lost flesh but her face is prettier than mine. Still, she does not have that sparkle in her eyes that says "I'm going to live."

"Okay, you go first," she says. "I'll be braver if I can keep my eyes on you."

I open my hem, pulling out the treasure I found last night and have been protecting from the elements for over ten hours. "Give me your face." Opening the Chickory wrapper up, I lightly paint her cheeks. The dye from the paper adds a blush to her pallor.

Spitting on my fingers, I blend it in so it looks natural and step back amazed at the instant transformation. "Beautiful. You look a picture of health now, Danka."

"My scar."

I take a little more mud and trace my finger along the cut. "It's healing very well," I assure her.

"It is?"

"Yes. You look very good indeed." We edge closer. "Don't watch the others; just tell yourself that you will fly over that ditch into my arms. That's all you need to think." I turn my back to her, leaving my hand behind me to hold hers until the last possible moment.

We don't have far to go; twenty, maybe thirty girls stand in front of us. The girl in front of me turns around. "You are going to make it," she says in Slovakian.

I stumble for words of encouragement but am at a loss. "You will too."

"Please take this." She takes my hand, passing something cold and round into my palm. "It was my mother's wedding band. I don't want them to have it," she whispers.

"I can't take this."

"You have to. Don't let them have it. Promise!" Her eyes are like steel beams, forcing me to swear I will protect her past.

"I promise."

She steps towards the guards. I do not know what to do with this gold in my hand. I can be killed for having it. I wipe my mouth, slipping the ring under my tongue, next to the elephant.

The thumb turns away. The girl whose family heirloom is hiding in my mouth moves toward the side of the condemned. She looks back wistfully. Our eyes seal our fates across the compound.

I will never know her name.

MY TURN ARRIVES. I step up to the tables.

"Halt!" My heart is pounding in my ears.

Their eyes are on my forearm—number 1716.

"From the first transport?" one of them says in German.

"Who can believe?"

Will this work toward my advantage? Or will it be my downfall?

The thumbs jerk for me to jump the ditch.

I march past them, my chin out, my shoulders straight, toward the ditch. There's no running start and only a few feet on either side for our take-off and landing. The ditch itself is a few feet wide and a few feet deep. Whoever falls in is covered by mud from the rain and has lost the last chance for life.

I fly over it with inches to spare, hugging the wall at the other side to give my sister plenty of room for her landing, but I cannot bear to look back and watch. Seconds stretch into the abyss of not knowing.

I wait, holding my breath, my eyes shut tight, listening, with my entire being hugging the wall, wishing it were my sister. I imagine that there is a thread between us that pulls her toward me. I do not think of her falling in the ditch. I think only of her being beside me.

Silence . . .

TWO HANDS SLIP around my waist, sending a little squeeze. I breathe again. Holding her hands to my belly, I pray I will never have to let go of them again. We do not speak, we do not rejoice; our victory is small in the face of so many failures. The sun is finally breaking through the clouds. It is pale and slight, but Danka and I lie on the damp ground, worn out from the hours of tortuous waiting. Our hands lightly touch, just enough to remind ourselves that we are still together. I take the ring and the elephant out of my mouth—two gravestones hidden under my tongue.

This is all that is left of her family. This ring is her immortality wrapped in gold and memory. Silently, I vow to keep it safe from the Germans as long as I am alive. We stand up as the sun begins its descent toward the horizon. Shadows lengthen across the field. There are still hundreds, maybe thousands, waiting in line to be selected.

Unable to watch or think about what has happened today, we wander through the empty camp in a daze. No one dares to speak to anyone. A teenage girl eats a lemon while her mother begs for a bite. Her eyes glare at her mother angrily as she devours the already squeezed pulp like a wild animal. Her teeth sink into the pale rind, ripping it apart. I turn away, dismayed. She eats the whole thing without sharing it with her mama.

*After the war, Rena had the ring made
into an initial ring: RK.*

What have they done to us? The piece of potato I find I eagerly share with my sister—how else can we survive if we do not care for one another? I do not understand the selfishness before me, but then it does not matter what I understand.

It is late at night when the last truck heads for the gas chambers. We are not excused. The death squad departs from camp, ignoring us. We stand waiting for a command, but for the first time in a year and a half we're not ordered to do anything. We go to our empty blocks. The block elder's not here; we can only assume she was among the thousands who were selected.

Bread is doled out. Our stomachs are grateful for the food, but our hearts are not.

Should I pray? Should I thank God for saving our lives again? How can I thank or praise a Creator who allows this to happen? This is not a miracle, to be alive—it is a tragedy. How can I praise the miracle that Danka and I live while thousands of our fellow prisoners are gassed and cremated just a few hundred meters from where we have life?

FOUR A.M.

"*Raus! Raus!*"

We take our tea and stand at attention for roll call. It will not even take an hour this morning. The smoke from the chimneys never ceases. A dull haze encompasses Birkenau. Ash fills the air, covering the roofs of the blocks and the ground we stand on. We march out with Emma, work all day, and return. Evening roll call takes a little bit longer; there are new, shocked faces to be beaten into submission. A new flock of Jewish girl-women who do not know about straight lines, silent attention, and gas chambers. The transports are coming. . . . The Nazis have been very busy.

FOUR A.M.
   "*Raus! Raus!*"
   Camp is full.[21]

∞

WINTER IS CLOSING in on us, and fall has slipped away. Yom Kippur passed us by without notice. A few of the new ones fasted; we know better. We stand in the early darkness of evening roll call. I am having trouble keeping alert to all the potential dangers; the hyperawareness that has served me so well is starting to fade from fatigue. I fear that with the onslaught of winter Danka and I are going to be in for real trouble soon. How long can we keep on going like this? Someday we're going to drop from sheer exhaustion or, worse. I am so helpless. Our fates lie in their whims.

Mengele is here again. He has made other appearances, but for some reason this night I notice it.

"Danka," I whisper, "the cold is here and last winter so many got frostbite. We have the shoes and socks from Erna and Fela, but how long will they last in the mud and snow? How long will we last working so hard?"

Danka knows what I'm going to ask before I ask it. "Please, Rena. I can't take a special detail ever again."

---

21. "January 1 [1944] . . . New male prisoners are given Nos. 171353-171430 and female prisoners are given Nos. 73983-74039" (Czech, 565). "Of 28,000 prisoners brought to the camp in 1942, barely 5,400 remained alive at the end of the year. In 1943, some 28,000 women prisoners died in Birkenau" (Strzelecka, 401).

"What can I do? I'm just hoping we get chosen. I'm not doing anything." I direct my eyes forward, but I cannot keep my tongue still. "Think about it," I whisper. "If we get chosen, and it's for inside work, we might make it. If we don't get inside, we're going to die for sure this winter. No one can survive as long as we have here. We have got to get a good job, with a roof over our heads." I smooth my stubble of hair and straighten the stripes of my dress out so they fall in uninterrupted lines.

"Rena," Danka hisses at me. She knows what I'm doing. I check us both, nodding to myself. We are hardy. We still look pretty good. There is still some meat on our bodies, and for some reason I still have a bosom. I stand with my chin out, eyes forward. Danka, unwilling to be left alone a second time, copies me.

His alabaster skin and glistening black hair gleam with care. His gray uniform has been neatly pressed and the pleat falls straight down his leg. I notice things like this. He steps closer toward our row. He doesn't know who we are. We have that one advantage; we are anonymous faces in a throng. We have used our anonymity to be invisible and escape his clutches; now we must stick out. Somehow he must see that we are good girls, clean and orderly, organized, all qualities the Germans admire, even in Jews. He has chosen us for life many times during camp selections. Only once has he chosen us for death and experiments. What will it be this time?

Mengele points at me again. Chin up, eyes forward, chest out, I hold my breath, stepping forward hesitantly.

He points to Danka.

I exhale. We move in behind the other girls already chosen. Dina is also in our ranks; I catch her eye.

Is this for life or is it for death?

MENGELE FINISHES HIS selection and orders an SS man to take us to quarantine. We march toward the isolation block—again. A feeling of dread washes over me the moment we enter the block. Danka's face is white. We move to the beds we slept on the last time we were in this place. Is this for life or is it for death? There is nothing I can do to save us. I sleep through the day, unable to bear the depression that seeps into my mind. Erika is not outside the door this time. . . . What if this is for experiments, like the other one? Danka and I speak sparingly, quietly, unwilling to discuss what might be.

"Rena?" Dina wakes me up. "What do you think this will be for?"

"I don't know, Dina."

"We've made it this far. It must be good." She has a naive hope that warms my heart.

"I hope so, Dina. For all of our sakes."

"We really deserve a break."

"They don't give breaks, do they."

"Maybe luck will be with us then." She leaves my bunk to go talk to Danka.

On the third day we receive new clothes again. These clothes are not long dresses with aprons, like the ones the experiment victims wore; these are simply another version of the striped dresses we have been wearing. The only difference is that they are cleaner.

"Rip off your old numbers. You will sew them on your new uniforms later!"

Hope trickles into my heart.

I slip the elephant and the wedding ring under my tongue; the nail file hides in my hand. Nobody knows where we're going, so I must take care that they won't be found. We dress as quickly as possible and line up, then march into the scribes' block to have our numbers written down. When we are let back outside it is under strict SS guard. There is no escaping like the first time. We march immediately outside the gates of Birkenau, down a road, past the train tracks.

We march for what seems forever—but everything seems far away when you're weak. I do not know where in the complex of camps we are heading; then ahead of us I see Auschwitz I. I reach out for Danka's hand. We are directed into a building outside the main camp though and led down a wide stairway into a basement. The room is large and remarkably warm. There are windows that let the sun in. There are real bunk beds set up in neat rows with fairly clean straw mattresses like we had in Auschwitz I.

SS and Staff
Quarters

Stabsgebaüde

(Rena's recollection of the layout of the basement where female prisoners worked and slept)

Corridor
for
Roll Call

Sewing
Room

Laundry
Room

Bathroom

Maria's
Bed

Edita's Room

Sleeping Quarters

Table

Diagram of the basement in SS staff quarters, as recollected by Rena.

"This is the new laundry detail," the guards announce to the block elder. She looks us over, shaking her head. Despite our new uniforms we must look terrible.

"I'm Maria," she tells us. "These are your new living quarters. The laundry is across the hall. You will be assigned positions tomorrow."

She leaves us alone, shutting the door to her room behind her.

Slowly we move toward the bunks to claim our new beds. Danka and I take the bottom so that we don't have to climb up anything in case we're tired at the end of the day. On the straw mattress, a sigh of relief escapes from my chest. There is a blanket for each of us; they're old, but they're not rags. Dina takes the bunk next to ours. We hug our blankets solemnly, not sure what to make of these luxuries. The beds hold two people rather than three or twelve, like human beings instead of herrings. It is warm. There is central heat in this building and only a few drafts. I have forgotten what warmth felt like.

"There's a toilet!" a girl announces excitedly. "And a sink!" I squeeze Danka's hand with a little pulse of hope. We are no longer in stables for horses; we are in a building for people. "There's even a shower!" We are in heaven.

STABSGEBAÜDE
Staff Quarters

From the distance through the iron bars
freedom is laughing at us. . . .
But the sun's still not shining.

—A song sung by the prisoners

WE WONDER WHAT is going on here, but anything is better than Birkenau, so we keep our questions to ourselves. We are put in a basement with seventy-five other Jewish girls who work as secretaries in the SS offices, the *Politische*.[1]

Our new detail is in the SS laundry, to replace fifty Polish Gentile girls. They were sent back to the Polish camp in Birkenau because the SS learned that the Polish men working in the SS kitchen were sneaking food to the girls. I feel sorry for those girls but at the same time am grateful for this chance at life.

Our first morning in staff quarters we are assigned to our new positions. Our block elder, Maria, is German. Her triangle is red; she's a political prisoner. Political prisoners are more likely to be kind, as they've been imprisoned for being against the Third Reich. Our friend Mania is chosen as the block scribe and works for Maria personally. Mania's sister, Lentzi, is placed in the sewing room.

---

1. Alfred Wetzler and Rudolf Vrba escaped from Auschwitz in April 1944 and wrote the following in their report: "[Of] the Jewish girls deported from Slovakia in March and April 1942, [there were originally] over 7,000. . . . Now there are only 400 of these girls left and most of them have been able to secure some sort of clerical post in the women's camp. About 100 girls hold jobs at the staff building [Stabsgebaüde] in Auschwitz where they do all the clerical work connected with the two camps. Thanks to their knowledge of languages they are also used as interpreters. Others are employed in the main kitchen or laundry" (Wyman, 5, 32).

Janka, who we knew in Auschwitz I, is in the hand-washing laundry. She's responsible for washing and ironing the delicate clothes of the women officers. She also takes the clothes to the quarters of the SS women. She is Maria's favorite because she's so young.

The only people who have not been sent back to Birkenau are the *Politische* secretaries; they are the lucky ones. They were chosen on the transport platform when they first came to camp and most have never lived in Birkenau. Edita is the only Jewish kapo that I know of in camp and is the head of all the secretaries. Aranka, who I know by sight from Bratislava, is one of the scribes. Rumor has it that when she was brought in from the transports to be shaved and disinfected the SS guards stopped to stare at her—that's how beautiful she is.

We still have roll call, but there is a roof over our heads now, and there are only a hundred and twenty-five girls to count, so it does not take hours. Our first morning in this heaven roll call is conducted in the hallway outside our sleeping area, across from the laundry. It is not four a.m. when they wake us; it is five a.m. We get a whole extra hour of sleep, and roll call does not last for over two hours in rain and sleet; it takes less than half an hour. There is no marching a kilometer or two to and from work either; we are only a few steps from the laundry.

"This is where you will work." Maria instructs us on how to run the laundry. "You will wear these shoes while working here and leave your other shoes on this shelf." The shoes we are shown are wooden and have straps across the arch just like the ones we wore when we first came to Auschwitz. "This is the hot water you will use to wash with." She shows us a large kettle on a coal-burning stove, which is already steaming. There are tubs with scrubbing boards in them and baskets of dirty clothes to wash.

Wardress Bruno enters the laundry to inspect us. We all immediately stiffen at the presence of the SS woman. She has a stern look and a formal, military manner. She points to a girl. "You will be responsible for the water in the kettle and keeping the coals hot."

So we begin our first day in the SS laundry. The stone floor is cold and the water sloshes against our calves and knees. We scrub long johns and undershirts against the washboards, rubbing them hard to remove the stains. It's hard work—nothing in Auschwitz-Birkenau is easy—but we are inside. There is so much water being dumped into the drains that they back up. We wade through the water as if we were fishermen instead of charwomen. Then we put the damp clothes in the baskets and someone carries them away.

"Halt! Roll call!" We leave the laundry, lining up in the hall, where we are counted and handed a portion of bread as we enter our sleeping quarters. The bread looks bigger than it was in Birkenau. We get a slice of sausage; it is small but welcome. Our legs hurt terribly after that first day but no one is complaining; there are no dogs, no SS men beating us unmercifully, no immediate deaths.

I rub my calves before lying down to sleep. I wonder if so much water is good for them and worry that they will become swollen or infected. I check my skin for abrasions and cuts; everything looks fine. Danka is already asleep. I roll over, pulling my blanket up under my chin, staring up at the bunk bed above me. My eyes droop under the weight of the past few days. For some reason, I want to pray but cannot remember any words.

If Mama were there, tucking me in, she would ask, *"Did you say your prayers, Rena?"*

"Yes, Mama." She pulls the comforter up under my chin. My bed is already warm from the hot brick she has smoothed over the sheets and let rest at my feet. There may be a harsh winter wind rattling our shutters but I snuggle down into down.

She kisses my cheek. "Sweet sleep."

WHEN WARDRESS BRUNO enters the laundry followed by a kapo, everyone stiffens and works more diligently than before. Her face is hard, her demeanor severe; she walks directly up to me as if she knows what she wants. "You speak German?"

"Jawohl, Frau Wardress." I straighten my shoulders and look forward but not directly at her.

"You will be responsible for taking the laundry out to dry. Pick two girls to help you carry the baskets."

"Jawohl." I point at my sister and Erna's cousin. "Danka and Dina." I call their names.

"Ilsa, they are in your charge," Wardress Bruno orders. There is an audible sigh of relief from amid the washers and sounds of sloshing water when she departs.

Ilsa is about fifty years old but wears a black triangle. I have trouble imagining her as a prostitute and have to stifle a smirk that creeps across my lips as I look at her red-orange hair and bowlegs.

"Take these baskets. I will show you the way to the drying place," she says in German.

"Danka, you and Dina hold the outsides," I instruct. I am afraid that the baskets will be too heavy for my little sister, so I decide from the very first that I will always be in the middle and step in between the two baskets heavily laden with wet clothes. We look at each other, reaching the handles simultaneously and hoisting them up, following Ilsa out of the cellar.

We step outside onto a road and follow it toward two buildings. My shoulders begin to ache. We pass the SS kitchen. My arms feel as if they're being dragged out of their sockets. We turn left into an open field beside another building. I stare and stare at the expanse before us. As I inhale deeply, the air bites my lungs. It is pure; there is no smell of burning flesh hiding in its odor. There are lines set up, with a little bag of clothespins.

"This is the *trockenplatz*, the drying place." Ilsa announces. We set the baskets down, put on our aprons, and obediently begin hanging the clothes up to dry. Then we wait.

There is a very handsome man who stands outside in front of a water pump that he operates. We each sneak a look at him while we work. There are SS going back and forth along the road regularly. I fidget among the clothes, smoothing them, making sure they are perfect and straight on the line. I am afraid there is something we are not doing that we might get in trouble for. Danka and Dina follow me, copying my obsessive antics. Ilsa informs us when it's time to return to the block for lunch. We take the clothes that are dry back to the laundry, and after our turnip soup return to the *trockenplatz* with fresh wet laundry. Finally Ilsa signals us that the day is over. We sort out which clothes are dry and which are not, carrying them back in separate baskets, but we bring in all of the clothes for the night. When we arrive in the laundry we leave the partially dry clothes in the baskets and place the rest on a table for folding.

We can see the Polish men working in the kitchen when we pass by each day, but because of Ilsa and what happened to the Polish Gentile girls, nobody dares to communicate with us. The man at the water pump, however, is so close to us that we manage to whisper to each other.

"What's your name?" he asks.

"Rena, my sister Danka, and our friend Dina. All three of us are from Tylicz."

"I used to ski there. It's beautiful. I'm Tadziu."

I can't help but wish that Ilsa would move farther away so Tadziu and I can have some conversation, but we are watched very closely these first few days. I guess we're on probation. The time lags as Ilsa watches us watch the clothes. We smile secretly at Tadziu. I think he is a shy man.

My fingers feel as if they are about to be peeled loose from the handles of the baskets, spilling the clean clothes across the dirt road; I struggle to keep them clenched. My shoulders ache. Ilsa is far behind us.

"Look at your kapo," Tadziu says to us as we put down our baskets. We look down the road and see her coming toward us on her extremely bowed legs. Her red hair gleams in the sun above her curving limbs as if she had a huge ball between her knees. She waddles towards us.

Tadziu teases, "Here comes innocence between parentheses!"

Like a bubbling gurgle of water, a sound wells up from inside of us, erupting quietly from our chests. I barely recognize what is happening to us. I can hear it; I can feel it, but it takes me a moment to identify. . . . We are laughing.

We are laughing in Auschwitz—though not too loudly.

The quake in my chest has not been caused from fright or sorrow but from mirth. Ilsa gets closer, and we struggle to stifle these strange sounds, which cause our eyes to squirt tears down the sides of our cheeks. But the closer she comes, the funnier she looks. We hide our faces, but every time we catch each other's eyes we start giggling all over again. It is terribly difficult to act austere and serious when all we can think about are Ilsa's bowed, parentheses legs and how innocent she isn't. The rest of the day we silently shake whenever we look at our kapo. Danka's face lighting up gives me a momentary sense of relief. We have not laughed in I don't know how long.

This laughter, which is so strange to us, is as valuable as bread; it eases our hearts of just a little pain and gives us something to smile about secretly.

Two weeks later Ilsa is no longer coming with us to the drying place; I guess that either she has completed her sentence and been pardoned or she's been moved to another place in camp. I become the one responsible for taking the clothes, and there is no one watching us for the first time since the beginning. Now when we carry the baskets out to the *trockenplatz* I stop and have Danka and Dina change places so they can switch hands and I can rest. I do not allow myself to exchange positions though.

We take the clothes out to hang no matter what the weather. Wardress Bruno believes that fresh air is essential for clothes, so even on inclement days we stand in the rain or sleet and watch the clothes get as soaked as we do. Only if it looks as if it will rain or snow all day do we stay inside and wash clothes to dry the following day; on days when it spits sporadically we hang the clothes up in hope that the sun will come out later. Hanging wet clothes in the cold nearly bites our hands off. We stick our fingers in our mouths to warm them, and then continue. Some days the clothespins with springs are too difficult for our fingers to press open and we have to use the ones with just slits in them. It is strange that after everything we went through to get inside work, here we should be, outside, with winter coming closer with each day.

I worry that the burlap dresses we wear are not nearly warm enough for the temperatures we will have to bear. The wind skates across the *trockenplatz*. Standing still is much colder than working hard labor. We have no gloves to warm our hands either. How strange to think of gloves! Last winter in Birkenau I would never have considered gloves or warm clothing. I cannot believe we survived it.

On the way back from the *trockenplatz* one night, the window to the SS kitchen opens and a friendly face asks, "Where are you from?"

We slow our steps down. "Tylicz, Poland," I answer in a low voice.

"All three of you?" He sounds glad that we're Polish.

"Yes, Polish Jews." I want to turn and face the person I'm speaking with, but that is impossible. I shift my eyes sideways without moving my chin.

"I'm an actor, from Warsaw. My name is Stasiu. Stop tomorrow in this same spot and I'll throw you a piece of sausage." I catch a glimpse of his face just before he moves from the kitchen window.

He's old, at least for Auschwitz—he must be in his forties. We pick up our pace as if nothing has happened. The next day we stop outside the SS kitchen just as the window cracks open. Danka and Dina switch places as I busily rearrange the clothes, making a hole in the center. A package lands neatly in the basket and I cover it up. Our hearts pound as we pick up the laundry and continue our trek. Inside staff quarters, while Dina and Danka unload the laundry, I disappear with the package, hiding it under our mattress, hoping and praying that nobody will catch me. We wait until dark; then, when everyone else is asleep, we divide the piece of sausage Stasiu sent us three ways and devour it.

∞

THERE IS A MEN'S kommando working in a field close to the macaroni factory, and I notice that one of them seems very interested in me. He's quite handsome. We steal glances. Danka and Dina have gone back to the laundry to take back some clothes that are already dry and fetch another basket while I guard the SS underwear.

"Where're you from?" the man asks when his kapo is out of sight.

"Tylicz." I hang up a pair of SS long johns.

"Warsaw." He works. I work. "How old?"

I have to think for a moment. Have I really had two birthdays in camp? They have passed unnoticed. "Twenty-three." We do not dare to exchange more words.

The next day I nod to Danka and Dina so they can see him.

Danka stares at him, smiling faintly. We hang the clothes, trying not to look too anxious for him to start the conversation—if you can call snippets of words passed across a field a conversation.

"My name is Marek." I hear his voice from between the legs of long underwear.

"Rena," I answer, busily smoothing the wrinkles from the undershirts already hanging.

Danka steps to one side of the clothesline. "Danka. Rena's sister."

"Dina." Dina and Danka hang something up together. There is a slight breeze catching the clothes and teasing them about in the air. Contact has been made, names have been shared. It is moments like these that help us feel alive. There is another living being who knows we are here; it is a relief to speak to anyone outside our own narrow prison. I am slapped gently by flapping clothes.

WE ARE HANGING the clothes up to dry when I notice a window at the top of the macaroni factory open for the first time ever and out comes a bag of macaroni. There is no one to see, no one to thank; it is a silent gesture. Quickly we cover it with the clothes already in the basket and smuggle it back into our quarters. Our hearts are pounding as we enter the block.

"Janka," I whisper to our young friend, "we have some extra food. Can you organize a pot full of water and slip it into the coals after roll call?"

Janka's eyes narrow craftily. She nods. There are coals left each night in the stove in the laundry room on which we can cook, if we can find anything to cook and if we are careful not to get caught. We stand at attention for roll call patiently, trying not to fidget, trying to stop our watering mouths and the rumbling in our stomachs. We march into our sleeping area, taking our portion of bread and breaking it in half. We lie down after our meal, feigning sleep. The sounds of deepening breaths and snoring filter through the dark.

I tap Danka. We roll quietly off our bunk and tiptoe to the door. We are the first to arrive at the stove in the laundry room. I empty the contents of the bag into the simmering water. We sit and wait. The door to the laundry room opens slightly. Silently, Dina enters. Janka slips through the portal as stealthily as a cat, then Deborah, Mania, Lentzi, Aranka, and a few others. Our excitement is impenetrable. "I got a bit of salt," one girl offers, pouring it into the steaming pot. We are smiling despite the danger we're in. We sit around the potbellied stove watching the kettle boil. It takes forever. The floor is cold beneath our buttocks, but we sit anyway, waiting.

I use my spoon to taste one of the noodles. "Done," I whisper to my co-conspirators in the dark. Dividing the noodles evenly into their waiting bowls, I figure, accurately, that there are five tablespoons for each girl, then pour the hot water on top, making sure everyone gets some. Danka and I are served last. The rest wait until we are all served; then in silent unison we begin to eat the warm, nourishing macaroni. We take our time. No one is urging us to hurry, so we linger over each spoonful slowly, as if we were at a dinner party in some wealthy family's house. The water the noodles were cooked in is delicious. It tastes like home.

Aranka nods to Danka and me before slipping back across the hall to her bunk. Slowly, soundlessly, the laundry room is emptied of its secret habitants. Janka stows the kettle so no one will find it in the morning, and together we tiptoe back to our beds, our bellies no longer rumbling but still hungry.

∞

DINA AND DANKA have returned to the laundry to get more clothes. I stand watch, eyeing the garments and Marek's work team with the same glance. He tosses a rock with a note wrapped around it in my direction. The note is full of niceties: *You're a pretty girl. Too bad we're not in the free world, but maybe someday we're going to be free. . . .*

"How many boyfriends did you have?" His voice slips across the field.

"Many," I tell him, trying to remember how to flirt, and then feeling bad that I have lied to him. It is not a bad lie. I had three boyfriends; that is almost many. "I was supposed to get married two weeks before I came here." I clip up two pairs of underwear and a pair of socks. When I glance back towards Marek, his back is to me; his kapo is nearby.

Marek is not in the field every day, and I miss him when he isn't sneaking words with me or risking his life to send me a note.

IT IS STARTING to get bitterly cold outside as winter arrives. "Do you think I should go ask Wardress Bruno for better clothes to work in?" I ask Dina and Danka as we hang the clothes up in a snow flurry.

"I'm afraid of her," Danka answers. She stomps her feet for warmth.

"I'm afraid of her too, but we've been here for a while and it's starting to snow. We have to take a chance. It's too cold for us to work without gloves and jackets." I rub my hands together to get them supple again so I can open the clothespins.

"You'll have to go on your own; she makes my knees turn to pudding."

So it is decided. I am going to approach the wardress with our request as soon as I get up the nerve. It takes a few days.

"Wardress Bruno?" My words chatter with nervousness. Her black hair and chiseled features frighten me; her blue eyes are serious and look as if they could be mean, but I have to go on. "I would like to report that it is getting quite cold on the *trocken-platz*. And could I request warm clothes for me and the two girls helping me?"

"Yes, I'll arrange that," she answers. "I'll take you after roll call." She dismisses me.

My jaw gapes open like a monkey's. She is not mean at all.

The next morning after roll call, true to her word, Wardress Bruno takes us to another building. She leads us upstairs to an attic, where we pick out skirts, thick stockings with elastic on the top to hold them up, jackets, boots, and gloves. I pick a black-and-white checked jacket, a man's shirt, and a woolen skirt, trying very hard not to think about where these clothes have come from. I try to remind myself that it is better for us to have them than for them to be sent to warm German bodies. In this way we are set to go outside, looking very much like human beings except for the white crosses painted across the backs of our coats and our numbers sewn on the left sleeves.

∞

MAREK'S DETAIL WORKS diligently all day long. We haven't had a chance to speak, but finally he edges his way towards me and tosses a stone. We are stealing words between us, looking as if we're working in case the SS are watching from the macaroni factory window or come riding their bicycles along the road.

Do you have any boyfriends now? the note says. I shake my head to answer no.

The next morning our conversation continues. "Have you had any intimate relationships with your boyfriends?"

"No." He is going to embarrass me for sure if he keeps asking these questions.

"You're a virgin?" He almost stops working. He is looking at me as if I'm not real.

"Yes!" I whisper proudly. He chokes on his laughter. He tries hard to keep working but is in a fit of chuckles. "I come from Warsaw, where I've never met a virgin yet." He has to walk away to cover himself.

"I think you're exaggerating!" I hide in the laundry, my face hot as an iron. Men! I decide to ignore him the rest of the afternoon.

To avoid his eyes I hang the clothes quickly so I am blocked from his view and duck behind the long rows of long johns bleaching in the winter sun.

He moves closer, digging busily. "You're blushing!" His voice peek-a-boos over the clotheslines. I shake my head and move farther away, hang an undershirt between his face and mine.

"We're in Auschwitz and you are embarrassed?" There is that strange sound in his voice—laughter.

I smile but do not allow him to see that I'm also amused by this thought. With everything we have been through, with everything we have seen, I am still self-conscious. "I'm glad I've given you something to laugh about."

"No one will believe it," he says. "Wait until I get back to the block—a virgin at twenty-three!"

The next afternoon he throws a third note. I stick it in the hem of my skirt and wait anxiously to read it until after roll call. Sitting on our bunk, I read it out loud to Danka and Dina: *When*

I was fifteen I lost my virginity. There was a married woman at a public swimming pool who asked me up to her apartment and she introduced me to it.

"He's making it up!" Danka giggles.

"What am I going to do tomorrow if he's there?" We smother our chuckles under the blankets, trying to fall asleep. I cannot wait to see him again, but I am too shy to face him.

IT IS EASIER to bear the weather with our new clothes. The gloves make a huge difference in our ability to hang the clothes up, but sometimes the rain still soaks us through to the skin. It seems so ridiculous to do nothing but stand in a downpour and guard clothes, but there is nothing else we can do. I eye the awning on the back porch off the SS kitchen with envy; if we could just stand there we would be a little dryer after a day of rain or snow.

"Should I ask Wardress Bruno if we can stand there when the weather is bad?" I ask.

"Wait a week, Rena," Dina suggests.

"That's a good idea. We just got the clothes; we don't want her to think we're taking advantage." The decision is made, but I am terrified to ask for anything else.

A week later it is snowing again though and that decides it.

"Wardress Bruno? I would like to make a report." I stand before the SS woman whose looks are so harsh.

"Yah?" She looks at me with semi-interest, as if I were more than just a number. After being a number for so long it is unnerving, and I must remind myself that one cannot trust the SS. She could change her mind about me in an instant. She has the power of life or death.

I begin my report. "We hang the clothes out for fresh air every day, rain or shine or snow."

"Yah?"

"There is an awning behind the SS kitchen. I can see the whole *trockenplatz* from there. If it would be acceptable to you, could we please have permission to stand on the porch when the weather is bad?"

"Yah, you can do that." She dismisses me. I breathe a sigh of relief. I tell Danka and Dina the good news—we have cover. It is just in time. Winter has arrived.

How strange it is that after all my hoping to get a job inside I should be standing outside, but I am simply grateful to be away from Birkenau with my sister, still alive.

The first snowy day after my request we stand under the awning all day. Sometimes I lean my elbows on the railing and scan the fields before me, where there are no fences. A train passes in the distance. I am careful not to make contact with anyone in the kitchen. This is my first day using the porch for shelter and I do not want to lose the privilege, so I keep to myself and my private thoughts.

The next day as we bring the laundry back from the drying place a stone lands at our feet. "Change positions," I whisper. Danka and Dina stop. We put the baskets on the ground and I retrieve the note adroitly.

We wait impatiently through roll call before I can read the note. Danka peers over my shoulder as I unfold the paper, but there are no words; it is a pencil drawing. We are slightly giddy about it and I am flattered that someone should take the time to sketch me: I am leaning forward and my skirt is hitched up a little too high around the curve of my legs.

"Does my skirt ride up that high?" I ask Danka.

"No, Rena, it doesn't." We giggle.

"He makes my legs prettier than they are too!" I wish I could hang the drawing up or hide it somewhere safe, but there is no place that is safe enough. Besides, it is signed: *Stasiu Artista*. He has also scribbled in the corner, *When you walk by the window tomorrow, lean back a little bit and slow down. I'm going to throw something to you.*

The next day we stop in front of the kitchen, and Dina and Danka exchange places while I look busy arranging the clothes. Smooth as clockwork the package lands in the underwear. I cover it up without a second lost, and we pick the baskets up without looking back.

After roll call we discover that the package Stasiu has sent is a bag of sugar. "Let's share it," Danka suggests. Dina and I nod in agreement; this is too precious to hoard selfishly. We whisper to twenty of our closest girlfriends to come to our bunk after everyone is asleep.

"We have a surprise for you," we tell them. "Bring your spoon."

Sitting with the bag of sugar in my lap, I take the spoon from the first girl in line, carefully leveling it off to make sure that everyone gets an equal amount. When it's all gone we rest on our bunks in the dark, licking the metal of our spoons over and over, trying to savor and squeeze out every last bit of sweet.

IT IS SLEETING. I have come to enjoy inclement days now because they give me a chance to whisper with my new friend, Stasiu Artista. Sometimes I yearn for a conversation that is face-to-face. One that is real and long and not dangerous. It's silly to want for something that is impossible, but I miss the days when I could flirt and walk down the road with a beau and just talk about whatever comes into our minds. That shouldn't be a crime, but it is.

"How did you like the picture?" Stasiu asks through the window.

"It was very nice, but you made the skirt too short. You were dreaming."

I hear a sound like soft laughter. "You are beautiful."

"My friend, I am alive, and here that is beautiful. Thank you for the compliment, though."

"How long have you been here?" he asks.

"March 1942."

"That's too long. . . ." His voice suddenly sounds very sad.

"How about you?" I hear him moving away from the window and fall silent.

It seems silly sometimes, especially when it's sleeting, to act as a sentry for clothes, but I have my orders. The afternoon wears on slowly. The gentle tapping against the tin roof above my head sounds like a lullaby. The crispness of the air seems to capture the smells from the SS kitchen, dangling them before my nose. Whether it is the smell of meat roasting or the sound of sleet I do not know, but suddenly I am transported back through time. How wonderful our house smelled the night before Sabbath—the goose, the *kugel*, the *latkes*. I long for real home-cooked food and

actual meals that take place at a table with white linens and silver-
ware, meals that last for hours because there is so much food and
there are so many friends and family enjoying genuine conversation and togetherness. *Mama has her white silk scarf draped over her*
head and lights the candelabra on the dining room table. She says the
Sabbath blessing and stretches her arms out over the flames and back
toward her heart—twice. Then, covering her eyes with both of her hands,
she prays silently.

Danka and I watch her with awe and anticipation. It is a solemn
moment, with nothing but the golden flickering light upon Mama's hid-
den face to indicate that time is passing. Her hands lower slowly, tears
shine on her cheeks. There are always tears sparkling in her eyes after the
Sabbath prayer—radiant. "Git Shabbes."

"Good Sabbath, Mama." Danka and I run into her arms. Papa
returns from temple and we sit down for a real feast. We are so blessed,
so loved.

Oh, for the tender meat of roast goose.

The note falls close to my feet. I reach down and pretend to
adjust my stocking while reaching for the message. I wish I could
just read it immediately without having to wade through the rest
of the afternoon until we get back to *Stabsgebaüde*. My palm itches,
but I tuck the note well into my jacket, ignoring the nagging desire I have to read it. Glancing quickly at the window, I see Stasiu
scuffling away. Once again I am alone with the skittering sound
of sleet.

That night we read Stasiu's note as if it were the day's newspaper; that is how important these communications are to us.

I have been here since 1939. The chef is number 45. He has been here
the longest of anyone I know who is still alive. We stare at his words,
seeing the naked truth. It is impossible to believe that years could
go by and we might still be here, but Stasiu is proof. We are proof. I
crumble his note while walking slowly to the toilet. It swirls down-
ward, dragging with it all prospects for a life of freedom.

∞

AFTER ROLL CALL, ten packages are given to us from the Red
Cross. There are no names on them as there were in Birkenau, but

Maria tells us, "Divide these up between you the best you can." We stare and stare at the packages, eager to tear open the brown wrapping paper to see the goodies inside.

"I think we should take a vote to decide who is going to divvy up the food," Mania suggests.

"I think Rena should do it," Janka volunteers. "She's very particular and honest."

"All for Rena, raise your hands." I cannot believe my eyes; every hand in the room is up. All one hundred and twenty-five girls vote for me. We open the packages as if this were a holiday, even though it's not a feast for so many. I put everything into separate piles: twenty cans of sardines, ten sweet cakes, ten loaves of wheat bread, and bags of sugar cubes.

"Somebody get a knife from Maria and someone else get a measuring tape from the sewing room so I can be exact." My hands shake. This is the biggest honor I have ever been given, more important than being chosen, the first Jew and the first girl, to recite a poem before our entire village on Poland's biggest national holiday when I was eleven years old.

We lay the measuring tape across the cakes; each one is about six and a quarter inches long. I divide the length of the cakes by one hundred and twenty-five and figure that each piece should be half an inch thick. With two girls holding the measuring tape taut, I mark off thirteen sections of cake and then carefully slice each piece at the premeasured mark. Our mouths water. We measure the wheat bread in the same way.

My hands tremble as I slice each section of cake. These are hungry people; everyone must receive exactly the same portions. I cannot show favor to anyone, not even my sister—not that I would even think of cheating another hungry person out of such precious food.

There are twenty tins of sardines and between six and eight per tin, and I figure that there are enough sardines for each girl to have one tablespoon. "It will be easier to divide the sardines up using our spoons so we do not lose the oil," I tell the girls. They stand in line, holding out their spoons as I meticulously scoop out the fish so that each spoonful is level. The sugar cubes are counted out as well. When it is all done, everyone takes her piece of bread, spoonful of sardine, and her nibble of cake and goes to her bed to eat in grateful silence.

If you knew there was a million dollars somewhere and you could take it, would you? These pieces of bread and cake are worth a lot more than that amount of money. I have never stolen from anyone in camp. Every scrap of food is a matter of life or death, and I can never bring myself to cheat another human being. I remember how it was in Birkenau—when I found even the tiniest morsel of food, even if it was a potato peel on the ground, I divided it with my baby sister. Even though it was burning my hand because I was so hungry, I always brought it to her to share. I consider myself an intelligent person, but I am so obsessive and prudent about food, it is ridiculous. This is what starvation can do to one.

THE GIRLS IN the SS offices are constantly complaining about the Jewish kapo, Edita. She's always reporting them for the littlest thing and then punishing them too severely. She is a tyrant and treats them more severely than some of the German kapos. None of us understands why she is so mean, but the secretaries come up with a way to get back at her.

"We have a secret mission," Aranka tells me. "Do you want to join it?"

I look into the faces of seven of the scribes. "For what?" I ask.

"We can't tell you. Have you got guts and are you strong?"

"Yes, I've got both. Is this something that will endanger my sister's life?"

"No," they assure me. "We're going to pin Edita down in her sleep and beat her." I nod. It sounds like a worthy cause. "You want to beat her or hold her mouth?"

"I'd better hold her mouth. I don't have the chutzpah to beat a person," I tell them.

"Tonight, then." We shake hands.

While the rest of the block sleeps, we sneak into Edita's room, gathering around her bed silently. Then, on the leader's signal, two girls grab her arms and two grab her legs as I pull my hands over her mouth and another girl covers her eyes. The two who are going to beat her begin to strike her over and over on the stomach, where no one will see the bruises. It's hard to keep the pressure on her mouth as she struggles to get free, but I press my hands into her face to prevent any groans or noises. When they are done pummeling her they nod to us, and we release our hold, dashing back to our bunks. Our covers are already folded back so we can jump into them, pull them up to our chins, shut our eyes, and look just like everyone else who is sleeping.

I force my breathing to be as slow and even as Danka's, but I am sure it is audible. What if she checks the room? What if she turns on the light and demands that the guilty parties step forward? I try to shut my brain off. What if we get caught? But Edita does not check our bunks. The next morning she walks stiffly out of her room without looking at anyone. Nothing is reported to the SS, and no one investigates because she doesn't tell anyone. She has learned her lesson. She stops berating the scribes and starts to act with a little shred of humanity toward her co-prisoners.

DANKA IS ON the outside basket and leans back as Stasiu throws us a piece of sausage and some bread. Out of the corner of my eye I see an SS man riding by on his bicycle. I swear that he's seen us, but we do not pause, look guilty, or do anything that will arouse more suspicion. We bury the food deep in the clothes and walk back to the laundry as quickly as possible. The whole way back we think that the SS man's going to come and catch us, and then we'll be done for. We are jumpy and irritable, our nerves frayed with fear. First there is the joy of having extra food, then there is the possibility of that food sending us back to Birkenau or worse. We would gladly give up the meal to avoid that end.

We hide the food as soon as we enter the block stairwell and, sure enough, the baskets are checked thoroughly, but no one accuses us of anything. After roll call I sneak back to the hiding place and share the sausage and bread with a few other girls. It doesn't taste as good as it did before; our fear has flavored it.

The next morning one of the Poles who delivers our tea whispers to me, "Stasiu Artista just got twenty-five lashes for stealing a sausage for one of you girls." I try not to show alarm. I'm glad he gave me the information because I can prevent the story from spreading and getting us in trouble. I also know that Stasiu has not given up our names to the SS officer who caught him. We are safe.

Three days later, as we march in from work, Stasiu signals me from the window.

"Change places," I whisper. We stop. Danka moves as the sausage lands in our basket, and Dina takes her place.

"You're going to get into worse trouble than before," I scold him. "You better not do that again!"

But he doesn't care. Every few weeks out comes a little bit of sausage, out comes an extra piece of bread—manna from heaven.

∞

IT IS SPRING. We do not allow ourselves to feel spring, but we cannot ignore the fact that it is here again. This is our third spring in captivity; except for the smell of the air, it has all but lost its meaning. All spring really means is that we have survived another winter. Marek and his detail are back working along the fence, and trains race by across the field. I enjoy the noise as they pass; it reminds me of freedom and far-off cities.

Danka and Dina and I hang the clothes up silently as a train passes us in the distance. I turn from my work to watch its journey, and for one moment my mind is transported beyond the walls and work fields of Auschwitz-Birkenau. There a woman bedecked in a white hat and white gloves, her chin leaning on her pristine wrist, is looking out the window, looking at me, looking through me as if I were not there. She is clean and refined. She looks as if she might be going to visit somebody and that the greatest burden on her mind is what to serve for dinner tonight.

I am so controlled always, never do I let the emotions catch up with me, but there is no stopping the tears pouring from the corners of my eyes. Where is she going? I ask myself. Why does she have a life and I have nothing?

"There is a world out there," I gasp, giving way to the deluge inside of me.

There is a song we sing in camp. It never leaves my mind for one moment, always I am singing it inside my head:

There used to be tangos, fox-trots, and fanfares
sung by dancing pairs.
There were tangos of dreams and lovers,
but now we're at war. Nobody writes songs.
It's a waste of our young years.
So sing this new song, our heads held high.
Sing, sister, behind the German iron bars
This tango of tears, suffering, and desperation what
the war means to us today.
Our hearts are crying hot tears.
Are we ever going to see the sun?
Are we going to see the beautiful world again?
From the distance through the iron bars freedom is laughing at us
and about freedom we are constantly dreaming.
But the sun's still not shining.

IT IS SO impossible, but there it is, just a few kilometers away. Even in Stabsgebaüde, even if I can't see it, the smoke is still belching from the crematoriums. We aren't out of it, and the Germans are so efficient, they're winning the war. We are surviving because we have a hope for living, but admitting to this hope is insane! In my heart I want to believe I will be free again someday because I don't have the strength to stand up and live without that hope. But death is too imminent; the crematoriums are too oppressive. Hope is only there because we cannot survive without it.

"What's wrong?" Marek's voice invades my sorrow.

"That train . . . ," I answer, my voice wavering and unsure, "there were people on it, all dressed up, sitting there as if there is no war . . . as if we're not even here." I disappear behind the clothesline to wipe my tears on SS underwear so no one will know that they have gotten to me, again.

∞

THE ROCK LANDS a few feet away. It is a simple note, just a few words: *Why don't we try to escape?*

And go where, Marek? I wonder. We are Jews, and nobody is for us anymore. Despite the spring my youth is gone. We work; we are temporarily safe, but I feel no passion for life anymore. I sit in the dark fighting the overwhelming urge to cry. One good, long boo-hoo—even that is not allowed. I clench my hands and jaw until the desire to weep recedes, like the ocean tide. Someday, if we survive, I will cry for a week, maybe more. But not today, not here.

MAREK'S WORK DETAIL is no longer by the macaroni factory. I notice his absence the way I do anyone's disappearance in camp: I fear that he is dead.

IT IS A WARM DAY. Summer is nearing and the clothes dry quickly. We have checked the shirts to see which ones should be folded and put in the basket. I bend down to pull a few tender shoots of grass to nibble on, when a shadow falls over me. Squinting my eyes, I look up at the horse and its rider. Her blonde hair has lovely, graceful curls that tumble across her shoulders. Her boots are like mirrors reflecting the sun. I have seen her before, riding across the fields of camp. She is quite beautiful, and I feel small and insignificant in comparison.

She allows her horse the reins. He shakes his head eagerly, lowering it toward the shoots of grass I was just gathering. Surveying the area for a moment, she allows him to graze. Then she pulls the reins up and clucks to her steed. They gallop off across the fields, her hair bouncing against her back. Pangs of memory shoot through me: I used to have long hair. . . . I used to have curls. . . . I used to sit on our plow horse. . . .

Danka and Dina return to the *trockenplatz.* "Wardress Grese was here," I tell them. We have seen her many times riding across the fields, and ever since she came to camp she has been whispered about because she is so beautiful.

"What did she want?" Danka asks nervously.

"I don't know. She certainly isn't going to tell me."

"Was she on her horse?"

"Yah." We hang up the new load of laundry.

Marek returns to the work detail by the macaroni factory and tosses me a note that is very long. I retrieve it, slipping it into my jacket. It must have been hard for him to organize a piece of paper so large. *I am an officer in the Polish army. I was trained to be a doctor in Belgium and then returned to Warsaw, where I received the post of an officer. I have some contacts in the underground who are willing to build a double floor in the train that takes clothes out of Auschwitz and into Germany. We can hide in this space, which will be small, but we can escape. You would have to leave your sister behind; we cannot risk more than one other person as one scream or cry could mean death for all of us. I would like to escape with you and make a life with you. I believe we can do this.*

I crumble the note, tearing it into little pieces, and go to the toilet to wash it away. Marek. So sweet, so eager, so naive. I swallow back the lump in my throat. I swallow the words of my friend.

I can't do this, I write back to him. *I cannot leave my sister in this place alone. Besides, I am not brave enough. Thank you for thinking of me, though.* I throw the stone across the field when no one is looking and turn away to hang the mounds of SS underwear that it is my duty to watch and clean and fold neatly.

I do not see Marek as often, but occasionally he sends word through the kitchen workers who bring our morning tea. I miss our correspondence and his voice drifting on the wind among the clothes. I miss his kind face across the field and his concern for my welfare. The trains still pass in the distance, but I refuse to look at them.

MALA IS THE messenger girl for the Birkenau camp. We have seen her many times walking from one office to another, exiting from the gates to take a message to one of the other camps. We all admire her, not only because she is beautiful but because her position is extremely important. Despite the fact that she's a Jew, they have given her almost free rein of the complexes and allowed her to keep her hair. She speaks seven or eight languages and takes messages from Wardress Drexler to the hospital, the SS offices, wherever they need her to go. We have always taken pride in her job; she is a symbol to us that we are of value, we are human. Still, even for her, with all her privileges, camp life was too much.

One morning she is not at roll call, and the men who bring us tea confirm that Mala has escaped with her lover. In hushed whispers all day we gossip and fantasize about how they did it.[2]

We speculate and imagine how they did it. "She must have had contacts in the outside world."

"Yah, sure. How else could they get out?" Late into the night, after we have eaten our portion of bread, we discuss their fates.

"He was Polish. He had the contacts."

"I heard his name is Edward."

"I heard they stole German uniforms from the laundry, and someone built a false floor under one of the trains shipping clothing out, for them to hide in." I remember Marek's plan.

"You know a lot." For weeks we whisper and pray that these two brave souls are never caught. In our hearts they live happily ever after, they escape from Nazi Germany and make it to England, or Switzerland, or America, anyplace in the free world where there is safety for a Jew and a Gentile. We stoke the flames of our own courage as Mala becomes our beacon of light. If she can reach freedom, someday maybe we can, too. If she is brave, we can be brave. Oh, to flee this place and be with one's love. We dream of it. We cling to it. It makes the free world seem real again. It makes us remember what freedom was like. And then it makes us sad.

"The SS punished the camps for Mala's escape," the men carrying the teakettle in the morning whisper. "The prisoners in Birkenau were forced to stand roll call for twenty-four hours. Many dropped from fatigue."

I thank God we are not in Birkenau anymore.

---

2. "June 24 [1944]. . . . Mala Zimetbaum (No. 19880) . . . escapes from Auschwitz II, together with Polish political prisoner Edward Galinski (No. 531) . . . who was brought to the camp with the first transport of Polish prisoners . . . on June 14, 1940. [Also on this date] six prisoners (male) . . . receive Nos. 189229–189234. [And] two female prisoners . . . receive Nos. 82064 and 82065" (Czech, 650).

∽

WE ARE JUST finishing hanging the laundry when Irma Grese appears again. This time she is on foot and wearing a beach jacket. She waltzes past us without the faintest sign of recognition, throws a blanket on the ground, and proceeds to remove the cover over her bathing suit. Nervously I check the garments swaying in the breeze. She lies down and begins to rub cream over her legs and arms. Danka's eyes widen in alarm. Dina steps back. I move away cautiously.

"You there!" I freeze at the sound of her voice. "Would you put some lotion on my back?"

I am shocked. I have never been *asked* to do anything by an SS; they always order their slaves. Not only that, but she has asked me, a Jew, to touch her! I move toward her, afraid that I might do something wrong, afraid to touch her gorgeous skin. Trembling, trying hard to still my hands, I gingerly smooth the cream over her shoulders and down her spine. Then I stand up, moving back toward the clotheslines, the safety zone, the place I know I belong. Busily we check the fabric for dampness, keeping our hands busy and our minds silent, pretending this SS woman's presence does not unnerve us.

I remember:

Danka and I wake up early on Sunday morning. Mama has cheese Danish for us in a little sack. We put on skirts to hide our shorts underneath, because Papa forbids us to wear shorts. She kisses us at the door, hands us our picnic, and tells us to have fun. We hike into the mountains until we reach the stream. Then we take off our skirts, folding them neatly and putting them someplace to stay dry while we play in the water and sunbathe. Around noon we open Mama's Danishes, still warm from the oven, or maybe the sun kept them warm, and eat them while languishing in the sun.

A wave of homesickness revolts in my stomach, making it flip-flop. How I miss lying in our forbidden shorts eating Mama's homemade sweets.

Throughout the afternoon Wardress Grese suns, then abruptly she dresses, folds up her blanket, and disappears down the road.

We watch her depart, folding laundry quietly into our baskets, each of us lost in her private thoughts.

THE MORNING TEA COMES and with it the news. "Mala and her lover have been captured." Rumors escalate through the day; everyone is whispering about what has happened. That night, after the lights are out, we discuss her fate in the dark.

"They were caught eating in a restaurant."

"They had changed into civilian clothes, but an SS was eating there and recognized Mala."

"She's too beautiful for someone not to recognize."

"They shouldn't have stayed in Poland."

"They should have fled the country."

"And gone where?"

"She's going to be hanged."

"They will torture them first."

"Poor Mala." We shudder. Our dreams are shattered.[3]

GRESE COMES OFTEN to the *trockenplatz* and always asks me to put lotion on her back while ignoring Danka and Dina. Sometimes she speaks to me, telling me about the war and asking me about myself. She is so congenial to me. Pleasantry from the SS is so strange. It is not rare—it's impossible. I do not know what to make of Grese's kindness, but I think perhaps she is lonely.

"How old are you?" she asks as I spread lotion across her shoulders slowly and carefully, making sure it is perfectly even.

"Twenty-three, Frau Wardress," I answer meekly.

"So am I." She is so matter-of-fact. I do not miss a beat. I do not fumble, stunned as I am by her words. We come from such different worlds, we are in such different circumstances—but we are the same age.

"Where are you from?"

"Tylicz."

---

3. Mala and Edward were captured on July 6, 1944 (Czech, 710).

"Never heard of it."

"It's very small . . . in the Carpathian Mountains."

She is quiet. I do not instigate conversation. I know my place. I am still a slave, no matter how friendly she seems.

"You know what's going to happen when the war is over and we've conquered the world?"

"No, I don't." My skin grows cold despite the blazing sun.

"All of you Jews will be sent to Madagascar." She doesn't use a mean tone of voice, she just says it matter-of-factly, as if she knows that without a doubt this is the way it will be. "You'll be slaves for the rest of your life. You will work in factories all day long and be sterilized so you can never have children."

My heart droops. Standing up slowly, I try to break away from hearing more without allowing her to see the bewilderment in my face. I have a feeling she does not approve of emotional weakness—no SS do—so I move toward the folds of underwear swaying in the summer breeze and hide.

There is a roaring in my ears, a train rushing through my head. Why don't I just die right now if I'm going to be a slave for the rest of my life? I stumble blindly away from her voice, fighting the dryness stinging my eyes. What's the point of going on if this is all there is? I hide my face between clean, white undershirts and shorts. I want to tear them off their lines and scream at the encroaching clouds darkening the sky above us. I want to end it all, make the endless monotony cease . . . make everything stop. I want to sleep forever and never wake up. Then I hear myself saying, Come on, Rena, you don't even know if you're going to survive tomorrow—why worry beyond that?

The train barreling through my head stops. My thoughts quiet and slow. The sky has not changed; the sun still burns brightly, and Wardress Grese still lies on her stomach as if she has said nothing to destroy my world. I could die tomorrow. I will worry about the rest when and if I make it that far. I hang up an undershirt, smoothing the wrinkles from the cotton, trying very hard not to think about Madagascar, while watching her beautiful body tan.

∞

IT IS HARVEST TIME. My birthday must be near, or maybe it has passed. I do not know. I only know that a farmer is crossing the field with his wagon full of cabbages, so it must be late August. He slows down his horse just a little as he passes us, then clucks and jerks the reins. The horse starts with a jolt and off roll five heads of cabbage. Danka grabs my arm with a squeeze.

"Dina," I say. "You and Danka keep watch while I nab a cabbage. Next you go, and then Danka." They nod in agreement, turning their backs to me, hanging up the clothes and keeping their eyes peeled for SS. I walk toward the bounty the kind farmer has left for us and quickly retrieve it, carrying it back obscured by my clothes and hiding it in one of the baskets. Within minutes we have obtained three huge cabbages, their leaves luscious and warm from the sun.

"What about the other two?" Dina asks.

"We have enough. We could get caught if we're too greedy. Besides, I'm sure some other hungry person will find them."

That night we dole out several leaves to our dearest friends while everyone else is asleep. They are sweet and crisp. The juice runs down our throats as we consume them. They are so fresh you can almost taste the earth they come from, and so full of vitamins that our bodies feel immediately revitalized, and the permanent holes that live in our stomachs are momentarily filled.

The next day I notice that the other two cabbages are gone. A few days later we see the farmer and his wagon coming across the field again. His head down, he slows the horse and then clucks, just as he did before. Off roll a few more cabbages. I cannot prevent the smile that emerges as I say a prayer of blessing to this man before nodding to Danka and Dina. This simple farmer does the same thing for us one more time during the harvest season, and always we share the bounty with our friends.

∞

AS THE FALL moves in on us again the news becomes more and more positive; hope begins to seep into our pores and our dreams. Morning tea is our favorite time of day because the men from the

kitchen who bring the kettle whisper news of the war to one or
two of us. We sip our tea sharing the latest information: the Allies
are pushing back the Germans; the Russians are closer; the Allies
are going to bomb the train tracks.

We wait each day for more good news, more hope, which
comes in on the radios smuggled into camp. This is food for the
soul, and even those weak from hunger feast on this free meal of
information, holding it close to their hearts as one would an extra
ration of bread. This is good because the portions are shrinking
once again and Stasiu is throwing less food, less often. The SS
seem more tense and irritable, so we must be extremely careful not
to annoy them. There are rumors that the laundry is going to be
moved. We've heard planes overhead.

The air is changing. The farmer with his cabbages no longer
crosses the *trockenplatz*, so harvest is over. September? October?
We hang the clothes out to dry in the cooling wind and whisper
about the events outside our world, wondering where the laundry
will be moved, wondering when and if the war will ever end.

At morning roll call we are told to line up and march out.
There is anxiety at first; we eye each other nervously. Danka grabs
my hand for a reassuring squeeze. We leave the basement guarded
by SS. Please don't let it be Birkenau, is the prayer each girl repeats in her heart. Anything but Birkenau. We head down the road
praying they will turn down another path. There is a fence and
watchtowers in the distance, but it is not Birkenau. Our fears are
quickly relieved. We assess our new compound: the fence is not
electric; there are eleven blocks.

We march into Block Four. "This is where you will sleep."
We enter our new living quarters hesitantly. The hair on my arms
is raised, my skin is prickly: these are the new blocks, the blocks
that Danka and I helped build when we were in Auschwitz and
Birkenau. The concrete holding the bricks together was sifted and
delivered by our own hands. We have forged our own prison.

Roll call in the new blocks is held outside, and then we are
marched out of the gates to a leather factory, where the laundry
has been relocated. Mullenders is our wardress. She is Dutch but
speaks German very well. "There are men working in the leather
factory," she tells us. "You will not speak with them or have any

dealings with them. If I catch any of you carrying on with them, you will be punished—severely!" Her cold eyes glare at us so that we catch her meaning.

It is whispered that in Block Eleven they are conducting experiments. Next to us, in Block Five, there are German soldiers known as the Brownshirts, hiding in case there is an enemy attack on camp. We can see them through the window of our block when we come back from work.

"They're waiting for the Russians," one of the girls tells me.

A bomb falls in a field, leaving a huge crater, but no one is even remotely injured. The transports keep coming; the gas chambers keep killing; the crematoriums keep burning. The first few days are depressing. We have lost our secret supply of food and miss contact with Stasiu Artista. The men from the kitchen who bring our morning tea do not risk sharing any news with us until the situation can be judged safe. We are lost without our daily routine. We hunger and thirst for news of the war.

THE OLD, ALL TOO familiar routine begins again. We wake at four a.m. We rise to harsh reminders: "*Raus! Raus!*"

The tea arrives. I stand in line to get my cup, but when it is my turn the server whispers, "Marek is downstairs waiting for you." He pours my tea and I move on. My head is pounding so hard that my ears ring. Danka watches my flushed face as I hurry into the basement.

He leans against a table in the hallway, opening his arms for an embrace.

"Marek! What are you doing?" I can barely whisper out loud, I am so nervous.

"You wouldn't run away with me, so I have come to you." He pulls me close to him. "I've wanted to hold you for so long."

"I must be losing my senses to be here with you. We could both be shot."

"It'll be worth it, if only for one kiss." He lowers his head and kisses me, but I am in no mood to kiss back.

"That was lovely." He sits on the table, pulling me onto his lap, holding me tight.

I cannot resist the warmth of human comfort, the longing to be held close and dear. I kiss him long and endearingly.

"That was really worth it!" He smiles. "And now you must get upstairs before anyone notices you're missing, and I must get back to serving tea before they notice my absence."

"Please be careful. I'll die if anything happens to you."

"Nothing will happen to me. I've been tortured and beaten by the Gestapo—what more is there?"

I do not answer him. Taking his scarred hands, I stroke the places where his fingernails once were.

"When we are free, will you marry me?"

"Marek, how do we know what will be?"

We kiss once more before I flee upstairs. Danka and Dina are waiting for me, and together the three of us run out of the block and into our positions for roll call. My face is glowing, my belly is wound up so tight I cannot even eat the portion of bread I saved from last night.

∽

FOUR A.M.

"*Raus! Raus!*"

We are woken with orders to line up for roll call; then we are ordered to march. Confused but obedient, we head out of the gates in neat rows of five. Using side glances, we look at one another warily, sending warnings like silent Morse code with our blinking eyes.

Our hearts sink as we approach the electric fences of Birkenau. The band is playing as we march beneath the sign ARBEIT MACHT FREI. The entire women's camp is standing at attention facing a platform.

"Halt!"

We stop, turning to face the gallows.

We wait. Camp waits.

Drexler steps up on the platform. "Today we will witness the execution of a prisoner who tried to escape. This is what you all have waiting for you should you even think about escape from Auschwitz!"

Mala is brought up on the platform. She is calm, undisturbed. Drexler continues talking about how foolish Mala was to think she could escape the Third Reich. "We will rule the world," she reminds us. I remember Wardress Grese telling me about Madagascar. We will always be slaves; there is no hope. There is no reason to fight against them. They are everywhere. Drexler's voice drones on, instilling fear and trepidation into our veins.

Mala is standing there holding her hands gently in front of her, a faint smile on her face. She looks victorious. There is no regret in her eyes. Her dress is extremely dirty. I am sure they tortured her, trying to extract information and the names of the underground who helped them escape. She does not look as if she told them anything, though. She has pride. Her chin is up; her eyes are unwavering.

We have stepped over so many dead bodies that death is something we have become immune to, but this execution disturbs us. Why do we feel so terrible? Why is this so much worse than the suicides on the wire, the selections, the endless murders? But they were dead faces devoid of hope, and here is Mala shining despite the darkness in camp. Her face never falls in despair. Why did it happen? Why can't just one of us stay in the free world and survive?

She is so beautiful. The sun in the sky isn't shining for us, but Mala is. She is our sun. She has tasted freedom and seen heaven in the world outside. There is no hope for us, we may not survive—but Mala, her chin lifted high, has escaped from all this madness. She has been the secret ray of hope, and now they're going to try to snuff our only light out.

They move her toward the noose, but in one adept movement she pulls a razor blade from her sleeve and slits her wrists. Her blood spills across the platform.

Taube tries to stop the bleeding. "*Scheiss-Jude*, you will die by hanging, not by your own hand!" He swears and curses her. She slaps him in the face, digging her fingers into his eyes.

"I'll kill you with my bare hands!" he yells, beating her body unmercifully. "Bring the cart!" he bellows, wiping his hands in disgust. A wheelbarrow flies toward the gallows, and prisoners carry her body to it.

"Take her to the crematorium at once. She is to die in the fire!"

Her crumpled body no longer cares where it goes. Her spirit is already hovering over this world. The cart races toward the death chambers; her arm, dangling just outside of the cart, gushes her life's blood upon the soil of Poland.

"Please let her die," we pray. "Please let her die before they put her in the ovens."

FOUR A.M.

"Raus! Raus!"

It is hard to wake up. The vision of Mala bleeding to death disturbed our sleep and rocked all dreams of freedom we had fostered from her escape. The kettle of tea waits like a cauldron of doom. Then the whisper cascades gently through our ranks, nourishing us with what little courage we have left.

"An SS took mercy on her and shot her before she was put in the oven." Our prayers were answered—by a German, of all things.[4]

∞

IT IS A WARM SUNDAY. We open the windows to let fresh air into the block. Standing at the windows, we stare at Block Five and the Brownshirts stare back at us.

Silently, we flirt. We are young and so are they; it is only natural. One of them holds a loaf of bread and points at it smiling and nodding. He runs downstairs and places a whole loaf of bread outside, then dashes back inside.

I run down to retrieve it. He has paused at the doorway and we look at one another from our separate worlds. I smile briefly and mouth *Danke schön* before disappearing back into our block.

"Look, it's a whole loaf of bread!" We can't believe our good fortune. "How many are there of us?" We divide the loaf up into twelve chunks and inhale it hungrily.

---

4. On September 15, 1944, the executions of Mala Zimetbaum and Edward Galinski are scheduled to take place simultaneously, in the separate men's and women's camps (Czech, 710).

BOOM! We jump. Air raid sirens wail across the camps.

"*Raus! Raus!*" our block elder yells. "Follow me! Quickly! Into the basement." We run downstairs. A door opens and we cram ourselves through it, bumping into one another. We try to turn around and move apart, only to step on each other's toes. Turning around to see if there is more room somewhere else, I see an SS officer shut the door. The latch clicks.

"Don't lock us in here!" somebody wails. "Don't forget us!"

The space is suffocating. We are all terrified. What if the building collapses and we're trapped inside? The whole structure is shaking, and we are crammed against each other in this small crawlspace. Flashbacks grab my mind—our first night in Auschwitz, the transport from Slovakia.

"Are you afraid?" Danka's voice anchors me back to the present.

"No," I lie to her, controlling the panic that tries to steal my breath. I put my arms around her, pulling her close. My heart is pounding so loudly, though, that I switch sides, holding her against the right side of my chest so she cannot feel it.

I cradle her like a baby in my arms. Her eyes look up at me for assurance as she wraps her arms around my neck. The ground beneath us rumbles. My legs are liquid, struggling to keep us both from collapsing to the floor. Nobody moves. One girl faints, and then another. There is a huge crash outside.

Silence.

What if the building above us has been destroyed and we are buried alive? They will not save us. We are Jews—refuse. No one will dig us out of this grave.

We lose all track of time and space, trapped as we are. No one speaks. No one can move. Another girl faints, her body hits the floor with a dull thump. My skin creeps eerily under my clothes.

Silence. Time stops.

THERE ARE FOOTSTEPS OUTSIDE. A key scrapes against the lock. Light sears into our widened pupils, causing them to retreat too quickly. We wince. Dazed and blinded, we struggle out of our cell. Each girl clutches a friend as our weakened knees buckle, and we stuggle up the stairs into daylight. There are ambulances and air raid sirens screaming across the complexes. We look out the windows, stunned.

Block Five is gone, flattened beyond recognition. Medical teams run this way and that, carrying stretchers. Frantically, the SS work to free their fellow soldiers from the rubble, but there is no one to save; all of the Brownshirts are dead. I stand at the window avoiding the tears smarting in my eyes. I am sorry that the soldier who brought us the bread is dead. I do not understand how I can feel this way about a German soldier, but I do. I conceal my sorrow. I do not love the Germans. I hate what they have done—are doing—to me, my sister, and my people, but I do not understand why somebody who was nice to us must die. I do not understand why anyone must die. None of it makes any sense at all.

EVERYONE IS DIZZY with the bombings; suddenly it seems as if the war might end someday, and we are filled with anticipation masked only by our servitude. Jusek, one of the men working in the leather factory, steals a few words with Danka one day as we are passing by. It is innocent, nothing more than what might happen in the free world when people feel hope. We go into the laundry not thinking anything more about it.

Wardress Mullenders stalks in behind us. Her eyes shift slyly. "Your number is up!" She looks directly at Danka and then exits. Danka's flushed cheeks go white. She leans against the wall, covering her face.

"Maybe she is just threatening to give your number up." I try to comfort my baby sister, but I'm scared. Mullenders has no softness toward us. She is cruel.

"What will happen?" Danka looks at me for direction. "Oh, God, what will happen to me?"

I do not answer. I do not know.

That night we enter the block and sit numbly on the bunk, trying to force the food down our tightening throats. There is a bit of commotion on the other side of the room, but we pay no attention. My mind is racing. What can I do to save Danka?

Dina sits down on the bunk and says matter-of-factly, "Danka will not be getting reported."

"I won't?"

"No. Everyone has pitched in with bits of jewelry, somebody even had a watch. We bought Mullenders off."

"What can I do?" I ask.

Dina shakes her head. "Nothing, Rena. It is done." The girls around us smile, their faces shining in the dark with pride and self-esteem.

This is how close we are. These girl-women with whom we have worked and lived for almost a year have saved Danka's life.

"RENA, WHAT'S WRONG with your voice?" Danka looks at me worriedly.

"I don't know."

"I think we need to do something about it."

"It'll go away, you'll see."

"You said that two months ago, and it's only gotten hoarser. Now it's getting cold again. I think this is something serious."

"There's nothing I can do about it, Danka." She's right though; it hasn't gone away. I almost sound like a man now; in another few weeks I may lose the ability to speak all together. Fortunately, there's little reason to speak out loud and no one inspects our throats or voices, but this loss of my voice is reason to be selected should an SS notice it.

"I heard what you were saying," a nurse who sleeps in our block says quietly. "We'll bring you something from the hospital. Saturday, after roll call."

On Saturday night, we chew our bread slowly waiting for the nurses to come. "Thank you for being so concerned," I tell Danka.

"I can't let you get selected," she tells me. "We have an oath."

I smile. We do have an oath, but it never occurred to me before that she's just as committed to my survival as I am to hers. She gets up off the bunk, slipping downstairs to wait. I watch her, amazed. This is my baby sister. When did she grow up?

We are deep into the night when four nurses arrive at my bedside. Silence is imperative; if any of us are caught we will all be shot.

The nurse in charge pulls a needle out of her pocket. "I am going to inject you with strychnine," she whispers. "Give me your arm."[5]

"It'll be okay, Rena." Danka strokes my brow. "You're brave. You can do this."

I try to look confident for my sister but cannot muster any feeling but fear. It is her eyes that are full of confidence and courage, and I lean on her strength, fighting the urge to panic.

The needle glimmers. The nurse's firm hand is cool on my skin as she prepares for the injection. The needle penetrates my flesh and immediately there is a burning fire raging through my body. My muscles spasm as I lurch to scream. Hands hold me down, pressing firmly on my mouth. The pain is excruciating. I try to remind myself to be silent, but there are moans escaping from my body which I have no control over. It is as if pins dance in my veins and puncture my lungs. I pant and heave, but cannot vomit.

"Get cold compresses! Water!" I hear the nurse order her assistants.

There is something wet on my skin.

Minutes . . . hours . . . I do not know how long I thrash and writhe in agony, incapable of controlling my limbs. The compresses seem to help. I scream when they change them. Danka's face is stained with tears.

In a fugue state I hover just above unconsciousness. The body sleeps fitfully, waking me with its sporadic twitching as the poison does its work. My mind is far away.

THE MORNING LIGHT in the block hurts my eyes. "How do you feel?" Danka's voice wakes me.

---

5. "At one time strychnine was used as a tonic and a central nervous system stimulant, but because of its high toxicity (5 mg/kg is a lethal dose in the rat) and the availability of more effective substances, it no longer has a place in human medicine" (Bartlett, 534).

"Terrible." I can barely mouth the words. She holds her finger up to her mouth, indicating for me to lie quietly.

"Something went wrong, I don't know what, but it was close. The nurse said you'll feel weak today, but tomorrow you'll feel better, and in a few days your voice should start to return to normal." She hands me a cup full of water. I gulp it thirstily.

"Thank . . . you."

"Shhh." Danka smiles. "Rest now."

It takes a few weeks, but slowly my voice does return to normal.

∞

THERE IS AN explosion outside. We all stop working. It doesn't sound like a bomb. There are no planes going over, but it sounds like it's just a few kilometers away. Mullenders runs to the door. We follow her slowly, glancing at one another carefully. There is smoke billowing up from the direction of Birkenau. We do not smile but our hearts grin. We wait, listening for more explosions and praying, though we do not know what we are praying for.

THE NEXT MORNING the news arrives with our tea. One of the crematoriums was blown up by the *Sonderkommando*.[6] We have finally struck a blow against our captors. We hope, feebly, that it is the beginning of the end, but the SS catch everyone in the Sonderkommando and kill them. Four girls have been arrested from the gunpowder factory; they helped smuggle the powder out. Those of us who continue to live sit silent shiva for our brave co-patriots.

∞

---

6. October 7, 1944 . . . there is a revolt by the Jewish *Sonderkommando*, with explosives smuggled by women prisoners. The plan to destroy all of the crematoriums was thwarted by the Germans, but the men in the Sonderkommando did successfully wreck Crematorium IV before the uprising was crushed (Rittner and Roth, 31).

DANKA HAS EXCRUCIATING pain due to a rotten tooth. On Sunday she and ten other girls finally get permission from our camp commandant to go to the camp dentist in Auschwitz. I stand by the fence watching my sister head out the gates of our camp without me to protect her, guarded by the SS who do not care whether she lives or dies. I am nervous being separated from my sister even though I know where she is going; too much can happen in a second and I am uneasy. I try to tell myself that I am being ridiculous and instead of pacing the block I go to the window and look out. It is a bright sunny day, but that brings me no peace. My mind is whirling with alarm and fear. There is a plane. I blink hard, staring into the sky. I cannot see it but I can hear it. The air raid sirens begin to whine.

Maria yells upstairs. *"Raus!* Get to the basement."

"My sister is out there!"

"Rena! Come on!" Dina shouts at me. I run across the room toward the stairs. The windows behind us shatter; glass shards shower down on our heads.

"Danka!" I scream. All is chaos.

In the basement we shiver with fear. I wish that Danka were in my arms like the last time. If I was with her at least I could do something . . . anything. I feel as if I'm going crazy with worry. I will never forgive myself if my sister dies without me. I squeeze my hands until I cannot make fists anymore. My God has abandoned me, left me cold; still I pray, but in the same breath I doubt his power. "Please don't let my sister die," I plead. "I cannot live without her. . . ." I try to mask my fear with bravado, but what will I tell Mama if something happens to Danka?

Finally the sirens stop and we are released from our dark and airless cell. I run up the stairs. Smoke is billowing into huge black thunderheads from the direction of Auschwitz. A girl returns through the gate. She is alone except for her guard.

"What happened?" I grab her collar. "Where's my sister?"

"I don't know. It was mayhem. Some people were killed."

"I have to get my sister!" My head pounds as the blood rushes into it; my vision goes black. Blindly, I run toward the gate to find my sister. I don't care about the guards in the towers. I do not care about anything but finding my sister.

"Grab her!" Dina yells. I feel firm hands gripping my arms, pinning me down. Out of my mind with grief, I try to shake them loose.

"I've got her!" Janka yells.

"Let me go!" I scream at them. They are the enemy. They are against me. I struggle to shake them off. I do not know how many girls hold on to prevent me from going through the gates and getting shot.

"Rena. Listen to me. You can't do anything. You have to wait here," Dina says.

Finally Janka's voice sinks through my insanity. "What if she is fine and you get shot trying to leave? What would Danka do without you?"

"Be still. She'll be back," Dina reassures me. "You'll see. Everything will be fine."

"I can't live without my sister."

"You don't know shes' dead. Wait before you get yourself killed. Get hold of yourself."

I gasp for air trying to listen to their cool, calm logic.

"I'm okay," I finally manage to say. "You can let me go. I won't run off, I promise." They move away slowly. Dina and Janka stay close by me as I pace back and forth in front of our block, remembering the Brownshirts, remembering how in Auschwitz people die for no reason.

There are some figures coming toward our complex. I stare and stare at their forms, trying to make out if one of them is Danka through the wire mesh. I think I see her but I could be making it up; I could be crazy and seeing things. I feel Dina's hand squeeze my shoulder.

"Is it her?" I am afraid that I have gone mad.

"That's her," Dina whispers.

"Thank you, God." But I am not sure if it is God's doing that she is alive. It could be simply luck, or a mistake. Chance is the only order in our universe.

They come through the gate and the SS guard leaves them. I hug and kiss my sister over and over, not allowing her time to explain.

"What's wrong?" she asks. "What did you think?"

"I thought you were among the dead! Promise me you'll never leave my side again." I lean, exhausted, against the block.

"I promise, Rena." She takes my hand, smiling into my worried eyes.

∞

HOW DID WINTER arrive again so fast? Is this really our third? Will next year bring a fourth winter, or death, or Madagascar?

"LINE UP!" SS MULLENDERS orders us. It is the middle of the day. We freeze, then move quickly into line.

"March!" she orders. We march out of the leather factory. It is not time to stop working, and we do not head back to the new blocks. "I want you to sing German marching songs." We open our mouths but no sound comes out.

"Sing or you will be punished!" She begins to sing, waving her whip at us threateningly. We join, our voices shaking in fear. She makes an unmistakable turn in the road. Birkenau looms before us. Our hearts are in our throats, but still she forces us to sing.

We march under the hated sign. We do not know immediately what the purpose of our return to Birkenau is, but we fear it worse than death.

"Line up! Face front!" she orders. "Keep your eyes open and face the gallows."

We line up with sinking hearts. We are, all of us, shaking uncontrollably. The whole of the women's camp is lined up facing a platform with four nooses. I stare and stare at the girl-women trapped in the camp, a sea of conquered spirits. Then I close my mind so that I cannot see anything else.

Ella, Roza, Regina, and Ester. We know their names from the men who bring us the tea. Their names are etched in our hearts. Two of them walk bravely toward the platform. They have been tortured. There are whispers among us. They never gave one name or contact of the many people who were involved in the sabotage. I wonder if I would have had the courage to do what they did: smuggle gunpowder out of the factory so that the Sonderkommando could blow up the crematoriums. I marvel at their strength. I weep inside, where no one can see.

"These traitors to the Third Reich are condemned to die by order of the Fuhrer, for espionage. You will watch these filthy traitors hang until they die, so you will be reminded what happens to enemies of the Reich! All caught closing their eyes will be shot for failing to learn this lesson!" Commandant Hossler yells.[7]

The girls go up on the chairs. The SS put the nooses over their heads. "Long live Israel!" They begin in unison to recite a Hebrew prayer. Their voices are cut short as the chairs are pulled out from underneath them. There is no God to save them.

I have to watch. It's the least I can do; it is how I honor them. We stand and wait until the last body has stopped its death dance in the air. They take the bodies down, loading them into a cart and wheeling them to the crematorium.[8]

"One of them is still alive," it is whispered through the rows.

"One of them is still breathing."

In a civilized world if the condemned survives hanging they are pardoned, but not in Auschwitz-Birkenau. We pray that she will die before she is put in the ovens.

Mullenders makes us march back to our camp singing more German songs. "Louder!" she orders. "Chins up!" We sing in our dry and cracking voices, our spirits trying not to break.

In the morning we wake slowly, depressed by the loss of our comrades. The kettle of tea arrives. We are in mourning for the girls who have died and not eager for news of the war today. One

---

7. "January 6 [1945] . . . In the evening four female Jewish prisoners, Ella Gartner, Roza Robota, Regina Safir, and Estera Wajsblum, are hanged in two separate executions. . . . The reason for the sentence is read by First Protective Custody Commander Hossler in Auschwitz; he screams that all traitors will be destroyed in this manner" (Czech, 775).

8. In November and December of 1944, demolition squads were created to dismantle some of the crematoriums and "no more selections are conducted among the prisoners. The prisoners die a 'natural death' from starvation, heavy labor, and the inconceivable living, hygiene, and sanitary conditions." In the camp registry 322 women, who died by violent means, were listed as having died because of "special treatment" (Czech, 756).

of the kitchen men whispers, "She died on the way to the crematorium." We breathe a sigh of relief. She did not suffer.

I get my tea. A note is slipped into my hand smoothly without a second's falter. It is from Marek: *They're going to march us out of camp. The Russians are very close. You must decide if you want to feign illness and stay in camp or march. I will help you either way and meet you in America. When you get out, go to America and find Charles Boyer. Tell him I sent you; he is a friend of mine from Belgium. He's such a famous actor even little children in New York know his name. . . .*

I fight back the tears. Children may know who Charles Boyer is, but I don't. America seems like such a far-off place.

WE GET MORE and more information that the Russians are coming and we are going to be freed. So we start talking about what we're going to do—should we stay or try to escape?

"They're going to leave all the sick in Birkenau and the rest will have to march to Germany," one of the girls in our block tells us.

"Well, then, we should pretend to be sick."

"I heard that they're planning to set fire on all four sides of the camp, lock the gates, and leave the electric wires on, so everyone will burn inside," one of the scribes tells us.

"So if we pretend to be sick we could burn to death?"

"That's what I heard."

"What should we do?" Danka asks me.

"I don't know. What are you going to do, Aranka? Act sick or march out?"

"I'm going to take a chance and march out. Maybe I can escape on the march."

"Maybe they're going to shoot you."

"It seems like our chances would be better of escaping on the march than locked inside a burning camp, though."

"All I know is that I don't want to die here. Let me die anywhere but Auschwitz." The voice is passionate. We all look at Janka. Her seventeen-year-old eyes have seen much in all of her years in the ghetto and camp. She has said what we all feel deep down inside. We will die if we must, but not here, not in the flames. We continue to work at the laundry every day, but Mullenders is jumpy and ill-tempered. Her regular morning speeches terrify us, but now we glare at her with hatred. We would not have dared to do so a few weeks before, but the songs she forced us to sing are still sticking to our tongues no matter how hard we scrub to rid our mouths of their taste. We know now that she will not have control over us forever and we hate her with a vengeance.

Our work days are not as long, and we discuss things more openly than ever before, worrying about what to do. It's not that we speak in front of Mullenders; that would be foolish. But when she moves away from us we whisper. Guesswork and rumors, guesswork and rumors—that is all we know. Nobody knows for sure whether staying or going is safer.

The morning tea arrives. I hold out my bowl, feeling a note slipped into my hand by the server.

"*Jekuje*, thank you for my tea," I say to him in Polish.

"You're welcome." He has kind eyes. What is it about these men in the kitchen that they will risk their lives to bring notes to us? Sometimes I am in such awe of their bravery. They do not know me; they are not blood relations, but they would die before they gave up my number.

I disappear quickly to read the note from Marek. It says, *How many girls do you want supplies for?* I show Danka the note. "How many should we try and help?"

"We have to help Dina."

"Yah, for sure. But who else?"

"Janka . . . Mania and Lentzi." I nod. We cannot help everyone, but we can help a few, and these are our friends who have helped us.

Clothes and food for six, I write to Marek. *Thank you.* The men with the kettle are preparing to leave. I slip the note to the one with kind eyes and move away.[9]

9. On January 17, 1945, the last roll call is held, counting 31,894 prisoners; 16,577 are women (Rittner and Roth, 14). "No. 202499 [is] the last number assigned to a [male] prisoner in Auschwitz." It appears that the last woman registered in Auschwitz was No. 89,325 (Czech, 785, 756). Fewer women registered in camp indicates just how many more women were selected for death when transports arrived in Auschwitz.

The day passes slowly. The weather is worsening. Clouds are everywhere, and it looks as if we'll be in for a snowstorm tomorrow. We hang up the boxer shorts and SS long johns on the lines inside. It suddenly seems so ridiculous, the days we spent watching the laundry in sleet and snow and rain. At least it's warm in the leather factory and the clothes dry quickly. The soup comes at noon. I receive another note: *Watch for the tea tomorrow. Don't forget—America.* I walk to the toilet casually and flush. We fold the underwear that has dried into our baskets and leave what has not dried hanging for the next day—if there is a next day.

∽

MORNING COMES. There is no work today. I get my tea and my instructions: *There is a kettle in the basement. Get everything out of it and leave.* I nod to Mania, who is the biggest and strongest of us. Danka knows to follow in a few minutes with Dina; then Janka and Lentzi will sneak downstairs. We must hide the food and clothes quickly, without anyone noticing. There is a loaf of bread for each of us, four bags of sugar, six pairs of pants, shoes, socks, and sweaters. I divide them up. Mania helps me. We conceal the clothes under our mattresses, hiding them for later.

"You're more robust, being a secretary and working inside. Can you carry two bags of sugar?" I ask Mania.

"Sure." She takes the bags under her arms. There is one little package wrapped in a rag that says *Rena* on it. I open it excitedly and find a chrome watch. Marek knows how particular I am. I smile to myself, fastening the band onto my wrist, remembering the last watch I wore. Pulling the sleeve down over my wrist, I return upstairs.

THE SS HAVE a lot on their minds, trying to destroy records, gathering things around camp. There are bonfires of paper that remind me of that dreaded night six years ago when the Nazis ignited our holy books outside the temple and shaved Papa's beard and ear locks. The flames are no longer newborn; they are aged and smile wickedly at those of us who have seen evil mature, unhindered.

Like Mengele's mask of beauty, no one will believe what this evil has cultivated behind these walls. They destroy the evidence so that there will be no proof, no records, nothing but our memories, if we survive, and they will try to obliterate those too. I look out the window of our block; the landscape is spotted with puffs of gray smoke and black cinders drifting up over the SS offices. For the first time since the beginning of our horror, the air smells like burning paper rather than burning flesh.

We wait through the day, putting our extra clothes on, changing our boots so that we are ready. This is almost as bad as being in quarantine. We have no clue as to what will happen to us, but at least it will be different. We're going to leave Auschwitz-Birkenau. There is a sense of anticipation for the unknown, but a sense of dread also hangs over us. We do not know when, but we know that soon they will come in and say "March out!" We are too tense to sleep. All day we wait. We try to rest. I clean my fingernails eight times.

"What time is it, Rena?" Danka asks from our bunk.

"Two o'clock."

"Where's the soup? They're late."

"They won't feed us today." A voice comes down from the bed above us.

"Why not?"

"They're saving the food for themselves." We're nothing but cover against the Russians. Expendable. They're not going to waste something as precious as food on us. We wait. We rest. It grows dark outside. No one brings our evening bread. Our block elder is agitated; she will have to march with the rest of us. Danka dozes. My eyes grow heavy, then jerk open; I'm afraid I'll miss something. The lights are still on in our block. There is stamping outside.

"*Raus! Raus!*"

We line up outside the block just as we always have. The SS count us and then give the orders. "March out!"

I look down at my watch. It is exactly one o'clock in the morning. It is January 18, 1945. We step outside the gates.

There are thousands of people before us. Bonfires speckle the landscape. Tramping through the well-packed snow, we march in neat rows of five, orderly to the end, leaving behind us the iron curse ARBEIT MACHT FREI: the words are branded on our souls. It is snowing. The blizzard has arrived.

Is this for life or is it for death?

We are the only women on the road, but there are men's bodies scattered across our path. Tramping and tramping, our legs ache with fatigue yet move as if they were mechanical. Stepping over bodies already covered with snow, we march for an hour, maybe two, before we are herded into a barn. Are the Russians near? Is freedom here? We collapse in the straw for a brief respite. Sleep is dark, dreamless.

"*Raus! Raus!*" We get up stiffly. A few do not wake. They are prodded, then shot. The snowdrifts are knee-deep and the wind is picking up; still, we do not have to break the trail as the men before us did. The sun rises in an overcast sky. It is a gray day. Our flesh is gray. Tramp, tramp; we step over three and four bodies at one time. Gunshots come from in front of us and in back of us, in front of us and in back of us. We're so numb to it that the bullets feel as if they're in our own heads. The snow is endless. It does not stall or slow down; it falls in sheets. I have blisters on my feet that would hurt more if my feet weren't so cold. When we stop for rest periods there is no food. We ration what food we brought with us; it is disappearing fast. The bread will be gone tomorrow and the sugar is too low. We eat snow.

"Why don't I take one of the bags of sugar, Mania? So you don't have so much to carry."

"I only have one bag left."

"How can it all be gone?"

"We've eaten it." She dares me to question her. I don't believe her but am too weak to argue. If we starve because of her selfishness, it will be on her head.

We tramp through white and red snow. We lurch over bodies.

We stop. In a barn, the six of us divide up the last of our bread and sugar. I'm so tired. It feels as if tomorrow will be the end for me. I wonder if I shouldn't just give up. It is almost as if I am hearing voices in my head while I lean against the thin barn wall. I stop my musing, listening for a familiar sound. Then I hear it—a family speaking Polish in the farmhouse connected to the barn. Their door is ajar. The voices tug at me, drawing me to them. I must

go see these people who were my people before this war. The SS
guards are outside.

I slip up to the kitchen, my knuckle raps at the door. "I am
sorry to bother you," I say in Polish, "but I have a sister and we're
both very hungry. We're from Tylicz. If you can spare one potato,
I'll give her half. If you give me two, I'll take one."

I hear the husband say, "We don't have enough to spare!"

"She's from Tylicz!" the wife exclaims. The family discusses
this briefly. Not wanting to endanger them, I wait outside, catching bits and pieces of their conversation. The door opens a crack.

A ray of warm, golden light drifts across my face. The wife's
eyes are moist with worry and fear. "Take these." She hands me
two hard-boiled eggs and two cooked potatoes. I hold them in my
hands, letting the warmth seep into my skin and the smell waft up
to my nostrils.

"*Jękuje. Bög zapłać.* May God reward you for this favor." I back
away from the door. "I will never forget you." That night we eat.[10]

I DO NOT know how long we have been walking or how far. I
cannot remember how many times the sky has grown light and
then dark, how many times my watch has done twenty-four revo-
lutions, or how many barns we have collapsed in. We could have
been walking for one day or ten. I do not know. I do not care. I am
so sick I want to die. I have such terrible diarrhea that I run to the
outhouse without asking. The SS must be tired of shooting people because they haven't shot me yet for leaving the barn without
permission. I try to sleep through the night, but we are freezing
and my stomach is empty.

"*Raus! Raus!*" Get up. Go to the outhouse. Stay there. They
have shot girls for trying to hide and escape. That is what I want.
I don't care anymore. The SS line everyone up. My hands support
my head, too weak to lift itself.

Someone is outside the door. Time to be shot. Time to die. It
will be a relief.

---

10. Polish villagers along the evacuation routes recover the corpses of prisoners and
bury over one thousand men and women in twenty-nine mass graves (Czech, 797).

"Rena." Danka's voice is outside the door.

I pull my pants up and tie them tight but fall back down on the seat, unable to stand up.

"What're you doing?" She opens the door.

"Go on without me. I'm staying here."

"No, you're not. You're coming with me."

"I can't walk, Danka. . . . Save yourself."

"Look at those bodies. Look at all those who are dead, but we're still alive. You're not going to die now. I'm not going to let you!"

"Janka!" I can hear the tremor in her voice. She is so brave. "Come help me." I cannot look in my sister's face. I am so sick of living. Their hands hoist me up between them. We stumble into formation.

Mustering all the strength and courage in the world, with Danka and Janka supporting just my elbows, I tramp through the snow again. The sun comes up cold against the barren landscape. Their hands are firm under my elbows. We walk as if there were nothing wrong with me. It is forever. Then, suddenly, my strength comes back.

"I can stand on my own two feet now," I manage to whisper.

"Are you sure?"

I nod. Janka lets go first. I do not stumble.

Slowly Danka releases her hold on me. They have walked the illness out of me. This is some miracle.

For hours we tramp over bodies, through snow. Gunshots fell those of us who are too weak to continue, but I am not one of those poor souls. Gunshots fell those still strong enough to escape, but we are not among them either. Do I wish that we had stayed in Auschwitz-Birkenau? Despite the cold, the hunger, no. I am glad that we will not die behind that sign, behind Hades' gates. We could be walking in circles the way the path is strewn with bodies; all looking the same: frozen, desperate. Free.

We arrive at a train depot.

"Get into the coal cars," they order. We can barely get in without help, but there is no help. Everyone is exhausted and too weak to climb into the empty cars. I help Danka in, who helps Dina, and so on; everyone has just enough strength to help one other person. We lean in the corner, finally able to rest. Then we start to shiver. The cold bares its fangs and digs into our flesh. I don't want to sit down because of the soot, but that concern does not last long. Overcome by fatigue, I collapse with the others onto the black, dirty floor.[11]

Air raid sirens begin to wail and planes swoop overhead as the SS and German people run into the railway station, leaving us outside. We huddle in the cars hoping the bombs will not kill us—hoping this ordeal will end. We pass out despite the sounds of war overhead.

QUIET.

I stir and crawl up the side of the car to look out at the people just starting to return to the platform. A lady holding her infant stands nearby. "Please, can you hand me some clean snow from the ground?" I ask in German. "We are so thirsty and the snow is too dirty up here to eat."

Her eyes register fear as she looks at the SS with their guns. She looks at her baby, shaking her head. I understand. The snow begins to fall again, and after a little while I am able to scrape a tiny layer of fresh clean snow off the ridge of the car before it turns black. This we melt in our mouths, trying to quench our thirst.

THE TRAIN STARTS. Wind whips our faces with bitter, subzero breath. I do not know what time it is. Every time I look at my watch I forget what the hands say, and I don't want to raise my cuff and give any reason for the cold air to touch my skin directly. For how long the train races through the night I do not know. We get

---

11. January 21, 1945, columns of female prisoners begin arriving in Wodzislaw in Silesia after marching thirty-one miles through blizzard conditions. We do not know which column Rena and Danka were in, but their march took anywhere from four to five days. The first column of women arrived on January 21 "half-dead, unconscious and feverish female prisoners" and were loaded "into open freight cars" (Czech, 796).

in and stay there until we are told to get out; it is dark and light somewhere in between.

"*Raus! Raus!*" We are ordered off the train. Our legs are cramped from sitting still and our joints don't bend easily as we leap into the snowdrifts below us. Four feet down.

We march again for a very long time through the dark. It is below zero. The snow is at our knees. No one has come before us to break the trail. There are no footprints to indicate that others have traveled this path; the bodies that strew the landscape are still warm. They are all girl-women. Where are they taking us?

Gunshots rip through the air like swatting flies on a hot summer day; still we march. I look at my watch, but the numbers have no meaning. There are lights ahead. We march toward the lights, through the snow toward the gate of another camp, Ravensbrück. The words cackle across the dawn—ARBEIT MACHT FREI. My heart collapses. We are not free.[12]

THERE IS NOTHING HERE; no blankets, no bunks, just lots of girl-women, and all the beds are occupied. We are so tired we curl up on cold dirt floors. I am so hungry that I sneak outside to find us food. There was a pile of potatoes we passed on our way through camp. Edging along the blocks, I scour the complex for the shadow I think will fill our bellies. There are no potatoes, only piles of bodies in the dark.[13]

∞

---

12. The trip to Ravensbrück is 677 kilometers, but it seems to have taken two days. "Almost half of the prisoners die on the way of hunger, of exhaustion from the long march, and of freezing" (Czech, 789). On January 23, 1945, the first column of women arrived in Ravensbrück. More columns arrived through January 27, and even after, as late as February 2, some of whom had walked for two weeks and more than 185 miles (Czech, 800–801).

13. January 27, 1945: Auschwitz is liberated by the Russian army at about nine in the morning. "Those troops found about 7,000 sick and exhausted prisoners—4,000 of them women" (Rittner and Roth, 14).

FOUR A.M.

"*Raus! Raus!*"

They wake us with watery tea and a crust of bread. I cannot remember when we ate last; then I recall the food from the Polish woman.

Is this for life or is it for death?

NEÜSTADT GLEWE

WE ARE IN RAVENSBRÜCK for a few days, or is it weeks? Somehow we find Erna and Fela, but this is no reunion. We are grateful to see our friends alive and wonder how much longer any of us have. There are so many of us and such little food that the SS decide to move some of us. The thumbs choose Danka, Dina, and me; I look around for the others. Erna and Fela, Janka, Mania, and Lentzi—they are not in our group. I don't know where they are. How quickly we go from having friends to losing them.

Danka, Dina, and I are piled into a flatbed truck, clinging to each other. Are they taking us to the gas? The flatbeds cross under the gates of Ravensbrück and turn west moving us farther into the interior of Germany. We lean against the wood sides of the truck, jostling into one another. The road is full of potholes and bumps. We avoid looking at the girl-women riding with us. We are too tired to care where they're taking us or why; we just want to rest and eat.

We arrive at Neüstadt Glewe, get counted, and are handed pieces of bread.[1] At least we don't have to sleep on the floor here.

---

1. Neüstadt Glewe is approximately 132 kilometers northwest of Ravensbrück. In her testimony to Yad Vashem, Raizl Tabakman Kibel recalled, "Even today I still cannot understand with what sort of strength and how I was able to endure the 'death march' and drag myself to Ravensbrück camp, and from there, after resting a week, or two, to Neustadt" (Gilbert, 775). There is very little documentation on the Ravensbrück subcamps. "All information on Neustadt-Glewe was destroyed when the fleeing Nazis tried to suppress evidence" (Saidel, 158).

In the morning we stand at roll call and quickly notice that there is no crematorium in this camp. There is a mound of bodies, though, about six feet high. The smell in camp is of decaying rather than burning flesh.

We are marched through the middle of town to work. The townspeople come out of their shops and homes to spit at us as we pass. The hatred in their eyes is dismaying. We are not human beings to them; we are lower than dogs. At the edge of town we are forced to dig trenches in an effort to stop the Allied forces. One would think the townspeople would be grateful for the work we do to protect them, but they spit at us that evening as well. We get another crust of bread and half a bowl of tea that night; that is all the food we are given. Rations are shrinking before our eyes. The Germans are losing the war.

For a month we are chased out of dreamless sleep and marched through town, and every morning, every night, we are spit at as we pass. We wake. We get counted. We march. We dig. We eat. We starve. We wonder if it will ever end.

FOUR A.M.

"*Raus! Raus!*" We stand at attention for roll call and are then dismissed.

"It isn't Sunday, is it?"

"I don't think so." Part of the camp continues to work at an airplane factory; the rest of us have nothing to do. Rumors circulate that we won't be working anymore.

"The Allies must be close," our whispers speculate. "Maybe the war is almost over." We hope this is true, but after the death march, we know better than to put any hope in this desire. They could move us again to another prison if they wanted to. They could march us to Madagascar.

The lull of not working and spending all day behind the fences is enough to drive me crazy. I notice that the pile of bodies lying behind the barracks in camp is getting larger, and I learn from the other prisoners that many of these women were arrested after the Warsaw Uprising. They are Jews and Poles, left to rot together outside without even a ditch to be buried in.

I go to the camp elder and say, "With no other work in camp to do, I was wondering if you might give us permission to bury the bodies of these few hundred women?"

"*Jawohl*," she says. "I'll give you a hand wagon. Choose nine others to help you. You start tomorrow morning. I'll assign two SS men to escort you." I make a note: she has a green triangle on her uniform. She is a murderer.

I ask for volunteers for this *leichenkommando*. Danka and Dina volunteer, as well as seven other girls. Covering our noses, we take the cart out to the mound of bodies. "We don't have gloves, so we must be careful," I warn the girls. "Only touch the arms and legs, and be very careful of any open wounds. We can't wash our hands before we eat, so we must be very careful so that we don't get sick." I take the arms while another girl takes the legs, and we swing a corpse onto the cart. It sighs as the last air is expelled from its lungs.

We falter. "*Schnell!*" the guards yell. "Come on!" We load the cart as quickly as possible, about fifteen bodies. Then we begin our march to the burial place. Across the road is a men's camp of Italian political prisoners.

"Not much longer! Not much longer!" they shout as we walk by. We do not have a radio in camp; the news of the world has been cut off from us. We stare at these wild-eyed men. They do not look crazy, just desperate for freedom. "Not much longer! Not much longer!" How long is not much longer?

The SS take us up a hill. The cart is heavy, and we strain our muscles to keep it moving. It figures they would choose a burial site that is difficult to reach.

"You will bury them here." The guards stop, pointing to the area where we should dig, then they move away to rest on their rifles.

I thrust my shovel into the soil. It's rock-hard. We try to dig deep, as we're supposed to, but it is impossible. I get in the hole to dig out the bottom. The soil is so unforgiving that it takes hours to dig the graves. Thoughts run through my head while I'm in the hole trying to dig a little deeper; the SS could just shoot us and we'd fall in having dug our own graves.

"Help me out," I call to the girls above. A hand reaches over the side; my sister pulls me out of the pit.

"I don't like seeing you in there," she murmurs.

"I don't like being in there." I mean it too.

This detail is difficult. We are so weak. But when we get all the holes dug and the bodies are put to rest in unmarked graves, we stand on the hill, the sun slowly sinking toward the horizon.

"Let's say a prayer for the women we've buried," I whisper.

There is a unanimous nod. Over the mounds of fresh dirt we say the *Kaddish*. The guards do not notice our stillness, our soft voices. It is very important to me to give these women who have died some sacred ground in recognition of their lives. The prayer makes us feel good, and there is not much that does that. We walk wearily down the hill back toward camp. We have worked hard today and buried only fifteen women, and the mound of bodies still in camp looks no smaller for all our effort. I am sorry that I volunteered us for this job.

"Do you think I could sneak some potatoes from the pile and get something to eat?" I ask Dina one Sunday afternoon. The portions are getting smaller, and we can no longer count on getting both soup and bread.

"I heard that the camp elder killed a girl for stealing a potato when she went out to get coal; she made the girl empty the bucket and there it was. She kicked the girl until she fell on the ground, threw a board on top of her, and jumped on the board until she was dead," someone tells me.

"Oh my God."

"Don't do anything to make this camp elder mad," another girl-woman adds. "She killed her husband and her in-laws. She's insane."

I shudder but am still enamored by the thought of trying to get two potatoes without getting caught. I am more capable than the girl who is now dead. I know I can do it.

THE MOUND OF bodies does not get smaller very quickly. The first week we bury about eighty bodies, but new ones have been added to the top of the heap.

The SS men who take us to the burial site are old and tired and mean. We do not fear them as much as we feared the younger, stronger SS men in Auschwitz-Birkenau, though. "I think we should devise a plan to overcome them. Knock them out," one of the girls in our kommando suggests.

"We could hit them on the head with our shovels and throw them in a really deep grave so they couldn't get out. Then we could escape!"

"Yah!" Their eyes dance with the thought of rebellion.

"I can't kill anyone," I whisper.

"Not kill—we'll just stun them."

"Think about it." I look at their fevered faces. "First of all, think how hard it'd be to make a hole that deep—we'd kill ourselves trying. Second, we're in Germany. There's not one German in this town who would help a Pole, let alone a Jew. Do you think it will be different elsewhere in this country? They hate us. If we were in Poland, it would be different. We might be able to count on our own people to help us escape. But we're not. We don't even know where we are. How far is it to the Polish border? Which way should we walk?" No one can answer my questions. "We would be caught and killed by villagers, or by the SS. Besides, my guess is we are far from any borders."

Their faces fall with disappointment.

"Maybe the Italians are right and it won't be long now," Danka adds. "Maybe we'll be freed soon."

"Maybe." No one really believes it, though.

We have started putting two or three bodies in each grave. Our strength is failing fast with the lack of food and the terrible conditions in camp. Pushing the cart up the hill is a chore we can barely accomplish. The chance of overpowering the old men is slipping away as quickly as our weight and our hope that liberation will come soon. The lower the pile of bodies gets, the worse it gets for us, because it is spring and the bodies are beginning to decompose. And there are fresh bodies on top now, too, so it's hard to tell until you touch one how long it's been lying there. Some of them we have to leave or they will fall apart. We're very careful not to disturb the very old, decaying bodies.

I wake, huddling in our bunk alone. Was it another nightmare that woke me? Rain falls on the roof overhead. The sky above us rumbles and clashes as violently as if God were at war rather than mankind. Where is Danka? She is terrified of thunderstorms.

Mama used to light candles and say a prayer during electrical storms in Tylicz. There are no candles here. I stare through the darkness, unable to tell whether Danka is in the block or not. Other eyes shine in the dark. Finally the storm overhead moves on. I wonder if its rain has fallen on Allied as well as German heads. The door creaks open and my sister steps inside. Like a mirage she glimmers in the dark. Her red hair, finally growing back after several months of not being shaved, frames her face.

"Where have you been?" I cannot tell if her cheeks are wet from tears or rain. She shakes her head, silent. "Danka, what were you doing?" I demand.

"Praying," she whispers hoarsely. "I was outside praying that the lightning would strike me dead so I wouldn't be hungry anymore."

WE BURY WOMEN all day and get in after roll call, after the bread has been handed out. There is nothing left. No food for those of us who have worked all day. I cannot bear my sister's hunger any longer and volunteer to get a bucket of coals for the block elder to put in the stove. Danka and Dina send me a warning glance. I ignore them both. At the pile of coal I check the vicinity, grab two potatoes, and thrust them under the coal in the bucket. Head forward, eyes down, I walk slowly across the compound.

Out of the shadows by the blocks I hear the camp elder's voice, "Let me see you empty that bucket on the ground."

I freeze and turn slowly around.

"Well?"

I dump the contents onto the ground. The potatoes could be covered by enough black dust to be masked amidst the odd-shaped lumps of coal that she won't see. . . .

She hits me in the left eye before I can even think to duck. "You stole potatoes!" She throws me on the ground, kicking me, stomping on me with her boots, trying to tear the flesh from my bones with her fingernails. I cannot see anything but the blazing hatred in her face; it is the face of Death itself. She loses her grasp on me for a second. I scramble away, fleeing across camp.

"Thief! Thief! *Scheiss-Jude!* Get back here you filthy dog!" Her harpy's voice follows my tracks like a bloodhound hot on the trail. I vanish behind the blocks, dodging searchlights and the madwoman's screaming voice. Under the cover of darkness I slip into one of the other blocks.

"I stole a potato and she's going to kill me for sure," I whisper into the dark.

"Come here." An anonymous voice calls out. Quickly, I crawl in between two bodies, and hide under their blanket.

Outside the wardress screeches, "Come out you miserable *mist biene*! Come out here! You can't hide forever. I'm going to get you!" It seems a lifetime until she quiets down. I wait for a little bit longer, just to make sure she's not hiding somewhere, and then slip out of the bunk I've hidden in. "Thank you for saving my life," I whisper to the girls whose faces I do not know, then creep back across camp, so the wardress won't know which block has hidden me. Blinded in my left eye, I thread my way through shadows and along walls until I reach our block. I slip in next to Danka. Her arms grab me. Squeeze tight.

"Oh, Rena. What's going to happen?"

"I don't know." We hold each other all night, sobbing, both of us shaking in terror. This is it. I am done for. That is all either of us can think about. There is nothing we can do but cling to each other for the last time. My teeth chatter from the chill of fear, the fear of death itself. Liberation is so close, and now this. Danka will be alone in the world after the camp elder gets through with me. We do not sleep at all. I will never survive roll call.

"*Raus! Raus!*"

My eye is swollen shut and black and blue and purple. Danka tries to put some dirt on it but it hurts to touch. We line up in the very back of the rows. The camp elder stalks across the front rows, screaming and cursing us.

"Anyone who knows who stole the potatoes last night should turn the prisoner in immediately. If I find out you are withholding information from me, I will kill you instead. Who knows who stole the potatoes?" No one moves. No one makes a sound. The SS women walk up and down the rows counting each prisoner, looking for me. Surely the camp elder saw my face and recognized me as the one from the *leichenkommando*. When she sees me she will kill me.

I try not to tremble, try to be brave for my sister.

"You'd better turn yourself in! You'd better come out!"

No one says a word; no one lets them know where I am. An SS woman comes down our row, counting us, inspecting us, looking for me.

Suddenly I feel very calm and warm. There is the slightest tingle on my cheek as if someone has touched my face. *Mama?*

The SS woman is just a few prisoners away, but I am warm and comforted. *Remember how you escaped Mengele. You told Danka you were invisible and you were.* The fear drains out of me through the heels of my feet into the earth, and I stand confident that I am imperceptible. *Mama is here, standing next to me. Her hand is over my eye.*

The SS woman looks at me, counts me, turns away. Danka sighs.

Protect me through the gate, Mama, I pray. I still have to march out with the bodies, and the camp elder is always standing there, counting the bodies, checking our numbers. I pretend to be rearranging the bodies in the back of the cart, making sure there is an arm obscuring my eye so she can't see my face and won't recognize me.

Every morning I feel a warm tingle on my cheeks as the SS walk right past my black-and-blue, swollen eye. Every morning I fumble with the bodies while we take them out the gate, and every morning I pass unseen under the nose of the camp elder.

How long can this go on? For six days I hide from the murderess, and she never sees my face. Do they not see me because they are blinded by prejudice and we all look alike to them? Or is this some greater mystery, larger than hate?

∞

2 MAY 1945

Four a.m. Five a.m. Six . . .

We step into dawn's light nervously, wondering what new trick this is that our captors are playing. There is no roll call. There is no one but us in camp, just one lone guard still in the watchtower. Not one SS woman, no wardress, no camp elder anywhere to be seen. We stand on the camp road gazing at the guard in the watchtower, wondering what to do. He is the only thing between us and freedom, and his gun is aimed directly at us. I look at my watch. It's ten o'clock. How long must we wait here when freedom is laughing just on the other side of these gates?

A mother and daughter decide they are hungry enough to brave getting to the pile of potatoes. They run across camp toward the only food left. A gunshot rips through the girl's heart. She collapses.

Her mother screams, rending her clothes and cursing God. No one dares to go comfort her. A second shot rips her throat out. *Lamentations.*

Their bodies taint that fatal pile of potatoes. The sweet taste of freedom grows bitter in our mouths.

The SS in the watchtower finally climbs down and disappears.

At eleven o'clock the Italians from the prison camp down the road shout outside our fences: "We're free!"

They have rubber gloves and wire cutters. "Come on! Storm the gates!" They sever the wires, breaking the electrical current and leaving a hole big enough for us to tear through. I grab Danka's hand, dragging her through the fence. We have bloody hands from the barbs we push out of the way. My sweater catches on the wire. I do not stop. It rips. I do not care.

Suddenly we are on the road. We blink, unable to believe our eyes. Soldiers dressed in dark green and olive, Russian and American soldiers are coming toward us.

"We're free!" We hug each other, crying. "We're free!" My heart is a stone in a river of tears.

The girls from camp disperse down the roads. There are girls going this way and that, all in confusion, all lost, trying to decide which way is home. Danka and a small group of girl-women watch me as if I should know what to do.

We walk for a little while until we reach a crossroads. Danka, Dina, and I stop and look down the two paths. One goes east, to the Russians and eventually to Poland; the other goes west, to the Americans. I do not know which way to turn. The sun is gold and brilliant, burning through the layers of obscurity in my mind. My fog begins to lift.

Mama is in the distance. Her babushka has fallen from her head; her arm is waving more slowly now. Which way should we go, Mama? . . . She is no longer running through the snow; the long winter has melted into spring. Go west, Rena. She pulls her babushka back up around her head and blows me a kiss.

Don't go, Mama. Wait for me. I brought you the baby back! . . .

Good-bye, Rena. You are a good daughter.

I stand in the middle of the crossroads waving to the vision that has kept me alive—Mama!

She stands there for one brief moment, her arm still in the air. Good-bye. Her image shatters into a thousand shards of light. My eyes wince with pain as if slivers of glass fallen from my eyes. The dream is gone. There is no one to go home to anymore.

Epilogue

TEARS STREAM DOWN HER FACE. I take Rena's hand. Squeeze. "You're done, Rena. You're done."

We sit quietly looking at the fire, our hands clasped across the generations. Her voice cracks when she finally whispers, "No one ever listened to the whole thing before."

She looks so innocent, so hopeful. "Do you think it will go away now? I was hoping I would tell it and never have to remember it again."

"I can't make it go away," I say. "I wish I could."

She shakes her head.

"Maybe sharing it with others will help it be less painful?"

Then, in true Rena fashion, a rush of good memories pours out of her. She doesn't want to make anyone go through what she did without giving us something positive. "Don't you think people will want to know about the kind American major who took us in and gave us a mansion on our first night of freedom?" Her eyes are brim full, but she still looks for a way to make us stop crying. I turn the microcassette recorder on again and lean back to listen until her voice becomes mine, once more. . . .

∞

GERMANY WAS DIVIDED in half between the Russians and the Americans, and we decided to walk to the American side. They weren't going to let us cross, but then I said, "Please, we were in Auschwitz and on the Death March." The major turned pale and told us to come through the barrier. Then he walked through the town looking for the biggest house he could find. It was a mansion—I had never seen such a large house except in movies. He banged on the door until the servants answered. Their masters had fled, of course, and the major ordered the servants to wait on us hand and foot. "Coffee! Chocolate! Anything they want. I want you to serve them breakfast in bed and bring them warm robes and towels." There were marble floors and oriental rugs. And a bathtub with claw feet. I had my first bath in over three years; no disinfectant, no SS, no men to shave me naked, just white bubbles and hot water, so hot to scald my skin off. I soaked up to my neck and sank my head beneath the surface. I scrubbed and scrubbed and scrubbed the years of dirt and filth and slavery from my skin. I scrubbed the lice and memories away. Danka couldn't get me to stop. I was mad with it—oh, to come out of that bath clean of all the past.

That night we slept in a real bed with real sheets, white and clean, like Erika and the kapos had, only even nicer because we had feather pillows and a balcony with two glass doors that looked out at a garden. Danka, Dina, and I slept in the same bed. There were other rooms, but we did not want to be apart in freedom. And this bed was so large, so warm and lush and comfortable. This was our first real sleep. It was deep but dark. I did not dream yet. That came later. But at four a.m. my body woke, wary and alert, waiting for the guards to start yelling: "*Raus! Raus!*"

I jumped from bed, no idea where I was. Paced the room, back and forth. We should be up. We should rush to use the toilet. We should line up to be counted.

"*Raus! Raus!*"

My whole body shivered. Outside the balcony windows the palest hint of light finally touched the sky. Only then did I stop pacing and wringing my hands. The sky was still gray but softer now, no longer a harsh metal sky to cut the heart to shreds.

Danka's arm slipped around my waist and squeezed me tight. This was freedom, a quiet room at dawn. Arm in arm we watched the world grow pink.

∞

WE WERE MOVED to a hospital for a few days and then to a displaced person's camp where we were nearly deported back to Germany because we had no papers. I gathered the girls we had been with in Neüstadt Glewe—Dina, Danka, and a few others—and we went to a major's office. He said he had no choice but to deport us. We fell on our knees, begging him to let us stay in Holland. "We were three years in Auschwitz. Please, don't forsake us. We suffered so much." We grabbed the major's knees and wept. "Please, don't do that to us. We have seen such horrors. Please don't send us back."

"All right. Enough of that." He tried to pick me up off the floor. "I won't deport you to Germany." He tried to show us out the door, but we were overcome. To receive such kindness after so many years of being treated like insects and trampled on, there is no way to describe our feelings—to be humans after so long of being told we were not. We fell on our knees again to thank him!

It was the Americans who sent us to the Red Cross and Relief Team Number Ten, where the commander, a Dutchman by the

Girls who made it from Auschwitz through the Death March and Neüstadt Glewe to Holland, with an unidentified Israeli soldier.

name of John Gelissen, put us to work helping Dutch people to get home. These were people like us, finally freed from the camps, but we saw no one from Auschwitz. We remembered how the girls from Amsterdam dropped like flies. How many of us had survived?

After a few weeks all the Dutch people had found their homes. The commander was at a loss what to do with us—we had no home, no family, and no country, either. So he gave us jobs. Danka and I sewed; the others cooked or cleaned. As long as we worked we could stay in Holland, so we worked hard. We worked so hard that when the commander discovered we had been hoarding bread under our beds, he was very understanding. It was so embarrassing, but we could not help ourselves—we had never seen so much bread in three years. And just in case things turned bad again, we hid loaves of it under our mattresses until it got moldy and began to smell.

He sat us all down. "You do not need to save your bread anymore. You will never lack for bread again," he promised. We nodded but were not convinced. I didn't want him to be mad at us, so every night I checked to make sure the bread we had hidden had not gotten moldy again, and after a month or so, we started to

John Gelissen and Rena Kornreich's
engagement picture

believe that there would be bread tomorrow and stopped storing the extra crusts under our mattresses.

The commander was very kind and good looking too! He took us dancing but danced twice as many dances with me as with the others, and so I began to fall for him. Danka adored John but did not think I should fall in love with a Gentile. I had already fallen in love with a Gentile once before though, so it seemed only right to fall in love with a Gentile again. Gentiles are not so different from Jews. We are both human beings. We laugh. We cry. We love. And on July 29, 1947, two years after the war, John Gelissen, commander of Relief Team Number Ten, married me.

We tried to start a family at once, but I miscarried. When Sylvia was born, I was so happy. I can't tell you. When they handed me this little perfect baby, my own baby, I counted all of her perfect fingers and all of her perfect toes. "I love you," I told her. "And I love you, John, and I love you, nurse, and I love you, doctor. I love the whole world even with the Germans in it." And I meant it too.

We followed Danka to the United States in 1954 and had four children total: Sylvia, Joseph, Peter, and Robert, and now we have three grandchildren, Shaun, Julia, and Zachary John. When we retired we went to the Blue Ridge Mountains of North Carolina, which reminded me of the Carpathian Mountains in Poland.

I found a good husband and have a good life, just like the elder woman who looked like Mama wished for me. Every year on May second John gives me white and red carnations, to celebrate the anniversary of our liberation. *This day is more important than your birthday*, he writes to me, *because without this day there would be no birthdays to celebrate. Love, John.*

∞

RENA KORNREICH GELISSEN died on August 8, 2006. She was surrounded by her family to the very end. For four years, John visited Rena's gravesite every day and used to joke that she finally had to listen to him talk. He joined his beloved Rena on July 10, 2010. They are buried together in Bethel, Connecticut. Every May 2—Remembrance Day—I send red and white carnations to be placed on their graves.

Danka and Rena

DANKA AND **ELI BRANDEL** were married in 1948 in Holland. After everything Danka had been through, all she wanted was to have a family of her own, but she had difficulty conceiving. The doctors in Holland could not help her. In 1952, Danka and Eli moved to America where she went to an obstetrician/gynecologist, who performed a procedure that Danka considered a miracle. She was able to conceive, but like her sister she too miscarried. Finally, Danka was able to carry a baby to full term and gave birth to a son, Norman, in 1955. It had taken seven long years. Soon after

The Brandel family (left to right: Norman, Danka, Sara, Eli)

Danka had Norman she told Rena that she had too much love to give and wanted to have another child. This was another hard pregnancy, and Danka nearly lost the baby, but in June 1957, Sara was born. She was named after Mama, Danka and Rena's mother.

> *Family was the most important thing to my parents, especially after losing most of their own. They were devoted, protective, and loving parents. Needless to say, they were overjoyed with their grandchildren, and spent as much time with them all as possible. Never having had the opportunity to know my grandparents due to the war, I didn't realize how much I missed of that special relationship until I witnessed my own children enjoying that special bond with their grandparents.*
>
> —*Sara Brandel Cohen, Danka's daughter*

Danka and Eli had five grandchildren: Andrew, Eric, Jamie, Jenna, and Adam. Danka passed away on November 21, 2012—she was ninety years old.

GERTRUDE (RENA'S OLDEST SISTER) immigrated to the United States in 1921. She married David Shane and had one son, Irvin. All of the family photographs from before the war come from Gertrude, who died in New York in 1994 at the age of eighty-eight. Rena has no idea what fate befell **Zosia** and her children, **Herschel** and **Ester Stuhr**. Despite efforts to locate the children in hopes they had been hidden in a Christian orphanage, Rena was never able to find her niece or nephew. Any information about their fates would be appreciated. It is believed that **Nathan Stuhr**, Zosia's husband, was lost in Siberia.

The fate of **Sara** and **Chaim Kornreich** is unknown. Rena believes that they were among the one and a half million Jews exterminated in the gas chambers of Auschwitz. According to **Alex** (**Joseph**'s son from Tylicz), the Jews forced to leave Tylicz for Florynka—Joseph, his family, and the Kornreichs—were transferred to the Grybow ghetto. Alex escaped from Grybow and fled to Slovakia, where he worked in the resistance. While working for the underground he heard reports that the Jews in Grybow were

Dina Dranger

forced into the Nowy Sacz ghetto or put into vans and gassed. Alex survived the war; he has one son and two daughters and lives in New York City.

Dina was separated from Danka and Rena in a military compound in Holland. She immigrated to France and married Emil Vajda, a highly decorated member of the French Resistance. Like Danka she had trouble having children but had one son, Daniel. **Erna** and **Fela Dranger** both survived Auschwitz and immigrated to Israel, where they each raised two children: Yaron and Akiva, and Rachel and Avishay. Of the twenty-five Jewish families who lived in Tylicz before the war, none live there now.

Erna Dranger

Fela Dranger

∞

DESPITE RENA'S AND DANKA'S best efforts to feed and help their friend, **Tolek Krukont** died in Auschwitz on September 24, 1942. After saving Rena and her father, Officer **Hans Joksch** (according to the rumor in Tylicz at the time) was transferred to the Russian front.

Because of the coat she found in "Canada," Rena believes that **Jacob** and **Regina Schützer** were exterminated in the gas chambers at Auschwitz. Rena never heard what became of their other daughter, **Cili Schützer,** and there is no mention of the rest of the Schutzer family in the digital repository now available online through the Auschwitz Museum. **Gizzy's** death *is* recorded; she died on October 23, 1942. The **Silbers**, the family Rena was staying with when she turned herself in, were able to escape from Slovakia to Switzerland and later immigrated to America.

After the Death March, **Janka** was separated from Rena and Danka in Ravensbrück. She survived the war and was married and settled in Germany. Rena does not know what happened to **Mania** and **Lentzi,** who were also separated from Rena and Danka in Ravensbrück. It is not known what happened to **Aranka.**

IN 2012, ON THE seventieth anniversary of the first transport, we learned the story behind **Adela Gross** and how she came to be on the first transport. Adela's cousin, Lou Gross, was only a toddler when Adela was sent to Auschwitz. The authorities came for her sister, but her sister was ill, so they took Adela instead. When they came back, the Gross family hid Adela's older sister and fled into hiding. Adela's sister survived the war, and every year Adela's family in Slovakia honors her memory by going to the train station in Poprad, where the first transport originated.

What became of the kapos **Emma** and **Erika** is unknown. But to Emma, Rena always wanted to pay a debt of gratitude—without Emma they might never have survived. Other women from the first transport have also reported a kind kapo by the name of Emma—her last name was never known.

∞

ANDRZEJ GARBERA saved many lives, including Rena's; he died a war hero at the age of twenty-three. In 1990, Rena returned to Poland for the first time since the war and was finally able to place flowers on his grave.

OF THE MEN prisoners who helped Rena and Danka little is known: **Heniek, Bolek, Stasiu** (Artista), and **Tadziu** (Wisniewski, the water-pump operator) were Polish citizens. While Rena never knew if they survived, she always wanted to thank them for helping save her life and her sister's.

Marek Sterenberg (camp serial number: 161910) arrived in Auschwitz on November 8, 1943 (Czech, 521). He did survive the Death March but never made it to America. He stayed in Poland and became a guard over Nazi prisoners, the very men who had tortured and brutalized him. In retaliation he took vengeance on his former captors. Marek was overpowered and disarmed by one of the SS prisoners and shot to death.

∞

OF THE SS RENA came into contact with, especially the lesser-ranking SS, little is known. The following information has been compiled for the reader's information from various sources, including two survivors' personal accounts.

"It is estimated that [**Carl Clauberg**] conducted sterilization experiments on about 700 women. In 1948 he was tried in the Soviet Union and sentenced to 25 years in prison. Freed in an amnesty in 1955, he returned to Kiel in the German Federal Republic, boasting of his 'scientific achievements.' Only after the Central Council of Jews denounced him was he arrested, in November 1955; he died in August 1957, shortly before his trial was to begin" (Czech, 810).

Josef Mengele was "accused of selections, fatal injections (phenol), shootings, beatings, and other forms of deliberate killing" and the suspicion was raised that "he threw newborn infants directly into the crematoriums and into open fires. . . . For over twenty years Mengele was able to evade all extradition attempts; he died in a swimming accident in Brazil in 1979" (Czech, 819).

"Heinrich Himmler . . . used terror and force against the opponents of the Third Reich and transformed his fanatical race ideology into concrete politics and organization—like the system of the concentration camps. . . . At the end of the war, Himmler tried to escape capture disguised as an army private; after his discovery and arrest, he committed suicide on May 23, 1945. . . .

"Rudolf Hoss (SS Lieutenant Colonel) . . . was named Commandant of Auschwitz in 1940. Characterized as an assiduous, petit bourgeois executive, he organized mass murder with technical and administrative meticulousness. Arrested in 1946, he testified at the Nuremberg Trial and was extradited to Poland in May of that year. In April 1947 he was sentenced to be hanged and was executed on the grounds of the camp [Auschwitz]" (Czech, 814).

"Among the SS supervisors, Mandel, Taube, Drexler, and Hasse distinguished themselves in their savage treatment of women prisoners" (Strzelecka, 396). **Margot Drexler** "was particularly feared by the women inmates, whom she beat and starved to death. She last worked at the Ravensbrück subcamp of Neüstadt-Glewe. After the war she tried to escape but was caught in Pirma-Bautzen in Czechoslovakia in the Russian zone in May 1945 and hanged in May or June of that year in Bautzen" (Clark).

Juana Bormann was known as "the woman with the dogs." We did not find out who she was until after Rena had passed away, but Rena would have been relieved to know that SS Bormann was convicted and hanged for her crimes against humanity.

Irma Grese was referred to as "the beautiful beast." She was tried with Bormann in the Bergen-Belsen war crimes tribunal and sentenced to death by hanging for torturing and assaulting prisoners (Gutman, 1990).

Maria Mandel was put on trial for war crimes and sentenced to death by a Polish court. She was executed in December 1947 (Rittner and Roth, 29). It is unknown whether her sister, Elisabeth Hasse, was ever held accountable for her actions or what happened to **Maria Mullenders**.

According to Caroline Moorehead, author of *A Train in Winter*, SS Unterscharführer, Reporting Officer, **Adolph Taube**, was executed for his war crimes—however, we have not been able to confirm which tribunal he was convicted at or where he was executed. There is no record of his cohort **Freidrich Stiewitz** ever being held accountable for their "calisthenics" or other murderous actions in Auschwitz-Birkenau.

Rena in Auschwitz, 1990

ACKNOWLEDGMENTS

When the first edition came out, Rena showed the book to the photo of Mama proudly and then called me crying. She was overcome with emotion, and in the midst of our conversation we both came to realize that God had finally answered her prayer when she saw the children going to the gas chamber. Today I hold that truth in my heart knowing that Rena's story has touched more than one person—it has touched thousands—to love instead of hate.

This edition could never have been made possible without the support of all the people who helped the first edition into print in 1995, so we would still like to thank the following people for their belief in us and their support: John, for his calm assurance throughout this project, making sure we took lunch breaks, providing Dutch jokes, and for being the wonderful husband he was; Danka, for surviving and letting us share her part in her sister's story; Corrine Johnson, for introducing me to Rena; Dr. Annette Allen, for the hours she spent discussing the initial drafts and her insight and help in refining the accepted manuscript; speed-reader extraordinaire Joanne Pankow, for proofing the manuscript twice in thirty-six hours before it went to our wonderful agent, Sarah Jane Freymann. Sarah Jane has been our champion since she first read the manuscript and is the main reason we have this revised edition in print today, but it was her heart for the project and her courage in believing in a first-time author and an old Polish lady "who doesn't speak that bad English" that brought Rena's story to our equally brave publisher, Beacon Press. Here we must thank not only our first editor, Deb Chasman, but also Helene Atwan, for wishing to bring out this revised edition, and Rachael Marks, for helping hone the new research and footnotes in this edition.

There are a number of new people we need to thank, as well. Chief Rabbi Lord Jonathan Sacks; Baroness Crowley; Sir Martin Gilbert; Dr. Piotr Setkiewicz, head of research at Panstowe Muzeum Auschwitz-Birkenau, for showing me Stabsgabaüde and the trockenplatz, and for speaking candidly about the place the first women at Auschwitz have in history; Dorota Nycz, document specialist, also at Panstowe Muzeum Auschwitz-Birkenau, for taking me into Block Ten, where Rena, Erna, Fela, Dina, and Danka were first housed in 1942; Crispin Brooks of the USC Shoah Foundation, for his support in helping me find records of women on the first transport in the Visual Archives Library, which inspired my first journey to Auschwitz on the seventieth anniversary of the first transport; to Gabriele and Andrew Braunsberg, for hosting us in Vienna, and Eliska Slavikova, in Bratislava; to Jem and her mum, for singing "It's Amazing" in a train station in Poland; to the young man who gave me a free coffee on the train to Auschwitz; to the Polish man named Marek, who picked us up hitchhiking on the road outside of Birkenau because there were no cabs and we were about to miss our plane; and to the many other people around the world who supported the 70th Anniversary Promise Vigils to raise awareness about the first transport and the first Jewish women in Auschwitz. To all of you a huge warm *dziękuję, Bóg zapłać.*

I would also like to thank Peter Dimock, who gave me editorial notes on early drafts of the digital edition and understood, even better than myself, the role I played as "Mama" in listening to Rena's story; Joanne Bloomfield, for her work on our website; and Fal, for all his work on the timeline and the beautiful poppies he painted. My heartfelt thanks to Gabriel Barrow, for typing the list of women from the first transport into a data file; and to Debbie Brandel (Danka's daughter-in-law) and Kat Furey, for helping me pore over the online digital archives to try to find the death dates of 998 missing girl-women. I could not have done it on my own.

Without Sylvia, Rena's daughter, proofreading the digital edition and helping edit it, and Sara, Danka's daughter, we would never have accomplished this new print edition. They are also the vital force behind our fan page on Facebook, where they are active voices sharing memories and moments from their mothers' lives. Our agent sent me a card back in 1995 that said, "There is nothing, nothing, nothing two women cannot accomplish before noon." We are three women! (And Rena's spirit oversees us all.) Sylvia lost her dear husband, Jim Lanier, before this new edition was published, but she would like to remember Jim with love and gratitude for all the support he gave her, and all of us, in bringing out the digital edition. Jim was our technical wizard. Sara would also like to thank her husband, Michael Cohen. Finally, I would like to thank my partner, Simon Worrall, for his painstaking proofreading, patience, and sense of humor. Because of all of these people, the world has access to *Rena's Promise* and that *is* a promise kept to our dearest Rena and Danka. We miss you with all our hearts.

BIBLIOGRAPHY

African American Lives 2. "Profile of Maya Angelou." PBS. Producer Henry Louis Gates Jr. Kunhardt Productions. 2008. http://www .pbs.org/wnet/aalives/profiles/angelou.html.

Bartlett, Neil, et al., eds. *McGraw-Hill Encyclopedia of Science & Technology.* 7th ed. Vol. 17. New York: McGraw-Hill, 1992.

Clark, Richard. *Capital Punishment UK Website.* 1995. http://www .capitalpunishmentuk.org

Collingham, Lizzie. *The Taste of War: World War Two and the Battle for Food.* London: Allen Lane, 2010.

Czech, Danuta. *Auschwitz Chronicle: 1939–1945.* London: I. B. Tauris, 1990.

Gilbert, Martin. *The Holocaust: A History of the Jews of Europe During the Second World War.* London: Collins, 1986.

Gutman, Yisrael, ed. *Encyclopedia of the Holocaust.* 4 vols. New York: Macmillan, 1990.

Hellman, Peter. *The Auschwitz Album.* New York: Random House, 1981.

Langer, Lawrence L. *Holocaust Testimonies: The Ruins of Memory.* New Haven, CT: Yale University Press, 1991.

Moorehead, Caroline. *A Train in Winter: An Extraordinary Story of Women, Friendship, and Resistance in Occupied France.* London: Harper Perennial, 2011.

The Partially Preserved Death Books (Sterbebücher) of Auschwitz Concentration Camp Prisoners: July 29, 1941, and December 31, 1943. Pánstwowe Muzeum Auschwitz, Digital Archives. http://en.auschwitz .org/m/index.php?option=com_content&task=view&Itemid= 31&id=529.

Posner, Gerald L., and John Ware. *Mengele: The Complete Story.* New York: McGraw-Hill, 1986.

Rittner, Carol, and John K. Roth, eds. "Prologue: Women and the Holocaust" and "Chronology." In *Different Voices: Women and the Holocaust.* New York: Paragon, 1993.

Saidel, Rochelle G. *The Jewish Women of Ravensbrück Concentration Camp.* Madison: University of Wisconsin Press, 2004.

Strzelecka, Irena. "Women." In *Anatomy of the Auschwitz Death Camp.* Yisrael Gutman and Michael Berenbaum, eds. Bloomington: Indiana University Press, 1994.

Wyman, David, ed. *Bombing Auschwitz and the Auschwitz Escapees' Report.* Vol. 12, *America and the Holocaust.* New York: Garland, 1990.

STUDY GUIDE

GENERAL QUESTIONS

1. In the introduction the coauthor asks: "So why is this history important to us today?" What is your answer to this question now? Has your answer changed since you have finished the book?

2. In the beginning of the memoir, the coauthor puts herself into the story. Her voice and Rena's voice flip back and forth between present time and the past and then, eventually, disappear as Rena's voice takes over. Why do you think the coauthor uses this technique? Is it effective for you as a reader?

3. The narrative voice also shifts from present to past tense in the beginning. If that was disconcerting for you, why? What might the coauthor have been trying to do by creating that sense of time shifting? As Heather's voice fades, we are left only with Rena's voice in the present tense. How does writing about Auschwitz in present tense change your perspective on the events you are reading about?

4. The coauthor mentions the use of footnotes as a kind of timeline to help the reader place Rena's story in history, as well as to support Rena's personal narrative. Discuss how that information affects your reading experience.

5. Men's and women's experiences in the Holocaust varied. What can you attribute to that fact? What would have caused these discrepancies? (The answer is in the footnotes.)

6. a) There are many themes in this story. If you could pick out one theme what would it be?

    b) There are some very subtle motifs you might have missed: the colors gray, white, and red, and the word *Lamentations*, which appears in the book. What might those colors and that word mean to you? What other motifs can you find, and what do they mean to you?

7. What were some of the key factors or qualitites that kept Rena and Danka alive through Auschwitz and Birkenau? Make a list and then find three different examples where one of those factors or qualities are written about.

8. In their book *A Path Appears*, Nicholas Kristof and Sheryl WuDunn reveal that both psychologists and neuroscientists have found evidence that altruism and generous behavior benefits the giver, not just the receiver, in terms of health, happiness, and longevity. What do you think compelled Rena to act so selflessly when it came to taking care of her sister? Was she acting out of the goodness of her heart, out of necessity, or as she was raised to act, or were there other factors?

9. Danka also helped Rena and saved her life during the Death March. How did their relationship help both to survive?

10. At the beginning of this book there are two quotes; one is from the Bible and one is from Maya Angelou. Discuss these quotes in relation to your own family history. Do you have experiences in your life or with your family that help you relate? Discuss your attitude toward other human beings as "strangers." What makes them different from you? What do you have in common? (This discussion can make for a good essay.)

11. Finally, Heather is regularly called a "Holohoaxer" by Holocaust deniers, and she works to preserve the truth of the Holocaust through this book, the website, and online forums. How would you respond to a Holocaust denier?

WRITING EXERCISES

1. *Voice, narrative, and empathy*: Pick one scene that you feel
   particularly strongly about and rewrite it from the perspective of one of the other people in the story (note: you cannot
   write it from Rena's perspective because you already know
   what she is thinking). Write the scene so you get to know
   who this person is, what he or she is thinking, and what
   motivates him or her to do what he or she does.

2. *Morality*: After 9/11, Rena expressed concern for American
   Muslims. She was worried that people would hurt them like
   the Jews were hurt in Europe. What do you think about her
   response? And what is your reaction to her statement "I do
   not hate. To hate is to let Hitler win"?

SENSORY EXERCISES

1. Imagine what a potato peel tastes like from Rena's descrip-
   tion and write down your perceptions. Then take a potato
   peel and eat it—remember she found hers in the dirt. How
   does it taste to you? Can you imagine it tasting wonderful?

2. a) Get together some stale bread, mustard, and weak tea (no
      sugar) and eat it for breakfast. Are you full? What does it
      taste like?

   b) Make some watered-down potato soup (eat it cold and
      with no seasoning). What's that taste like? (Rena told me
      my potato soup was too good for this exercise, even when
      it was watered down.)

   c) Make some macaroni, and when it is done, sip the water.
      For years after Auschwitz, Rena would secretly sip her
      pasta water and think how wonderful it tasted. How does
      the noodle broth taste to you?

3. Finally, write about hunger. Have you ever been as hungry
   as Rena describes? Think about that time in your life and
   examine it for the physical sensation. How did you feel mentally and emotionally?

Note: Give time to each portion of food, to taste and consider what it was like to eat almost nothing but that stale bread and watery soup (which is going to be better than what she was served) for three years and forty-one days.

GROUP EXERCISE

(This exercise works best with the early portion of the Auschwitz chapter.) Have your reading group or class line up and march outside. No one should be allowed coats, etc. Make them move quickly. Before exiting the building make sure they understand that any giggling, talking, etc., is punishable by "death." Simulate "roll call" by using a mean voice and glaring at them. Order them to line up in rows of five, five wide, five deep (you can make it smaller if the group has just a few people in it). Have them stand for five minutes at full attention and remind them of how many hours every day Rena stood just like this, no matter what the weather. Then order them to line up for a mock selection. Using a stop watch or by counting "one-one thousand, two-one thousand, three-one thousand" give each person three seconds to stand in front of you before giving him or her the thumbs-up sign, allowing them to return to the building. Make sure everyone is selected for life. You will be able to tell which students believe you will select them, and that allows for interesting discussion: why did you think I would select you? Often I hear reasons like "because I am Muslim," "because I am short," "because I am thin," or "because I failed the last test." Give participants time to process this experience through writing and discussion.

If you don't have a group, stand still for ten minutes by yourself and allow yourself to imagine what it was like to do that for two hours twice a day. Pick a day when the weather is inclement. How do you stand still for so long? What do you have to do (mentally and/or emotionally) to stay still?

UNITS

You can download more study guides for complete units online under the Education tab at www.renaspromise.com.